The Emergence of Private Authority in Global Governance

The emergence of private authority has increasingly become a feature of the post-Cold War world. In *The Emergence of Private Authority in Global Governance*, leading scholars explore the sources, practices, and implications of this erosion of the authority of the state. They analyze and compare actors as diverse as financial institutions, multinational corporations, religious terrorists, mercenaries and organized criminals, and assess the potential for reversal of the situation. The themes of the book relate directly to debates concerning globalization and the role of international law, and will be of interest to scholars and students of international relations, politics, sociology, and law.

RODNEY BRUCE HALL is Assistant Professor of International Politics at the Department of Political Science of the University of Iowa. He is the author of *National Collective Identity: Social Constructs and International Systems* (1999).

THOMAS J. BIERSTEKER is Director of the Thomas J. Watson Institute for International Studies and the Henry R. Luce Professor of Transnational Organizations at Brown University, Providence, Rhode Island. His previous publications include *State Sovereignty as Social Construct* (Cambridge University Press, 1996, coedited with Cynthia Weber).

The Emergence of Private Authority in Global Governance

Cambridge Studies in International Relations is a joint initiative of Cambridge University Press and the British International Studies Association (BISA). The series will include a wide range of material, from undergraduate textbooks and surveys to research-based monographs and collaborative volumes. The aim of the series is to publish the best new scholarship in International Studies from Europe, North America and the rest of the world.

CAMBRIDGE STUDIES IN INTERNATIONAL RELATIONS

Series list continues after index.

The Emergence of Private Authority in Global Governance

edited by

Rodney Bruce Hall
University of Iowa

and

Thomas J. Biersteker
Brown University, Providence, Rhode Island

CAMBRIDGE
UNIVERSITY PRESS

9034417
KSG- ISP 426

PUBLISHED BY THE PRESS SYNDICATE OF THE UNIVERSITY OF CAMBRIDGE
The Pitt Building, Trumpington Street, Cambridge, United Kingdom

CAMBRIDGE UNIVERSITY PRESS
The Edinburgh Building, Cambridge CB2 2RU, UK
40 West 20th Street, New York, NY 10011-4211, USA
477 Williamstown Road, Port Melbourne, VIC 3207, Australia
Ruiz de Alarcón 13, 28014 Madrid, Spain
Dock House, The Waterfront, Cape Town 8001, South Africa

http://www.cambridge.org

© Rodney Bruce Hall and Thomas J. Biersteker 2002

First published 2002

Printed in the United Kingdom at the University Press, Cambridge

Typeface Plantin 10/12 pt   *System* LATEX 2$_\varepsilon$ [TB]

A catalogue record for this book is available from the British Library

ISBN 0 521 81861 3 hardback
ISBN 0 521 52337 0 paperback

For our teachers,
Hayward R. Alker and Friedrich V. Kratochwil

but man, proud man,
Drest in a little brief authority,
Most ignorant of what he's most assur'd,
His glassy essence, like an angry ape
Plays such fantastic tricks before high heaven
As make the angels weep
    Shakespeare, *Measure for Measure*, II, ii, 117

Contents

Figures

Tables

Contributors

THOMAS J. BIERSTEKER is Director of the Thomas J. Watson Institute for International Studies and the Henry R. Luce Professor of Transnational Organizations at Brown University, Providence, Rhode Island.

A. CLAIRE CUTLER is Associate Professor of Political Science at the University of Victoria, Victoria, British Columbia, Canada.

CATHLEEN FOGEL is a Doctoral Candidate in Environmental Studies at the University of California, Santa Cruz, California.

RODNEY BRUCE HALL is Assistant Professor of International Relations in the Department of Political Science at the University of Iowa, Iowa City, Iowa.

MARK JUERGENSMEYER is Professor of Sociology and Director of Global and International Studies at the University of California, Santa Barbara, California.

STEPHEN J. KOBRIN is the William H. Wurster Professor of Multinational Management in the Department of Management at the Wharton School of the University of Pennsylvania, Philadelphia, Pennsylvania.

RONNIE D. LIPSCHUTZ is Associate Professor of Politics at the University of California, Santa Cruz, California.

BERNEDETTE MUTHIEN is a Doctoral Candidate at the University of the Western Cape, South Africa, and Program Convener at the African Gender Institute at the University of Cape Town.

LOUIS W. PAULY is Professor of Political Science and Director of the Center for International Studies at the University of Toronto, Toronto, Ontario, Canada.

SASKIA SASSEN is Professor of Sociology at the University of Chicago, Chicago, Illinois.

IAN TAYLOR is Lecturer in the Department of Political and Administrative Studies, University of Botswana, and Research Fellow, Department of Political Science, University of Stellenbosch, South Africa.

PHIL WILLIAMS is Director of the Matthew B. Ridgeway Center for International Security Studies and Professor of Political Science at the University of Pittsburgh, Pittsburgh, Pennsylvania.

Preface

This volume arises out of a workshop entitled "Private Authority and International Order" convened at the Thomas J. Watson Institute for International Studies, Brown University, Providence, Rhode Island, 12–13 February 1999. The workshop was organized by Rodney Bruce Hall in consultation with Thomas Biersteker, while Hall was a postdoctoral research fellow in international relations theory at the Watson Institute. The original objective of the workshop was to explore the devolution of state authority, so central to the work of the late Susan Strange, and to do so across issue areas that included, but transcended, the international political economy. At the end of her life, Strange was studying the sources and consequences of the "retreat of the state" and the devolution of authority and sovereign perquisites of public authority to private actors operating in the international political economy. The workshop was organized to explore these phenomena in the realms of international security and international organization, and to generate analytical categories and methodologies to study it.

During the course of the workshop lively debates ensued regarding the nature and consequences of private authority in the international system, as well as the long-term implications of the emergence of private authority for the future of global governance. Workshop participants were persuaded by the fruitfulness of the discussions and agreed that a collection of essays should be assembled to capture the most salient issues that emerged in the discussions. The purpose of this volume is to examine the emergence of private authority in the international system, and the extent to which this phenomenon is significant in international organization and international security, in addition to international political economy.

Subsequent to the workshop, we found topical and analytical gaps in the research design of the project. The editors subsequently commissioned the essay on transnational corporate networks by Stephen Kobrin, and the piece on the operations of contemporary private mercenary armed forces by Bernadette Muthien and Ian Taylor in an effort to strengthen the research design and comprehensiveness of the resulting volume. The organization of the volume into three subtypes of private authority – "market authority," "moral authority," and "illicit authority" – is a result of discussions of the editors who met at the end of May 2000 at Brown University to draft the concluding chapter summarizing the most theoretically significant findings of the volume.

The workshop discussion constituted two very intense, frenetic, and full days of intellectual activity, and we gratefully acknowledge the debts we have acquired to participants, and to other contributors to the discussions whose work is not collected in the present offering.

The following scholars contributed papers to the original workshop, many of which have subsequently been published elsewhere, and thus are not included in this volume. Special thanks in this context go to Peter Andreas formerly of the Center for International Affairs of Harvard University, Ian Robert Douglas formerly of Bristol University, Craig N. Murphy of Wellesley College, Richard Price of the University of Minnesota, and Peter Uvin of Tufts University. We are also grateful to Abbott Gleason, James Ron, Dietrich Rueschemeyer, Nina Tannenwald, and Robert Wade of the Watson Institute at Brown University, for serving as panel discussants during our workshop and for immeasurably enriching our understanding with their participation in the discussions. Douglas Blum of Providence College played a similar role, and we thank him for contributing to the lively workshop discussions. Special thanks go to Craig Murphy who had originally intended to help edit and contribute to this volume, but was forced to withdraw due to the weight of the burdens attending his time-consuming duties as the current president of the International Studies Association. The volume bears, nonetheless, the always beneficial marks of his prescient commentary and advice. We also wish to extend our thanks to the staff of the Watson Institute for the exceptional logistical support and service that makes a workshop run smoothly, especially Leslie Baxter, Susan Costa, Sheila Fournier, Jean Lawlor, Patricia Monahan, and Nancy Soukup.

Both editors would like to extend special thanks for the financial support of the Board of Overseers of the Watson Institute, who financed the workshop, Hall's research budget, and his postdoctoral fellowship. Hall also acknowledges the financial support of his colleagues in the Department of Political Science at the University of Iowa for providing research assistance in the 1999–2000 academic year during which his contribution to this book took shape. And Hall particularly wishes to extend thanks to his former research assistant, Jonathan Acuff, who cheerfully took on the tedious but exacting tasks of standardizing the notes of each contribution, and of extracting a master bibliography from the collection, in addition to many related tasks, each of which he performed flawlessly.

RODNEY BRUCE HALL AND THOMAS J. BIERSTEKER

Part I

Introduction: theorizing private authority

1   The emergence of private authority in the international system

Rodney Bruce Hall and Thomas J. Biersteker

Traditional notions about authority in the international system derive from Weberian conceptions of the state and of the domain of international politics. There is a presumption within much of international relations theory, consistent with Weber, that the domain of the domestic is fundamentally different from the domain of the international. For Weber, the essence of the state is its ability to claim "the monopoly of the legitimate use of physical force within a given territory."[1] Because of their claims to legitimate authority, most states "can rely on the habitual obedience of their citizens by establishing legal codes in which the threat of physical coercion is only implicit."[2]

According to most traditional accounts, however, this ability to rely upon legitimate authority for habitual obedience is largely absent in the international system. International politics take place in a realm where anarchy allegedly reigns. States act in their own interest and sometimes employ force to achieve their objectives. The absence of a global state has led many observers to deny the very existence of authority, defined as legitimized power, operating within the international arena.[3] States are both the source, and the exclusive location, of legitimate, public authority. This applies to the operations of states both in the realm of domestic affairs, and in the international arena. Until recently, therefore, most explanations of international behavior have concentrated on the coercion employed by states or on the self-interested motivations of individual states, to the virtual exclusion of the recognition by states of the legitimacy and authority of rules and norms operating within the international system.[4] Not only have states been asserted to be the principal actors in the international arena, but they are also considered to be the only legitimate actors in international relations. The authority they exercise over their subjects in the domestic realm conveys to them a legitimacy and agency to interact with other states in the international society of states.

However, during the latter decades of the twentieth century, it became increasingly obvious that there were a growing number of theoretical and empirical challenges to these traditional conceptions about authority and the international system. The concept of anarchy in the international system has been challenged and reconsidered from a variety of different perspectives.[5] Rather than a simple Hobbesian state of nature, there is a growing recognition of degrees of order and institutionalized, patterned interaction within the international system. Forms of governance without the presence of formal state or interstate institutions have been identified in the international arena.[6] International regimes, conventions, norms, and ideational convergence facilitate aspects of global governance. The boundaries between the domestic and the international have also begun to blur, as issues that were once solely under the purview of domestic law and politics, such as environmental standards and labor regulations, are both influenced by, and increasingly affect, international law and politics.[7]

At the same time, a growing number of actors – actors other than the state – appear to have taken on authoritative roles and functions in the international system. Many of these new actors have often been closely associated with the practices associated with the phenomenon of globalization. They include, but are not restricted to, the apparent authority exercised by global market forces, by private market institutions engaged in the setting of international standards, by human rights and environmental non-governmental organizations, by transnational religious movements, and even by mafias and mercenary armies in some instances.

While these new actors are not states, are not state-based, and do not rely exclusively on the actions or explicit support of states in the international arena, they often convey and/or appear to have been accorded some form of legitimate authority. That is, they perform the role of authorship over some important issue or domain. They claim to be, perform as, and are recognized as legitimate by some larger public (that often includes states themselves) as authors of policies, of practices, of rules, and of norms. They set agendas, they establish boundaries or limits for action, they certify, they offer salvation, they guarantee contracts, and they provide order and security. In short, they do many of the things traditionally, and exclusively, associated with the state. They act simultaneously both in the domestic and in the international arenas. What is most significant, however, is that they appear to have been accorded a form of legitimate authority.

While power and authority are closely related, authority is used here to refer to institutionalized forms or expressions of power. What differentiates authority from power is the legitimacy of claims of authority. That is, there are both rights claimed by some superior authority and obligations recognized as legitimate on the part of subordinates or subjects to that authority. Having legitimacy implies that there is some form of normative, uncoerced consent or recognition of authority on the part of the regulated or governed, "the normative belief by an actor that a rule of institution ought to be obeyed."[8] This consent is the product of persuasion, trust, or apathy, rather than coercion. People, institutions, and states recognize the authority of tradition, the authority of expertise, the authority of moral claims, and sometimes even the authority of a "natural" inequality. These forms of authority "import some general claim on human trust into a social relationship in order to introduce an additional pressure for conformity beyond that which the relationship itself can exert . . . if obedience is the counterpart of power, trust is the counterpart of authority."[9]

There is an implicit social relationship between those who claim or exercise authority and those who are subject to, or recognize, authority. The relationship is a public one, to the extent that claims and recognition of claims of authority involve an open, visible process among different agents. As R. B. Friedman observes, "there must be some public way of identifying the persons whose utterances are to be taken as 'authoritative.'"[10] Being public does not, however, imply that a state or public institution must be involved, or be wielding authority, even though they might participate in recognizing it in certain situations. It does, however, imply that the social recognition of authority should be publicly expressed. This opens the possibility for the emergence of private, non-state based, or non-state legitimated authority and the idea that "authority does not necessarily have to be associated with government institutions."[11]

While we proceed from the notion that the sphere of the "private" can be defined in terms of what is *not* in the realm of the "public," this reciprocal, mutually defining relationship between public and private is only a starting point for us. We do not intend to reify this distinction. Rather, we will attempt to transcend the liberal tendency to associate the private sphere "with the individual and freedom of markets and economic exchange, while the public sphere is associated with state authority and legitimate compulsion."[12] We recognize how problematic this dualistic identification (of the private sector with the market and the public sector with legitimate authority) can be in actual practice. Our conception of "private authority" is intended to allow for the possibility that private sector markets, market actors, non-governmental organizations, transnational actors, and other institutions can exercise forms of legitimate authority. We find it telling that at the beginning of the twenty-first century there are so many examples of sites or locations of authority that are neither states, state-based, nor state-created. The state is no longer the sole, or in some instances even the principal, source of authority, in either the domestic arena or in the international system.

There is a recognizable issue domain over which the relationship of authority is typically recognized, although the boundaries of this domain are often imprecise and subject to forms of contestation. Nevertheless, authority entails both a social relationship between author and subject, and a definable domain of action. The consent to authority is socially constructed through a variety of different political and rhetorical practices – ranging from behavioral consent to routines, norms, and public declarations of recognition.

With the advent of globalization, a great deal of attention has been focused on the authoritative role of the market and on market-based actors or institutions. Susan Strange has written that, while realists traditionally have overemphasized political structure, changes in information, communications, and financial technologies have "altered the basic relationship in any political economy – that between authority and market."[13] Strange contends that non-state actors, such as enterprises, transnational social institutions, international organizations, and non-governmental organizations, are increasingly acquiring power in the international political economy, and, to the extent that their power is not challenged, they are implicitly legitimated as authoritative. Ian Hurd has made a similar argument, maintaining "[t]o the extent that a state accepts some international rule or body as legitimate, that rule or body becomes an 'authority.'"[14]

Authority can be exercised not only by intergovernmental institutions like the International Monetary Fund, but also "by creditor banks in negotiating debt rescheduling, or by firms choosing new locations for production and employment."[15] The mobility of capital and the competition among states as potential recipients of global capital have created a situation in which markets increasingly have the "authority to reward or punish according to their judgment of how any government manages its money supply, its fiscal deficit, its foreign debts, or, through deregulation of cozy banking cartels, improves the efficiency of its banks and its local credit markets."[16] States are often complicit in the creation of the market as authoritative. When state leaders proclaim that the "forces of the global market" give them little room for maneuver or independent policy choice, they are participating in the construction of the market as authoritative. They are not only ceding claims of authority to the market; they are creating the authority of the market.

While some suggested that the market itself is becoming authoritative, others have concentrated on the authority of private, market actors like firms, regimes, and institutions. Claire Cutler, Virginia Haufler, and Tony Porter have investigated the nature and functioning of private authority in the development of transnational private regimes.[17] They define a transnational private regime as "an integrated complex of formal and informal institutions that is a source of governance for an economic issue area as a whole."[18] Their work explores other forms of organized interfirm cooperation that are also accorded the trappings of authority.

The essays included in this book review the debates about the nature of private authority in the international political economy. Claire Cutler summarizes and extends the research she and her colleagues have conducted over the past few years in the chapter that immediately follows this one. Stephen Kobrin, Louis Pauly, and Saskia Sassen define the parameters of the debate about the nature of the market as authority in the succeeding three chapters. However, this book takes the discussion of the concept of private authority one step further, beyond the international political economy, by exploring the authoritative dimensions of other private, non-state, and non-market based actors in the contemporary international system. Essays by Mark Juergensmeyer and by Ronnie Lipschutz and Cathleen Fogel consider the moral authority of transnational religious movements and non-governmental organizations. Chapters by Phil Williams and by Bernedette Muthien and Ian Taylor describe the actions of influential private actors such as mafias and mercenary armies, which are surely more problematic locations of authority, but which are actors behaving in an apparently authoritative manner in some contexts. In the pages that follow, we consider the emergence of private authority in the international system in general terms, in markets, as market actors, in transnational movements, and among mafias and mercenaries. This is the first comparative exploration of the notion of private authority in issue areas beyond the realm of international political economy. In addition to forms of "market" authority, the volume considers the "moral" authority exercised by non-governmental organizations or transnational religious movements, and the "illicit" authority of mafias and mercenaries.

We are interested in the extent and the nature of the emergence of private locations of authority in the international system, and their implications for the future of international order and global governance. Many of these issues are related to the identification of the boundaries of state and (interstate) public authority in a contemporary international system characterized by the globalization of neoliberal ideas and practices. Where (and how) are the boundaries of public authority being challenged, and by whom? To what extent are these challenges profound or insignificant? One salient analytical cut into the emerging issue of private authority in the international political economy is the debate about whether the state is complicit in the transfer of its once sovereign prerogatives (such as the setting of exchange rates, the maintenance of a stable currency, or trade management).

Where evidence exists that functions that were once the exclusive, sovereign prerogatives of the state have devolved to the responsibility of private actors, the question of state complicity arises. In such cases, is the state complicit in the devolution of its authority to private actors? Has the state delegated authority, enabled authority, or simply allowed authority to slip away, and for what purposes? Or is the state merely impotent to do much about this devolution of authority? Has the state no mechanism with which to combat the collusion and coordination of firms with interests in minimizing state authority through the development of "private regimes"?[19] If the state is complicit in the transfer of authority to private actors, is it because state managers wish to escape domestic accountability for painful adjustments, which the requirements of macroeconomic policy coordination suggest are indicated and necessary?[20] Is neoliberal globalization reorganizing rather than bypassing states, sometimes with the participation of states in this process?[21] Or is convergence among state policies inadequate to support a claim of "disciplinary neoliberalism" in the international system?[22] Or, to take the question a step further, has the state been captured, perhaps through the "indifference" of domestic polities,[23] by powerful actors within domestic society, whose interests the captured state promulgates as economic, monetary, and trade policy?[24]

These questions have important implications for some of the central debates within contemporary international relations. Disagreement about the dynamic nature of sovereignty – about the evolution (or non-evolution) of sovereignty – illustrates well some of the central disagreements between structuralist and constructivist theorists.[25] Constructivists and poststructuralists tend to view sovereignty as a dynamic social institution the character of which is not only historically and socially contingent, but which is also a constitutive element of the international system.[26] It is worth noting, in this context, that both of the editors of this volume have contributed to these arguments.[27] Committed structuralists, however, continue to see sovereignty as an essentially static concept, even at times an overemphasized concept.[28] Given that the concept of sovereignty involves claims about authority, identity, and territory, the idea that "authority" in the international system could be wielded by private, rather than public, actors has enormous implications for theorizing about the social institution of sovereignty, its salience, its changing meaning, and its endurance. The future of the sovereign state, and the resilience of its status as the principal unit of analysis of the international system, is as much an empirical as a theoretical question. The work of the contributors to this volume significantly enhances our understanding of these empirical issues.

Another issue of longstanding contention in international relations theory concerns the vitality, salience, and legitimacy of the state itself. Within the realm of international political economy, scholars as diverse as Saskia

Sassen, Susan Strange, Matthew Horsman and Andrew Marshall, and Ethan B. Kapstein have argued that neoliberal globalization is a challenge to the legitimacy of states. They have suggested that social (as opposed to civil and political) citizenship is in abeyance; that, while firms may have full citizenship within the nation-state, the withdrawal of social rights from the modern welfare state has resulted in the degradation of individual citizenship.[29] Other scholars, however, have argued that these assertions may be overstated,[30] and that firms seek investment in states with stronger, not weaker state capacities to provide an attractive, stable climate for investment.[31] Still others have argued that the impact of external economic pressures is largely determined domestically, and that the effect of such pressures varies with the strengths or strategies of domestic elites and institutions.[32] Once again, the empirical and conceptual work contained in the chapters that follow add significantly to our understanding of the changing nature of the state as an institution.

Our book is organized around the exploration of three different types of authority identified above: market authority, moral authority, and "illicit" authority. We begin, however, with a review of the most significant work undertaken to date on the concept of private authority. Claire Cutler (chapter 2) summarizes the most significant findings of her collaborative work with Virginia Haufler and Tony Porter, and provides an essay that extends their work on private authority beyond the realm of the international political economy. She encourages us to break from traditional approaches to international relations and to explore the salience of private subnational and transnational socioeconomic forces. She draws upon materialist ontologies in her analysis, and her insistence on the recognition of the historical contingency of social action mirrors recent constructivist scholarship on the historical contingency of sovereignty. Cutler's theoretical insights about the nature of authority suggest that two of its most prominent features are its public nature and its identity as a social construct.[33]

Market authority

In chapters 3, 4, and 5, Stephen Kobrin, Louis Pauly, and Saskia Sassen offer three insightful and interestingly divergent perspectives about the nature of market authority. In some of his previous work, Kobrin has argued that globalization has replaced vertically integrated hierarchical firms functioning within national economies with "a global, postmodern, networked mode of organization where the very concept of geographically based economies may not even be relevant."[34] In chapter 3, Kobrin describes how the "external sovereignty" of state actors has been diminished. He conceptualizes sovereignty as the state's capacity to exercise jurisdictional authority over its own affairs, and explains the reduction in sovereignty by the fusion of markets in high-tech industries brought on by prohibitive research and development costs. This confronts national governments with a tradeoff between efficiency and autonomy, and it appears that most national governments are opting for the former.[35] One possible outcome for state authority, he argues, is an evolution in the meaning of sovereignty that might result in the emergence of a neomedieval system of overlapping "subnational, national, regional, international, and supranational authorities."[36] A logical consequence of Kobrin's analysis is that the emerging authority of private institutional actors in technology and finance leaves states with a choice between *de facto* surrender of sovereign authority, or economic and technical marginalization. This implies a pyrrhic victory for those who "choose" sovereign autonomy.

In chapter 4, Louis Pauly raises important questions about whether globalization radically diminishes state power. Pauly directs our attention to the sources of neoliberal globalization, arguing that we are in the midst of an expansion of a specifically "American" vision of liberalism throughout the world. The power of this vision and the leverage provided by the expansion of the American economy has generated a grand neoliberal discourse on the blessings of markets and market solutions to national and global problems. However, Pauly reminds us that resistance to this project is only now emerging in discernible forms. He advises us to study the origins of the transnational economic order for clues that while "the logic of markets suggests globalism . . . the logic of politics remains deeply marked by distinctly national identities" (p. 78 below). Pauly also takes issue with "the language of inevitability" (p. 80 below) in the writings of both proponents and opponents of globalization, and argues that it is hardly inevitable that transnational capital actors will increasingly, or continue to, exercise a "determinative influence over a widening range of [national] economic . . . policies" (p. 81 below). For Pauly, there is nothing new in the fact that capital mobility exercises constraining effects on national fiscal, monetary, and macroeconomic policies. "[W]hat is new," he argues, "is the widespread perception that all states, all societies, and all social groups are now . . . affected" (p. 81 below).

Pauly finds the state to be complicit in some of the devolution of its authority to the vagaries of the market, because markets have always served as a way to "obscure distributive issues" (p. 82 below) in democratic societies. Markets help to diffuse the blame for negative economic outcomes for the losers in domestic society, and the United States appears to be extending this arrangement to the international arena. There is good evidence to support the argument that the nearly universal global relaxation of capital controls and attendant moves to market-based decision-making procedures in the formulation of national economic policy have generated confusion among those who suffer the consequences of such policies about just who is to blame. Matthew Horsman and Andrew Marshall have consequently concluded that "the nation-state can no longer be held accountable on the very issues which so directly and persistently affect the daily lives of those that it purports to represent, mirror, sponsor and protect. Once the citizen discerns this trend, the exercise of authority by the state is undermined and authority necessarily shifts."[37] Pauly, while recognizing the problem of legitimacy,[38] does not agree that these conclusions necessarily follow. If history is any guide, he argues, national citizens lay responsibility for financial crises and for their resolution squarely at the door of national governments. This suggests that governments failing to respond with any and all means, including capital controls and even economic closure, would not remain long in power. Because markets ultimately require stable political and institutional foundations, Pauly insists that it remains the case that "markets [a]re a tool of [state] policy, not a substitute for it" (p. 86 below). Like hegemonic stability theorists,[39] Pauly argues that the system requires a crisis manager to guarantee the stability of markets, and we can be certain that some state or international institution would always step in to fill this role should a crisis arise. When markets fail, "[a]gents of legitimate public authority" take back "regulatory power, or . . . markets collapse" (p. 87 below).

Saskia Sassen has argued that citizenship for the average person has been devalued by globalization, both in terms of the tangible, social benefits of citizenship, and in terms of the right to affect policy at the polls, or the political benefits of citizenship.[40] If consumptive power and capital are the new criteria for a full franchise, this situation disenfranchises the poor, who lack these assets.[41] Sassen retains her concern with issues of global economic justice in chapter 5, but she also articulates an analytical perspective that differs in important respects from that of both Kobrin and Pauly. She maintains that the global economy simultaneously transcends the authority of the national state, yet is at least partly implanted in national territories and institutions. She suggests new analytical methods for studying the relationship between globalization and state sovereignty. She points out that economic globalization materializes partly in national territory, and she develops a description of the international system in the era of globalization that comprises an entire set of governance mechanisms. Some of these are centered on the state, and some within a burgeoning private legal framework that is developing within national legal frameworks, but threatening to manifest itself independently.

According to Sassen, globalization is partial and particular, rather than universal. It is a system of power that is generating new norms, thus striving to generate legitimations and legalities. While globalization generates a new space for crossborder transactions, Sassen finds it more interesting to focus on how the governance of this crossborder space is moving from national legal frameworks to the interstate system than to concentrate on the volume, speed, density, and novelty of transactions. The new strategic actors in the system, and the new bases of systemic legality, are all private actors: firms, accountancy agencies, and standards setters. Sassen contends that the globalization of liberalism and the "privatization" of economic processes involves the relocation of regulatory functions from public to private authorities.

Sassen agrees with Pauly that the state is at least complicit in this process. She describes how governmental institutional structures are transformed in the process of working with intermediaries. Changes are often manifest initially as minor alterations in national legal codes such as, when in response to currency crises, financial service firms generate changes in state depository systems to normalize these institutions with international standards. From these examples, Sassen illustrates how a focus on the proliferation and consequences of information technologies may obscure the more interesting issues of how private actors employ these technologies in the work of producing and reproducing the organization and *management* of a global production system and a global marketplace.

The emphasis on mobility of capital and the deterritorialization of economic transactions in so much of the globalization literature obscures the extent to which the apparatus of private governance of the global economy is strongly territorialized or geographically "embedded" in global cities and export processing zones. Sassen reminds us that, while economic activity has indeed become spatially dispersed, the high-level management and control functions of these activities are increasingly contained within what Sassen has elsewhere referred to as "global cities,"[42] which she characterizes as strategic sites for the production of these specialized functions to run and coordinate the global economy. Global cities such as Tokyo, New York, London, and Sao Paulo are the sites from which the larger production function is geographically dispersed. It is decision-making by private actors in these financial centers that can lead to changes in the national institutions and laws of states seeking access to their financial products. This is the basis of their private authority.

In redirecting our attention, back to distinctions between the locations of production and the locations of authoritative decision-making, Sassen helps us to understand why crossborder financial flow statistics are not always useful, either for understanding globalization conceptually, or for studying changing authority relations. She indicates that authority relations have changed qualitatively, though some analysts might dispute this claim. Nevertheless, Sassen sees an emerging governance role for private firms and supranational organizations in the international economy. Her analysis raises two fascinating questions, the answers to which might help illuminate the emerging structure of authority relations. The first question is: how is authority constructed and constituted by the discursive justifications of the state in the process of ceding its sovereign perquisites to private and other supranational actors? The second question is how (and whether) the content of state authority has changed.

Pauly's analysis raises an equally important and related question. He contends that, while it is easy to delegate authority to financial markets in relatively good economic times, when downturns come, states, as the only agents of legitimate public authority, will take back regulatory power. They will do so in their own interest, to avoid financial market collapse and attendant social unrest. Pauly appears to argue that private authority is a contingent and fleeting phenomenon, visible only until the next major global economic downturn. However, to the extent that intermediaries between private actors and the state generate institutional changes within states, might these, per Kobrin's analysis, lead to macrostructural changes of the global financial architecture itself? The question then becomes whether the state can ever take back regulatory authority once it has been surrendered.

Moral authority

As Claire Cutler argues in chapter 2, private regimes entail both "formal and informal institutions that [are sources] of governance for an economic issue area as a whole" (p. 29 below). Non-governmental organizations are private actors that can serve important epistemic and legitimation functions in formulating transnational policy decisions, regime rules, principles, and decision-making procedures. Beyond the realm of the international political economy, non-governmental organizations associated with transnational social and religious movements provide other sources of authority that not only legitimate challenges to the existing international order, but also suggest alternative conceptions of the bases for future orders.[43]

In chapter 6, Ronnie Lipschutz and Cathleen Fogel draw upon Lipschutz's earlier work on non-governmental organizations as sources of transnational civil societies[44] to argue that NGOs function as private authorities in the emerging privatization of environmental regulations.

Lipschutz and Fogel illustrate how private organizations serve as sources of "eco-labeling" certification and establish standards of "sustainable forestry" recognized by firms (p. 133, 134 below). Lipschutz and Fogel illustrate the manner in which NGOs, as well as multi- and transnational coalitions and alliances, corporations, and corporate associations have taken upon themselves "normative, functional and instrumental responsibilities."

Provisionally, we can see at least three different ways in which private authority is exercised by NGOs. First, there is the authority of the agenda-setter. One might object that this is "power" granted to, or gleaned by, certain privileged NGOs by virtue of the locations of their headquarters, the placement of their primary officers, and/or their access to governmental decision-makers. However, this objection deals only with the lobbying activities of a minority of NGOs. Further, this objection fails to recognize that the success that some NGOs enjoy in these lobbying efforts is due in no small part to their success in manipulating the choices and policy preferences of average citizens at the grassroots level of organization. If the perspectives and policy prescriptions of some NGOs did not enjoy popular support, and the genuine popular legitimacy by which power becomes authority, no lobbying success would be enjoyed in most states.

The second way in which private authority is exercised by NGOs is by virtue of their authorship, or expertise. Many NGOs provide expert advice as part of their effort to influence policy preferences. To the extent that they are seen as credible providers of technical expertise or information that is difficult to acquire, compile, organize, or analyze, they may enjoy the authority that accompanies authorship. One good illustration of this is Amnesty International's annual human rights report, which amasses, organizes, and analyzes evidence of human rights violations in remote, repressive, difficult-to-reach countries, as well as accessible and ostensibly open and democratic ones.[45]

A third way in which private authority is exercised by NGOs is associated with their emancipatory and normatively progressive social agendas, or their ostensible objectivity or neutrality as non-state actors. This is a form of "moral authority."[46] For the purposes of our discussion, as convenient shorthand, we will refer to the authority that accrues to those with expertise, as well as that which accrues to those who act in an emancipatory or normatively progressive fashion as "moral authority." However, we will also apply the term to movements whose transcendental religious ideas and aspirations may be deemed normatively regressive by those reared in the culture of the secular democratic West, and/or may lead them to acts of religious violence that are normatively repulsive to most people. We do so because those social actors who generate transnational religious movements are advancing a claim of transcendent moral authority as a justification for their actions and designs.

In this context Mark Juergensmeyer in chapter 7 provides an analysis of the resurgence of private violence in the form of terrorism, particularly the private violence of transnational religious networks. Juergensmeyer's contribution builds on his earlier work, which conceptualized the causal significance of religious networks for authority relations in a national context.[47] Here, he examines the issue transnationally. In his earlier work Juegensmeyer identified the rise of religious nationalism as a response to the challenges of the post-Cold War world, and as an assault on Enlightenment ideology and the secular political bases of national identity. Juergensmeyer sees these movements as a response to the weakening political, ideological, and economic bases of the secular national state.[48] Thus there are grounds for theorizing that these movements are an attempt to invoke the private authority of transnational belief systems to fill the ideological and political vacuum created by the delegitimation of these state structures. Ironically, Juergensmeyer sees a resuscitation of the declining ideology of nationalism by its ancient foe, religion, as an unintended consequence of these efforts.

In chapter 7, Juergensmeyer reassesses the increasingly transnational character of religious violence and retheorizes religious terrorism as the public performance of violence, rather than merely as a symbolic act of delegitimation of the secular national state. The state is delegitimated to the extent that very public, destructive, and consequently highly visible acts of terrorism demonstrate the inability of the secular national state to protect the citizenry and, consistent with the requirements of Weberian empirical statehood, to exercise a monopoly over the legitimate use of physical force. Highly visible religious violence is, in this context, relevant to the issue of private authority because it is a very clear public demonstration of a highly "private" capacity for violence, with claims to a higher authority than that of the state.

Juergensmeyer's findings are fascinating, in part because they are based largely upon primary source interviews with participants in acts of terrorism, such as with the men serving sentences for convictions for the 1993 bombing of the World Trade Center in Manhattan. His interviews provide him with evidence that some transnational religious networks employ terrorist violence as public demonstrations of non-state (private, in our lexicon) power. Had both towers of the World Trade Center collapsed onto neighboring buildings rather than imploding, as they did in the 2001 attacks, as many as 200,000 people might have lost their lives. This figure is highly symbolic, as it is roughly the number of people who lost their lives in the US atomic bombings of Hiroshima and Nagasaki in 1945. In the ideology of the attackers, a loss of 200,000 American lives in the World Trade Center would constitute a symbolic retribution, and restore the lost pride of marginalized people by attacking a highly visible symbol of American power. In the anti-Zionist ideology of this particular Islamic terrorist network, the choice of targets was doubly symbolic as they viewed the World Trade Center as a center of a Jewish financial conspiracy victimizing Arabs and adherents to Islam.

There is a strongly visionary stance to these transnational movements. They are predicated on epistemological foundations that are not merely transnational but, in the view of their adherents, transcendent. Ramsey Yousef, who is in prison for conspiring to bring down twelve American airliners (and their passengers and crews) in a single day, is a member of a vaguely transnational group with a distinctly transnational identity, who see themselves as part of a global confrontation of Islam with "the infidel." Juergensmeyer notes similarities in the Japanese cult, Aum Shinrikyo. Osama Bin Laden, who remains highly sought by US authorities, serves as an example of a form of transnational religious terrorist-entrepreneur, funding terrorist operations all over the globe that he does not directly control. Juergensmeyer notes that even religious nationalist groups (with an interest in imposing their regimes on specific territories) have transnational networks of support. Thus transnational religious networks can serve as sources of private authority due to their capacity to incite passionately committed, highly dramatic, and visible (however destructive) social action on the part of globally far-flung subjects of their authority.

Illicit authority

Chapters 8 and 9 explore the nature of private authority associated with forms of organized violence. We refer to the form of private authority exercised by mafias and mercenaries as "illicit" authority because the activities of these groups violate domestic and international legal norms. However, these groups often enjoy a legitimate social recognition to the extent that they step into a power vacuum left by a weak state and provide public goods that the state fails to provide. In chapter 8, Phil Williams explores challenges to state authority by transnational criminal organizations (TCOs) in both the domestic and the international arenas. Several states, not least Russia, appear helpless to collect adequate tax revenue or stem endemic corruption that hinders the provision of social services and the administration of the rule of law. Many functions that one would expect the sovereign state to perform are instead executed by domestic organized criminal associations, who may thereby legitimate themselves in the eyes of a domestic populace as an alternative center of social organization. The inability of other states to discern where the government begins and where the mafia ends in a state the size of Russia has its own implications for the salience of private authority for international order. Evidence that TCOs are developing strategic alliances to avoid domestic and transnationally coordinated efforts to curtail their activities suggests an even greater challenge to state authority, which bears further study.[49] Williams's chapter explores the challenge of TCOs to state authority in this context.

In chapter 10, Bernedette Muthien and Ian Taylor provide an analysis of the emergence of corporate mercenaries[50] and "private" policing, and consider the implications of these phenomena for shifting authority relations and the decline of state control over the means of violence.[51] As private actors acquire the resources and the motives to contract for security services at home and abroad, for both defensive and offensive purposes, they acquire the capacity to back "private authority" with physical force. The implications of such developments for the Westphalian conception of state sovereignty are sobering.

Phil Williams's work on TCOs intersects with the work of both Kobrin and Sassen in highly interesting and germane areas. His work is oriented toward explaining the transnationalization of criminal organizations, and he studies the covert side of social and organizational phenomena that are more overtly evident in Kobrin's work. Williams provides us with a study of illicit, network-based, transnational criminal enterprises, in contrast to Kobrin's analysis of the global networks of wholly licit, transnational corporate and financial enterprises (TNCs). Williams suggests that TCOs share many characteristics and emulate many of the "business practices" of their more legitimate TNC counterparts. The aim of TCOs is profit, the same as TNCs, but their means is crime. They diversify their enterprises and their assets, just like TNC conglomerates. Colombian drug cartels have, for example, diversified from cocaine into heroin, and Williams suggests that it becomes very easy to speak of the Cali drug cartel as the world's most successful transnational firm to the extent that their profit margins and aggregate profits engender the title. Transnational criminal organizations are engaged in the formation of strategic alliances in ways that appear to emulate the recent strategies of TNCs.

Like Saskia Sassen, Williams emphasizes the role played by "global cities," which he portrays as breeding grounds for criminal cosmopolitanism. Global cities are often embarkation points for immigrant communities drawn to them by many of the negative, as well as positive, externalities associated with the globalization process. These immigrant communities, he suggests, are natural environments for the birth of illegal enterprises, since they are often composed of marginalized people who develop self-support mechanisms within their culturally isolated communities by illicit means, if licit means are unavailable. Immigrant and diaspora communities provide opportunities for both recruitment and cover for these illicit activities. He reminds us that TCOs rely upon the capacity of immigrant and diaspora communities to launder their profits through a thriving global financial services system that is headquartered, as Sassen reminds us, in global cities.[52] Thus, though TCOs threaten the state capacities of certain countries, they scarcely constitute a threat to the international financial system. Moreover, Williams suggests that the relationships between TCOs and states are not uniformly adversarial. He provides us with a taxonomy of the attitudes of states toward TCOs, which appear to range from hostility and opposition, to tacit acceptance and even active collusion. His taxonomy and analysis of the relationships between TCOs and those states on the more permissive end of this spectrum has important implications for the nature of the emerging private authority of TCOs.

In their analysis of the resurgence of private political violence, Bernedette Muthien and Ian Taylor examine the reappearance of mercenaries and private armies. They have become increasingly conspicuous in Africa, where problems of state capacity and state legitimacy have often been most severe in the late twentieth century. Their account of the evident willingness of transnational market actors to back their designs with private military force potentially provides us with a frightening glimpse of a future characterized by the creeping substitution of the authority of the sovereign state with that of private actors. This most graphic of illustrations of the nascent emergence of private authority in security affairs underscores the importance of examining the emergence of private authority in international issue areas beyond the realm (however important) of international political economy.

In the concluding chapter of this volume, chapter 11, we summarize many of the most theoretically salient findings of our contributors. We examine the sources and bases of market, moral, and illicit authority, and we also generate a subtypology of each of the three major forms of private authority discovered in the work of our contributors. We attempt to provide preliminary responses to several of the questions raised in this introductory essay, and conclude with discussions of the conditions under which market authority, moral authority, and illicit authority might be reversed, and the implications for future research.

NOTES

1 Max Weber, "Politics as a Vocation," in H. H. Gerth and C. Wright Mills (eds.), *From Max Weber: Essays in Sociology* (London: Routledge & Kegan Paul, 1948), pp. 77–78.
2 Michael Joseph Smith, *Realist Thought from Weber to Kissinger* (Baton Rouge and London: Louisiana State University Press, 1986), p. 25.
3 Helen Milner, "The Assumption of Anarchy in International Relations: A Critique," *Review of International Studies*, 17 (1) (1991), 67–85.
4 Ian Hurd, "Legitimacy and Authority in International Politics," *International Organization*, 53 (2) (Spring 1999), 379–408.
5 Nicholas Onuf and Frank F. Clink, "Anarchy, Authority, and Rule," *International Studies Quarterly*, 33 (2) (1989), 149–73; Milner, "Assumption of Anarchy"; and Michael E. Brown, Sean Lynn-Jones, and Steven E. Miller, *The Perils of Anarchy: Contemporary Realism and International Security* (Cambridge, Mass.: MIT Press, 1995).
6 Friedrich Kratochwil, *Rules, Norms, and Decisions: On the Conditions of Practical and Legal Reasoning in International Relations and Domestic Affairs* (Cambridge: Cambridge University Press, 1989), and James N. Rosenau and Ernst-Otto Czempiel (eds.), *Governance Without Government: Order and Change in World Politics* (Cambridge: Cambridge University Press, 1992).
7 Robert Keohane and Joseph Nye, *Power and Interdependence* (Boston: Little Brown, 1977).
8 Hurd, "Legitimacy and Authority," 381.
9 Leonard Krieger, "The Idea of Authority in the West," *American Historical Review*, 82 (2) (April 1977), 259.
10 R. B. Friedman, "On the Concept of Authority in Political Philosophy," in Joseph Raz (ed.), *Authority* (Washington Square, N.Y.: New York University Press and Oxford: Basil Blackwell, 1990), p. 64.
11 Ibid.
12 A. Claire Cutler, "Locating 'Authority' in the Global Political Economy," *International Studies Quarterly*, 43 (1) (March 1999), 64.
13 Susan Strange, "Territory, State, Authority, and Economy: A New Realist Ontology of Global Political Economy," in Robert W. Cox (ed.), *The New Realisms: Perspectives on Multilateralism and World Order* (Tokyo: United Nations University Press, 1997), p. 9.
14 Hurd, "Legitimacy and Authority," 381.
15 Strange, "Territory, State, Authority, and Economy," p. 4.
16 Ibid., p. 11.
17 A. Claire Cutler, Virginia Haufler, and Tony Porter (eds.), *Private Authority in International Affairs* (Albany, N.Y.: SUNY Press, 1999).
18 Cutler, Haufler, and Porter, "Private Authority and International Affairs," in Cutler, Haufler, and Porter, *Private Authority and International Affairs*, p. 13.
19 Cutler, "Locating 'Authority' in the Global Political Economy," 62.
20 Louis W. Pauly, *Who Elected the Bankers? Surveillance and Control in the World Economy* (Ithaca, N.Y.: Cornell University Press, 1997).
21 Arguments to this effect stem from analysts as diverse as the Marxists to more mainstream classical and liberal political economists. See, for example,

Leo Panitch, "Rethinking the Role of the State in an Era of Globalization," in James H. Mittelman (ed.), *Globalization: Critical Reflections. International Political Economy Yearbook*, vol. 9 (Boulder, Colo.: Lynne Rienner, 1996), pp. 83–113; Thomas M. Callaghy, "Globalization and Marginalization: Debt and the International Underclass," *Current History*, 26 (613) (November 1997), 392–96; and Pauly, *Who Elected the Bankers?*

22 Louis W. Pauly and Simon Reich, "National Structures and Multinational Corporate Behavior: Enduring Differences in the Age of Globalization," *International Organization*, 51 (1) (1997), 1–30.

23 Stephen Gill, "Globalization, Democratization, and the Politics of Indifference," in Mittelman, *Globalization*, pp. 205–28.

24 Robert Wade and Frank Veneroso, "The Asian Crisis: The High Debt Model Versus the Wall Street–Treasury–IMF Complex," *New Left Review*, 228 (March/April 1998), 3–24.

25 The salience of modern Westphalian sovereignty to the structure and to the patterns and practices of international politics within the contemporary international system go back at least as far as John Ruggie's early critique of Kenneth Waltz. See John Gerard Ruggie, "Continuity and Transformation in the World Polity: Toward a Neorealist Synthesis," *World Politics*, 35 (2) (January 1983), 261–85.

26 See Cynthia Weber, *Simulating Sovereignty: Intervention, the State and Symbolic Exchange* (Cambridge: Cambridge University Press, 1995); Jens Bartleson, *A Genealogy of Sovereignty* (Cambridge: Cambridge University Press, 1995); Thomas J. Biersteker and Cynthia Weber (eds.), *State Sovereignty as Social Construct* (Cambridge: Cambridge University Press, 1996); and Rodney Bruce Hall, *National Collective Identity: Social Constructs and International Systems* (New York: Columbia University Press, 1999).

27 See Biersteker and Weber, *State Sovereignty*, and Hall, *National Collective Identity*.

28 Note especially Krasner's comparatively lonely, but unrepentantly structuralist argument: Stephen D. Krasner, *Sovereignty: Organized Hypocrisy* (Princeton, N.J.: Princeton University Press, 1999).

29 See, for example, Louis W. Pauly, "Capital Mobility, State Autonomy, and Political Legitimacy," *Journal of International Affairs*, 48 (2) (Winter 1995), 369–88; Susan Strange, *The Retreat of the State: The Diffusion of Power in the World Economy* (Cambridge: Cambridge University Press, 1996); Saskia Sassen, *Losing Control? Sovereignty in an Age of Globalization*, 1995 Columbia University Leonard Hastings Schoff Memorial Lectures (New York: Columbia University Press, 1996), pp. 31–58; Mathew Horsman and Andrew Marshall, *After the Nation-State: Citizens, Tribalism and the New World Disorder* (London: Harper-Collins, 1994); Ethan B. Kapstein, "Workers and the World Economy," *Foreign Affairs*, 75 (3) (May/June 1996), 16–37.

30 See Robert Wade, "Globalization and Its Limits: Reports of the Death of the National Economy Are Greatly Exaggerated," in S. Berger and R. Dore (eds.), *National Diversity and Global Capitalism* (Ithaca, N.Y.: Cornell University Press, 1996), pp. 60–88.

31 Peter Evans, "The Eclipse of the State? Reflections on Stateness in an Era of Globalization," *World Politics*, 50 (1) (1997), 62–87.

32 Linda Weiss, *The Myth of the Powerless State* (Ithaca, N.Y.: Cornell University Press, 1998); Stephan Haggard and Sylvia Maxfield, "The Political Economy of Financial Internationalization in the Developing World," *International Organization*, 50 (1) (1996), 35–68; and Geoffrey Garrett, "Global Markets and National Politics: Collision Course or Virtuous Circle?," *International Organization*, 52 (4) (Autumn 1998), 787–824.

33 Cutler, "Locating 'Authority' in the Global Political Economy," 62–63.

34 Stephen J. Kobrin, "The Architecture of Globalization: State Sovereignty in a Networked Global Economy," in John Dunning (ed.), *Governments, Globalization and International Business* (Oxford and New York: Oxford University Press, 1997), p. 154.

35 For a penetrating analysis of the social tensions created by this tradeoff, see Dani Rodrik, *Has Globalization Gone Too Far?* (Washington, D.C.: Institute for International Economics, 1997).

36 Kobrin, "Architecture of Globalization," p. 162.

37 Horsman and Marshall, *After the Nation-State*, p. 217.

38 See Pauly, "Capital Mobility, State Autonomy, and Political Legitimacy."

39 See, for example, Charles Kindleberger, *The World in Depression, 1929–1939* (Berkeley: University of California Press, 1986), and Timothy J. McKeown, "Hegemonic Stability Theory and Nineteenth-Century Tariff Levels in Europe," *International Organization*, 37 (1) (Winter 1983), 73–91.

40 See Sassen, *Losing Control?*, pp. 36–39. Following T. H. Marshall's notion of the "social citizenship" of the welfare state, Sassen argues that, unlike civil and political citizenship, social citizenship is under pressure by globalization (ibid., p. 37). We argue that political citizenship may be under pressure as well. See T. H. Marshall, *The Right to Welfare and Other Essays* (New York: Free Press, 1981).

41 Horsman and Marshall, *After the Nation-State*, p. 261.

42 See especially Saskia Sassen, *The Global City: New York, London, Tokyo* (Princeton, N.J.: Princeton University Press, 2001 [1991]), and Sassen, "Global Financial Centers," *Foreign Affairs*, 78 (1) (January/February 1999), 75–87.

43 For treatments of widely diverse transnational social movements, see Benjamin Barber, *Jihad vs. McWorld: How Globalism and Tribalism Are Reshaping the World* (New York: Ballantine Books, 1995); Arjun Appadurai, *Modernity at Large: Cultural Dimensions of Globalization* (Minneapolis and London: University of Minnesota Press, 1996); Mark Juergensmeyer, *The New Cold War? Religious Nationalism Confronts the Secular State* (Berkeley: University of California Press, 1993); Craig N. Murphy, "Seeing Women, Recognizing Gender, Recasting International Relations," *International Organization*, 50 (3) (Summer 1996), 513–38.

44 See especially Ronnie D. Lipschutz, "Reconstructing World Politics: The Emergence of Global Civil Society," *Millennium: Journal of International Studies*, 21 (3) (Winter 1992), 389–420, and Lipschutz with Judith Mayer, *Global Civil Society and Global Environmental Governance* (Albany, N.Y.: SUNY Press, 1996).

45 See, for example, Peter Willetts (ed.), *"The Conscience of the World": The Influence of Non-Governmental Organizations in the UN System* (Washington, D.C.: Brookings Institution, 1996).

46 Rodney Bruce Hall, "Moral Authority as a Power Resource," *International Organization*, 51 (4) (Autumn 1997), 591–622.

47 See Juergensmeyer, *The New Cold War?*

48 Mark Juergensmeyer, "The Worldwide Rise of Religious Nationalism," *Journal of International Affairs*, 50 (1) (Summer 1996), 1–20.

49 Phil Williams, "Transnational Criminal Organizations: Strategic Alliances," *Washington Quarterly*, 18 (Winter 1995), 57–72, and Williams, "Transnational Criminal Organizations and International Security," *Survival*, 36 (Spring 1994), 96–113.

50 See, for example, Simon Sheppard, "Foot Soldiers of the New World Order: The Rise of the Corporate Military," *New Left Review*, 228 (March/April 1998), 128–38.

51 Janice E. Thomson, *Mercenaries, Pirates and Sovereigns* (Princeton, N.J.: Princeton University Press, 1996).

52 Note, for example, the recent evidence of penetration of Russian TCOs' money laundering activities into one of the largest, best-capitalized transnational banks headquartered in New York.

2 Private international regimes and interfirm cooperation

A. Claire Cutler

This chapter focuses on the development of private international regimes as institutionalized manifestations of private authority. Private international regimes may, of course, emerge in a number of issue areas and involve a multiplicity of non-state actors, as many of the chapters in this book illustrate. However, the focus here is specifically on the emergence of such regimes through the cooperation of firms, business and industry associations, and other corporate actors. This focus is significant because contemporary developments in domestic and global political economies are enhancing the authority of private institutions, actors, and processes. In many states, the privatization of government activities, the deregulation of industries and sectors, increased reliance on market mechanisms in general, and the delegation of regulatory authority to private business associations and agencies are expanding the opportunities for the emergence of private and self-regulatory regimes. Indeed, "[p]rivate actors are increasingly engaged in authoritative decision-making that was previously the prerogative of sovereign states."[1] Corporations, "singly and jointly, construct a rich variety of institutional arrangements that structure their behavior. Through these arrangements they can deploy a form of *private authority* whose effects are important for understanding not just the behavior of firms, but also for analyzing the state and its policies."[2]

The paper is less concerned with the nature of the relationship between private international regimes and states, although this is clearly a challenging and pressing concern which is addressed more generally in the concluding chapter. Rather, the main concern is to frame or to distill *private international regimes* as instances of global governance relations or of private international authority. This raises three sets of considerations: analytical, theoretical, and normative. The first set relates to the analytical task of identifying private international regimes as a subset of the more general category of private international authority. Here I am concerned with establishing the indices and scope of private international authority, and clearly assume working definitions of both private international authority and private international regimes. I am also concerned with developing some sort of understanding of the incidence of private international regimes and their nature and general character.

The second and third sets of concerns relate to the theoretical and normative dimensions of private international regimes. They raise the task of conceptualizing private international regimes as authoritative institutions and as manifestations of legitimate authority relations. This is, perhaps, the most troubling exercise. There are major obstacles to theorizing about private international authority in general, and private international regimes in particular.[3] Moreover, the normative implications of private authority are profoundly disturbing. Very basically, the democratic, formalistic, and legalistic associations of authority with states and the public sphere obscure the growing authority of private institutions, actors, and processes. As a consequence, efforts to hold private institutions accountable in any democratic way are bound to flounder, for that which goes unrecognized is difficult to regulate. Indeed, the move of private authority to obscurity is at root an ideological move inspired by the "liberal art of separation"[4] that serves to isolate and insulate increasing aspects of existence from public scrutiny and review. The legally formalistic associations of authority with the state function ideologically by depicting the world not as it *is*, but as it *ought* to be.[5] Legal formalism identifies state/public authority as the only legitimate authority, rendering non-state/private authority a theoretical and empirical impossibility. As an ontological *non sequitur*, private authority is thus not part of the discourse of responsible or accountable governance.

An adequate understanding of these obstacles and implications is absolutely crucial to evaluating the possibility of reversing the trend toward privatized authority, which is addressed in the conclusion to this chapter. Indeed, this chapter argues that overcoming these theoretical obstacles requires a critical examination of the conventional wisdom in the fields of both domestic and international political and legal theories. It requires moving beyond political theory and international theory as "problem-solving" theories to embrace them as "critical" theories in the manner contemplated by Robert Cox. Problem-solving theory "takes the world as it finds it, with the prevailing social and power relationships and the institutions into which they are organized, as a given framework for action." It claims to be value-free, but Cox argues that it is in fact deeply ideological because it takes the existing order as a given and in so doing serves the sectional and class interests that are satisfied with that order. In contrast, critical theory "stands apart from the prevailing order of the world and asks how that order came about." It reasons historically and dialectically and is concerned "not just with the past but with a continuing process of historical change."[6] Understanding the historical and dialectical manner in which private international authority and private international regimes emerge and develop provides important insight into what appear to be rather contradictory trends. As a number of chapters in this volume illustrate, forces of globalization that appear to be linked to the emergence and operation of private international authority serve, in some cases, to deterritorialize or delocalize authority relations, but in other cases to territorialize and localize authority.[7] The deterritorializing tendency of market authority, for example, is emphasized in the chapters by Saskia Sassen and Stephen Kobrin. In contrast, other incidences of market authority remain firmly embedded in the territorial state, as the chapter by Louis Pauly suggests. Critical theory assists in understanding variations over time in different manifestations of private international authority.

In addition, critical theory examines the material, institutional, and ideational dimensions of private international authority, and provides understanding of the complex nature of its operation. The highly institutionalized private international regimes that form the focus of this chapter are thus to be differentiated from the more informal and even diffuse moral authority of NGOs, as discussed in the chapter by Ronnie Lipschutz and Cathleen Fogel, or indeed that exercised by religious terrorists, addressed in Mark Juergensmeyer's contribution.

Finally, critical theory is inspired by emancipatory goals – principal objectives being the clarification of alternate world orders and the promotion of change in social relations.[8] This alerts us to the inescapably normative dimension of private international authority, which is highlighted most clearly in the Lipschutz and Fogel chapter. The normative implications of illicit private international authority, addressed in the chapters by Phil Williams and Bernadette Muthien and Ian Taylor, are significant. Illicit private authority provides a profound challenge to democratic and formalistic theorizations of authority.

This chapter seeks to develop our understanding of private international authority by situating *private international regimes* as the most institutionally developed form or instance of private international authority. The discussion will first define private international regimes, identify significant empirical examples, and offer a few insights into the reasons for their proliferation. It will then turn to explore the theoretical and normative dimensions of private international regimes, highlighting the challenge that they and other forms of private international authority pose for conventional understandings of authority.

Private international regimes and private international authority

There is a prior interest which raises theoretical and analytical issues that must be addressed before defining private international regimes. This concerns whether it makes sense conceptually and theoretically to adopt the regime framework developed for the analysis of interstate regimes for the study of non-state regimes. This is a troubling question that raises some of the central challenges to the theorization of private authority that are considered in the next section. However, a brief review of the nature and evolution of the analytical foundations of the concept of "international regime" illustrates that there are no obvious barriers to its adoption in the study of non-state authority.[9]

Paradoxically, regime analysis emerged as an analytical attempt to address inadequacies in the then conventional approaches to international organization, including their state-centricity and excessive legalism and formalism. Indeed, regimes came to form a central analytical focus for the study of international organization.[10] Regimes also became part of the conceptual framework for the developing field of international political economy. There analysts such as Stephen Krasner, Robert Keohane, Mark Zacher, Oran Young, and others adopted the regime concept as a useful corrective to studies that neglected the role of non-state actors in international relations.[11] Some, such as Robert Keohane and Mark Zacher, embraced the concept of regime robustly, and the next decade and more witnessed a proliferation of regimes studies.[12] While others, such as Susan Strange, though critical of the way in which the state had "colonized" the study of international relations, remained deeply skeptical about the political role of regime analysis,[13] the analytical framework of regimes came to form a central place in international relations scholarship, at least in North America. As the field developed, so too did the study of regimes. A number of European scholars embraced the concept and contributed to the proliferation of regime studies and of valuable cooperative theoretical and empirical analyses.[14] However, the promise of broadening the analytical net to include non-state actors, particularly of the corporate kind, was not fulfilled.[15] Regime analysis became progressively more state-centric in focus as the role of corporations was filtered through the lens of state power.[16] Regime analysis, like the study of international organization and international political economy, was "captured" by a neorealist synthesis of realism and neoliberalism, becoming about as state-centric as neorealism.[17] As Miles Kahler notes, neoliberals had challenged the excessive state-centricity of realism. However, "[n]eoliberalism was redefined away from complex interdependence toward a state-centric version more compatible with realism."[18]

In addition, the analytical focus on regimes became more formalistic, at least in the work of some leading regime theorists. Robert Keohane defined international regimes as "institutions with explicit rules, agreed upon by governments, that pertain to particular sets of issues in international relations."[19] The focus on states, explicit rules, and compliance drew regime theory closer to its roots in formalistic and legalistic international law, factoring out attention to informal and *ad hoc* normative arrangements. As Andrew Hurrell notes, the "apparently growing stress on explicit, persistent, and connected sets of rules brings regime theory and international law much closer together."[20] The focus on explicit rules and institutional structures thus detracted from the analytical bite of informal practices and loosely institutionalized norms and practices.[21]

The association of regimes with states, state power, and formal institutions and rule structures might appear to be overwhelming, and is evident in the general currency of certain theories. Hegemonic stability theory, for example, associates international regimes with the provision of public goods, which only governments/states are in the general habit of providing, and with institutionalized state responses to market imperfections and failures.[22] However, while the concept of regime is interpreted predominantly in state-centric and formalistic terms, it need not be. "[S]ets of implicit or explicit principles, norms, rules, and decision-making procedures around which actors' expectations converge in a given area of international relations" can logically extend to the activities of business associations, firms, cartels, and the like, whether formalized in explicit rules and institutions or not.[23] Indeed, one might begin by noting that authority has both analytical and normative dimensions, and one might draw upon the insights of regime analysis in developing the analysis of these dimensions.[24] This section addresses the "analytical element of how authority is structured, how it operates, and how it is recognized and distinguished from other forms of influence," while the next deals with the normative aspects "of how authority is justified, who or what gives legitimacy, and why the authority of someone is accepted as such."[25] When one differentiates between *cooperation* and *authority*, there is evidence to suggest that corporations often cooperate, but without a sense of obligation or duty.[26] "Authority requires a basis in trust rather than calculation of immediate benefit, and therefore cooperation must involve the development of habits, norms, rules, and shared expectations – cooperation must be institutionalized."[27] A critical factor is that participants regard the rules and practices to be obligatory. The obligatory element is in turn related to acceptance of the legitimacy of an authority, as well as a general sense of the efficacy of authority. Legitimacy involves the respect accorded "an authority," such as a specialist, a scholar, or an expert whose authority derives from specialized knowledge and practices that render such knowledge acceptable, and appropriate, as authoritative. It also involves the respect accorded those "in authority," such as political leaders, generals, or representatives who possess an explicit or implicit grant of authority from the state.[28] Efficacy involves general compliance with rules and practices.[29]

Moreover, to be authoritative, cooperation must be institutionalized. However, the degree of institutionalization is highly variable. Empirical studies reveal a high degree of variation in the scope and depth of institutionalization of private regulatory arrangements. Six general types of cooperative arrangements may be identified as authoritative arrangements, both in terms of their acceptance as legitimate by the participants and in terms of the latter's general compliance with their precepts. They are organized in terms of increasing degrees of institutionalization, suggesting that interfirm cooperation moves in a linear fashion from low to high degrees of institutionalization. However, this is not necessarily the case. Nor is there necessarily a relationship between the degree of institutionalization and the strength of the cooperative arrangements. The types of cooperative arrangements may be delineated as follows:

1. *Informal industry norms and practices*: This is the loosest form of interfirm cooperation, which often evolves through repeated practices in industries and firms that acquire authority over time. The tacit understanding that emerged in the 1960s in the Eurobond market restricting issuers to blue-chip companies or to governments is one such example. There are other examples in the emergence of international commercial law.

2. *Coordination service firms*: These are firms that operate to coordinate the behaviour of other firms, like multinational law, accounting, management, and insurance firms, stock exchanges, debt-rating firms, and financial clearinghouses. These firms often operate on the basis of rules and practices established by business associations, which are discussed below.

3. *Production alliances, subcontractor relationships, and complementary activities*: Strategic partnerships, joint ventures, and networks are identified as three types of production alliances. They involve arrangements between firms that would otherwise compete with each other, but that decide to cooperate in the joint production of goods or services. Networks comprise extensive and complex subcontractor relationships among firms. These are increasingly common today. A good example is the

way in which Nike Inc. is organized on the basis of subcontracted facilities.

4. *Cartels*: Cartels are formal and informal arrangements between producers to coordinate their output and prices. Cartels are certainly not novel arrangements and bear likeness to production alliances. However, production alliances are regarded as generally legitimate, while cartels are censured by antitrust legislation. The maritime transport industry has long been regulated by cartels.

5. *Business associations*: Corporations often cooperate through the formation of business and industry associations, which today often operate transnationally. Such organizations may operate as self-regulatory associations, developing norms and procedures that bind their members. They also may operate as representative associations, acting on behalf of members in their dealings with governments and like. Business associations, like the International Chamber of Commerce, are an important source of norms and practices, many of which may evolve into rules of customary international law.

6. *Private international regimes*: A private international regime is defined as "an integrated complex of formal and informal institutions that is a source of governance for an economic issue area as a whole."[30]

Private international regimes differ from the other types of private corporate authority identified above by the pervasiveness and breadth of their activities. They may also incorporate other types of private authority. Private international regimes may be created by "negotiation and interaction among firms within a particular industry sector or issue area, and generally incorporate a number of business associations, both national and international. They formulate rules and procedures for dealing with conflicts among participants, and between participants and their customers."[31]

Private international regimes are thus important forms of interfirm cooperation, embodying the most extensive institutionalization of rules and procedures governing regime members and, in some instances, nonmembers as well. "The interfirm cooperation represented in international regimes operates on multiple levels in complex ways, and often involves extensive interaction and cooperation with the state. Indeed, one of the important analytical goals in studying private international regimes is to understand the degree to which the private actors in a regime are independent of the public ones."[32] In addition, hierarchical integration in particular industries may be a significant source of private authority and could be used as a measure of institutionalization itself. For example, informal industry practices may be developed by coordination service firms and later be adopted by industry and trade associations. They may also be adopted by and enforced by states in response to the representations of self-regulatory business organizations. Clearly, this sort of linear progression is not characteristic of all sectors, industries, or issue areas, and an important analytical concern is identifying variations in the integration and institutionalization of private authority. A related concern involves deciding when looser forms of interfirm cooperation may be regarded as having crystallized into a private international regime.[33]

The concept of private international regime has been fruitfully used to analyze the regulation of the internet, the international minerals industry, industrial production standards setting, the regulation of intellectual property, the insurance industry, and the maritime transport industry.[34] In addition, while not explicitly identified as private international regimes, issue areas including the early cotton industry, cartelized industries in the period between the two world wars, and debt-rating industries might also constitute private international regimes. These studies illustrate that many private regimes rely on informal norms and practices. Moreover, they suggest that, "because there is no objective criterion that can establish a required threshold at which private institutions are comprehensive enough to be considered regimes, their existence is often difficult to establish irrefutably."[35]

A good empirical example of a private international regime is the transnational merchant law regime.[36] Known variously as the modern law merchant regime, transnational commercial law, and the law of private international trade, the regime governs international commercial relations of a private nature.[37] It has been in existence for over a millennium, although it has taken very different institutional forms over its history. The medieval law merchant order was a private, self-regulatory regime that operated outside local legal systems and political economies. Medieval merchants devised laws through private means and enforced them in private merchant courts that were independent of local legal systems. With the emergence of states, first in their mercantilist and later in their capitalist formations, the merchant order disappeared as an autonomous legal system as its laws and courts were incorporated into national legal and judicial systems. There international commercial relations became juridified, as states sought to systematize and rationalize international commercial relations.[38] Today, in a curious twist of Weberian state authority, the juridification of international commercial relations is intensifying, but at the hands of predominantly non-state, corporate actors through their exercises of private authority. The modern law merchant regime forms a highly institutionalized order in which both public and private authorities interact to create and enforce international commercial laws.[39]

Significantly, merchant autonomy over law creation and over international commercial arbitration (the latter is also addressed in the Sassen paper) is creating a highly privatized legal order that delocalizes and deterritorializes commercial transactions and law. However, states remain intimately involved in the enforcement of international commercial agreements, serving to relocalize and reterritorialize the transactions at the point of dispute settlement. This curious mix of private and public authority, which operates to delocalize/deterritorialize and relocalize/reterritorialize international commercial relations, provides an excellent illustration of the dialectical operation of a private international regime.

Other examples of private international regimes may be found in the dispute settlement orders emerging under the General Agreement on Tariffs and Trade/World Trade Organization, the Canada–US Free Trade Agreement, and the North American Free Trade Agreement.[40] In each case, privatized international commercial arbitration has replaced the adjudication of international commercial disputes in national courts of law. The operation of these regimes centers around multinational law firms which, as "merchants of norms," exercise profound moral authority, in addition to market authority through their monopoly of privatized dispute settlement processes.[41] The international commercial arbitration world operates like a private club, the entry to which is limited to those schooled in Western legal science and which perpetuates a normative regulatory order that privileges neoliberal market discipline. Similar privatized regimes are emerging in the fields of taxation and accounting, suggesting that the expansion of privatized authority is an ongoing process.[42]

In seeking to explain the emergence of private international regimes, analysts have focused on market-based explanations, drawing upon efficiency incentives, transaction cost analysis, and public goods theory.[43] For example, the emergence of the law merchant order is explained by some as comprising institutional responses to the transaction and information costs and insecurity experienced by traders engaging in trade over wide geographical regions.[44] Other, power-based explanations of the emergence of private international regimes focus on the regulatory influence of firms dominating markets and issue areas.[45] More historical explanations focus on the significance of broader trends like globalization, rapid technological change, and the expansion of markets in enhancing the influence of corporate actors.[46]

These examples indicate that interfirm cooperation is increasingly taking on the "mantle of authority"[47] as the contraction of government authority and the expansion of private regulatory authority are generally accepted by societies. The apparent expansion of private international regimes reflects a changing balance between public and private authority with broader implications of a normative and ideological nature, to which I will now turn.

Theorizing private international regimes

In positing that interfirm cooperation is increasingly "taking on the mantle of authority," I am arguing that firms are basically functioning like governments. This raises both theoretical and normative concerns. First, it raises major issues for democratic and representative theories of governance. Indeed, as mentioned at the outset, there are significant theoretical obstacles to conceptualizing private authority, which clearly apply to private international regimes as well. Liberal theories of the state and of international law associate political authority with the public realm of government.[48] Only public authorities are entitled or empowered to prescribe behavior for others because only public authorities are accountable through political institutions. Private entities, such as corporations or business associations, are not entitled to act authoritatively for the public, because they are not authorized by society and are thus not subject to mechanisms of political accountability. Indeed, their accountability (legally and financially) is to their private members. Thus, under democratic theory, only elected representatives and their delegates may function authoritatively in prescribing and proscribing behavior.

Similarly, under liberal theories of international law, the only legitimate "subjects" of the law are states and their designated representatives. This means that only states and their designates may initiate claims under international law and be the subject of legal rights and duties.[49] Corporate liability exists only as a derivative of state liability under the legal doctrine of state responsibility.[50] Corporate personality is thus filtered through the persona of the state. However, this poses major problems of ensuring accountability for corporate actions, a concern of growing significance in the areas of environmental damage and injury to consumers from faulty or defective products sold in countries with inadequate consumer protection laws. States are often unwilling to assume responsibility for the actions of corporations, particularly if the latter can disclaim liability for the actions of subsidiaries doing business abroad. Moreover, it is increasingly more difficult to determine corporate nationality and to identify the appropriate legal jurisdiction to which to attribute responsibility in cases of transnational corporations the operations, holdings, and directorships of which are widely dispersed. These factors are effectively rendering transnational corporations and their actions "invisible" under international law.[51]

The attribution of public functions to private actors directly challenges democratic and liberal theories of governance and law. Indeed, to impute political authority and accountability to corporate action "would be to turn representative democracy on its head."[52] It threatens to undo "the liberal art of separation" that underlies separations between state and civil society; public and private; government and market; politics and economics.[53] However, the normative statement that only duly elected and representative governments "ought" to be capable of exercising political authority must not be confused with the empirical fact that corporations "are" increasingly functioning authoritatively in ruling themselves and others:

[t]his obstacle [the "public" nature of authority] is only convincing, however, if one accepts that the normative statement that private power "ought" not be regarded as legitimate and binding establishes the *a priori* validity of the empirical statement that private power "is" in fact not regarded as legitimate and binding. The public dimension of authority is only an obstacle if one accepts that private power does not *in fact* operate in an obligatory way.[54]

Formalism thus threatens to obscure the actuality of private authority. Moreover, while imputing "public" authority to "private" actors may well threaten the conflation of the public and private domains and thus undermine central tenets of liberal political theory, some of the most interesting and innovative studies of international regimes have had no difficulty in casting their analytical nets so as to catch the activities of private actors.[55] This suggests that there is a growing asymmetry between the theory and the practice of international relations: the theory makes an impossibility of private authority and private international regimes, while the activities of non-state actors grow increasingly authoritative. This asymmetry is not new to international law. Major ruptures of the political order are often only later reflected in legal theories, as in the shift from the medieval to the modern and then postmodern political economies.[56] Indeed, a source of innovation in legal theory comes from changing practices of the participants, states or otherwise. Today this asymmetry is a reflection of deeper processes of globalization at work that are producing a disengagement of law and state and enhancing the authority of non-state authority more generally. As one legal analyst notes, "[i]n so far as our stock of theories of law assume that municipal legal systems are self-contained or that public international law is concerned solely with external relations between states, such theories just do not fit the modern facts."[57] The proliferation of transnational, regional, and nascent legal orderings reflects "new kinds of legal order" linked together by one theme – "the disengagement of law and state."[58]

The erosion of the public/private distinction also raises normative concerns. The question here is whether private interests *ought* to be the yardstick for international regimes. There is nothing natural, organic, inevitable, nor inherently meaningful in the distinction between the public and private spheres. In both politics and law they emerged as part of the analytical foundations of the bourgeois state and political economy and owe their currency to dominant corporate and class interests.[59] As such, they function ideologically and instrumentally to advance the interests of corporate capital within states and the interests of transnational capital between and among states. For example, private authority in the maritime transport industry, in addition to structuring commercial expectations and actions, "also operates politically to ensure that certain activities do not engage public regulation, scrutiny, and review. Private protectionism in the form of maritime cartels and private associations ensure limited entry to those who are not members of the maritime 'club' by creating 'invisible' barriers to entry. Indeed, the distributional consequences of rules that purport to operate in the common interests of providing greater certainty in transactions . . . are rendered invisible by their private and, hence, 'nonauthoritative' origin."[60] The maritime transport regime is a private international regime that privileges the interests of transnational shipping, insurance, and financial industries and preserves the interests of the most powerful maritime states. It thus gives rise to troubling normative implications that are only obscured by liberal legal and political fictions surrounding the properly "public" nature of authority.

However, while the concepts of private authority and private regimes raise important normative concerns, they do provide a useful corrective to excessively formalistic approaches to the study of international relations. They have an advantage that is particularly relevant to understanding the contemporary transformations associated with globalization. In focusing on informal and often only loosely institutionalized forms of governance, the concept of private authority is able to comprehend certain fundamental changes in legal ordering that are associated with the deepening of neoliberal discipline more generally. The privileging of private ordering and self-regulatory arrangements among corporations through autonomous processes of dispute resolution and the private arbitration of trade and commercial disputes, through special corporate tax arrangements, and through increasingly delocalized financial relations is minimizing the development of explicit rules of law and enhancing the influence of private, *ad hoc*, and discretionary practices. This is working a revolution in our notion of the "rule of law" and rendering the analytical focus on explicit rules and institutions highly formalistic, if not irrelevant. As William Scheuerman argues, both a unifying corporate elite and the compression of time and space are obviating the need for explicit, pre-dictable, and fixed legal rules.[61] Instead, the corporate world wants and is generating private, *ad hoc*, and discretionary standards. No longer are many transactions complicated by the distances of space and the lapse of time. Simultaneous transactions thus narrow the need for fixed rules, while the unity provided by a uniform legal culture continues to pro-vide an element of stability in expectations. The preference today among commercial actors for "soft law" rather than "hard law" reflects this same trend in the transformation in the "rule of law" and the creation of a more permissive rule structure that permits cheating when necessary.[62] Indeed the modern law merchant regime operates to globalize both highly institu-tionalized authority and the moral authority of marketized and privatized legal regulation.

The concepts of private authority and private regimes can thus be very powerful analytically, theoretically, and ideologically. Analytically, they "render visible the activities of transnational corporations, business associations, and organizations that structure commercial activity and determine outcomes in terms of controlling market access and market shares . . . and regulating the entire process of transacting."[63] Theoreti-cally, they assist in clarifying the processes driving the generation of global authority relations. Ideologically, they assist in revealing the private inter-ests being served by political orders and legal regimes and raise the vexing problem and challenge of enhancing corporate accountability, reminding us that "[t]heory is always *for* someone and *for* some purpose."[64]

The investigation of these purposes in the various forms that private authority takes is a profound challenge and is inextricably linked to is-sues of legitimacy. Arguably, the authority exercised by corporations and markets is easier to accept in cases in which one detects the devolu-tion, delegation, or even the silent permission of governmental author-ities. In privatizing industries, services, and sectors, governments may be silently complicit in the occupation of the field by private corpo-rate or market authority. Clearly, the global cities Saskia Sassen ana-lyzes need the support of a governmental framework in order to survive, suggesting that the dialectic between deterritorializing and reterritorial-izing authority varies over time. Moreover, as the chapter by Louis Pauly suggests, governments might be quite prepared to reoccupy the field if they deem it necessary. However, when one considers other forms of private authority, it becomes more difficult to reconcile the infusion of private ordering into public domains or issue areas. Arguably, the moral authority of emancipatory NGOs, addressed in the chapter by Ronnie Lipschutz and Cathleen Fogel, can still be accommodated as exceptions to the conventional notions of the legitimacy of public and state-based international authority. However, as one moves away from the legal into the margin of the legal or the domain of the illegal, legitimacy problems become more acute. The moral authority of religious terrorists, addressed in the chapter by Mark Juergensmeyer, pushes beyond conventional notions of legitimacy, as too do the private armies discussed by Bernadette Muthien and Ian Taylor. Clearly, overtly illegal authority, like that of the mafia addressed by Phil Williams, poses the most significant challenge to the legitimacy of private authority. If private corporate authority turns representative democracy on its head, illicit authority threatens to empty it of meaning. Such is the most extreme challenge of private international authority.

NOTES

1 A. Claire Cutler, Virginia Haufler, and Tony Porter, "Private Authority and International Affairs," in A. Claire Cutler, Virginia Haufler, and Tony Porter (eds.), *Private Authority and International Affairs* (Albany, N.Y.: SUNY Press, 1999), p. 16.
2 A. Claire Cutler, Virginia Haufler, and Tony Porter, "The Contours and Significance of Private Authority in International Affairs," in Cutler, Haufler, and Porter, *Private Authority and International Affairs*, p. 333.
3 See ibid., pp. 365–69, and A. Claire Cutler, "Locating 'Authority' in the Global Political Economy," *International Studies Quarterly*, 43 (1) (March 1999), 59–81.
4 Michael Walzer, "Liberalism and the Art of Separation," *Political Theory*, 12 (3) (1984), 315–30.
5 See Judith Shklar, *Legalism* (Cambridge, Mass.: Harvard University Press, 1964).
6 The now familiar distinction is made by Robert Cox in "Social Forces, States, and World Orders: Beyond International Relations Theory," in Cox with Timothy Sinclair, *Approaches to World Order* (Cambridge: Cambridge University Press, 1996), pp. 88–89.
7 For further discussion of the contradictory nature of forces of globalization on the balance in relations between state and society, see Anthony Giddens, *The Consequences of Modernity* (Cambridge: Polity Press, 1990); Frederic Jameson, *Postmodernism or the Cultural Logic of Late Capitalism* (Durham: Duke University Press, 1991); and David Harvey, *The Condition of Postmodernity: An Enquiry into the Origins of Cultural Change* (Cambridge, Mass., and Oxford: Blackwell, 1990).
8 For more on the emancipatory nature of critical theory, see Andrew Linklater, "The Question of the Next Stage in International Relations Theory: A Critical-Theoretical Point of View," *Millennium: Journal of International Studies*, 21 (1) (1992), 77–98, and Mark Hoffman, "Critical Theory and the Inter-Paradigm Debate," *Millennium: Journal of International Studies*, 16 (2) (1987), 231–49.
9 When Virginia Haufler, Tony Porter, and I first began the project on *Private Authority and International Affairs*, we in fact defined it as a study of private

international *regimes*. However, our first workshop revealed that the analytical focus on regimes was simply too narrow to capture the complex, rich, and variable types of the activities that ordered the corporate world. Most participants were dissatisfied with what they regarded as regime analysis's excessive preoccupation with the state. As a result, we broadened our focus to that of private international authority in order to capture the phenomenon of non-state authority and its tremendously varied manifestations.

10 For further discussion of the analytical foundations of regime analysis that dates from that time, see Friedrich Kratochwil and John G. Ruggie, "International Organization: A State of the Art on the Art of the State," *International Organization*, 40 (1986), 753–75. For a less positive view of regime analysis in that same volume, see Martin Rochester, "The Rise and Fall of International Organization as a Field of Study," *International Organization*, 40 (1986), 777–813. For a contemporary assessment of the contribution of regime analysis to the study of international organization, see Rochester, "The United Nations in the New World Order: Reviving the Theory and Practice of International Organization," in Charles Kegley (ed.), *Controversies in International Relations Theory: Realism and the Neoliberal Challenge* (New York: St. Martin's Press, 1995), pp. 199–222.

11 This is not intended to be a literature review of regimes theory. However, the classic originating text is Stephen Krasner's edited volume on *International Regimes* (Ithaca, N.Y.: Cornell University Press, 1983), which was a special issue of *International Organization*. It included articles by a number of authors who went on to develop regimes theory as the analytical foundation for international political economy.

12 Robert O. Keohane, *After Hegemony: Cooperation and Discord in the World Political Economy* (Princeton: Princeton University Press, 1984); Mark W. Zacher with Brent Sutton, *Governing Global Networks: International Regimes for Transportation and Communications* (Cambridge: Cambridge University Press, 1996); Thomas Risse-Kappen (ed.), *Bringing Transnational Relations Back In: Non-State Actors, Domestic Structures and International Institutions* (Cambridge: Cambridge University Press, 1995); Volker Rittberger with Peter Mayer (eds.), *Regime Theory and International Relations* (Oxford: Clarendon Press, 1993).

13 Strange, "*Cave! Hic dragones*: A Critique of Regime Analysis," in Krasner, *International Regimes*, pp. 337–54.

14 See Andreas Hasenclever, Peter Mayer, and Volker Rittberger, *Theories of International Regimes* (Cambridge: Cambridge University Press, 1997), and M. A. Levy, O. R. Young, and M. Zürn, "The Study of International Regimes," *European Journal of International Relations*, 3 (1) (1995), 267–330.

15 See Virginia Haufler, "Crossing the Boundary Between Public and Private: International Regimes and Non-State Actors," in Rittberger with Mayer, *Regime Theory and International Relations*, pp. 94–111, for the theory's neglect of corporate actors and authority.

16 I deal with this matter more fully in "Private Authority in International Trade Relations: The Case of Maritime Transport," in Cutler, Haufler, and Porter, *Private Authority and International Affairs*, pp. 283–329. See also Stephen

Krasner, "Power Politics, Institutions, and Transnational Relations," in Risse-Kappen, *Bringing Transnational Relations Back In*, p. 279, for the conditioning role of the state.

17 Miles Kahler, "Inventing International Relations: International Relations Theory After 1945," in Michael W. Doyle and G. John Ikenberry (eds.), *New Thinking in International Relations Theory* (Boulder, Colo.: Westview Press, 1997), p. 36.

18 Ibid., p. 35.

19 Keohane, "Neoliberal Institutionalism: A Perspective on World Politics," in R. O. Keohane, *International Institutions and State Power: Essays in International Relations Theory* (Boulder, Colo.: Westview Press, 1989), p. 4. For a very good summary of debates over the definition of international regimes and the benefits and costs of different versions, see Hasenclever, Mayer, and Rittberger, *Theories of International Regimes*, ch. 1.

20 Hurrell, "International Society and the Study of Regimes: A Reflective Approach," in Rittberger with Mayer, *Regime Theory and International Relations*, p. 54. Also, for the view that international regimes and international law have much in common, see A. Claire Cutler, "The 'Grotian Tradition' in International Relations," *Review of International Studies*, 17 (1991), 41–65, and Robert J. Beck, Anthony C. Arend, and Robert D. Vander Lugt, *International Rules: Approaches from International Law and International Relations* (New York and Oxford: Oxford University Press, 1996), ch. 7.

21 It is noteworthy that regime theorists of a more constructivist bent offered the promise of a less formalistic approach. Certainly the work of Oran Young, Friedrich Kratochwil, and Alexander Wendt is notable in this regard. However, the focus remained very much on states. For a good review of constructivist approaches and a useful bibliography, see Hasenclever, Mayer, and Rittberger, *Theories of International Regimes*, ch. 5.

22 But see Haufler, "Crossing the Boundary Between Public and Private," and Adrienne Héritier (ed.), *Common Goods: Reinventing European and International Governance* (Boulder, Colo.: Rowman & Littlefield, 2002), for examples of private actors providing public goods.

23 Stephen Krasner, "Structural Causes and Regime Consequences: Regimes as Intervening Variable," in Krasner, *International Regimes*, p. 2.

24 Cutler, Haufler, and Porter, "Private Authority and International Affairs," p. 5, drawing upon Stephen Lukes, "Perspectives on Authority," in Joseph Raz (ed.), *Authority* (Washington Square, N.Y.: New York University Press and Oxford: Basil Blackwell, 1990), pp. 203–17.

25 Cutler, Haufler, and Porter, "Private Authority and International Affairs," p. 5.

26 See Robert O. Keohane, "International Institutions: Two Approaches," in Keohane, *International Institutions and State Power*, pp. 158–79, for the distinction between regime-governed behaviour and cooperation.

27 Cutler, Haufler, and Porter, "Contours and Significance of Private Authority," pp. 334–35.

28 For the distinction between "an authority" and those "in authority," see R. B. Friedman, "On the Concept of Authority in Political Philosophy," in Raz, *Authority*, p. 79.

29 These matters are developed more fully in Cutler, Haufler, and Porter, "Contours and Significance of Private Authority," pp. 362–65.

30 Cutler, Haufler, and Porter, "Private Authority and International Affairs," p. 13.

31 Ibid., p. 14.

32 Ibid.

33 Not unlike how the practices of actors can over time crystallize into customary international law. See Peter Malanczuk (ed.), *Akehurst's Modern Introduction to International Law*, 7th edn. revised (London and New York: Routledge, 1997), ch. 3, for the variety of indicators used to determine if a practice has attained the status of law.

34 These, like the six categories discussed above, are all examples taken from Cutler, Haufler, and Porter, *Private Authority and International Affairs*.

35 Cutler, Haufler, and Porter, "Contours and Significance of Private Authority," p. 355.

36 See A. Claire Cutler, *Private Power and Global Authority: Transnational Merchant Law and the Global Political Economy* (Cambridge: Cambridge University Press, forthcoming); Cutler, "Global Capitalism and Liberal Myths: Dispute Settlement in Private International Trade Relations," *Millennium: Journal of International Studies*, 24 (3) (Winter 1995), 377–97.

37 See generally Norbert Horn and Clive Schmitthoff (eds.), *The Transnational Law of International Commercial Transactions* (Deventer, Netherlands: Kluwer, 1982).

38 See Cutler, *Private Power and Global Authority*, and Cutler, "The Privatization of Global Governance and the New Law Merchant," in Héritier, *Common Goods*, where juridification is defined as the utilization of law to legitimate increasingly more claims to authority coming from both state and non-state actors.

39 See A. Claire Cutler, "Public Meets Private: The International Unification and Harmonization of Private International Trade Law," *Global Society*, 13 (1) (1999), 25–48.

40 See *International Organization*, Special Issue: The Legalization of World Politics, 54 (3) (Summer 2000); A. Claire Cutler, "Globalization, Law, and Transnational Corporations: A Deepening of Market Discipline," in Theodore Cohn, Stephen McBride, and David Wiseman (eds.), *Power in the Global Era: Grounding Globalization* (Basingstoke: Macmillan, 2000), pp. 53–66; and William Scheuerman, "Economic Globalization and the Rule of Law," *Constellations: An International Journal of Critical and Democratic Theory*, 6 (1) (March 1999), 3–25.

41 Yves Dezalay and Bryant Garth, *Dealing in Virtue: International Commercial Arbitration and the Construction of a Transnational Legal Order* (Chicago and London: University of Chicago Press, 1996).

42 See Sol Picciotto and Ruth Mayne (eds.), *Regulating International Business: Beyond Liberalization* (Houndmills and Basingstoke: Macmillan, 1999); and William Bratton, Joseph McCahery, Sol Picciotto, and Colin Scott (eds.), *International Regulatory Competition and Coordination: Perspectives on Economic Regulation in Europe and in the United States* (Oxford: Clarendon Press, 1996).

43 See Cutler, Haufler, and Porter, *Private Authority and International Affairs*. This analysis bears some likeness to the distinctions between interest-based and power-based theories of international regimes identified by Hasenclever, Mayer, and Rittberger, *Theories of International Regimes*.

44 Paul Milgrom, Douglass North, and Barry Weingast, "The Role of Institutions in the Revival of Trade: The Law Merchant, Private Judges, and the Champagne Fairs," *Economics and Politics*, 2 (1) (1990), 1–23.

45 This is part of the explanation for the emergence of international commercial arbitration. See Dezalay and Garth, *Dealing in Virtue*.

46 The chapters in Cutler, Haufler, and Porter, *Private Authority and International Affairs*, illustrate the validity of all three types of explanations. Indeed, variation across issue areas and industries precluded drawing any overall conclusions as to the relative importance of the three sets of considerations.

47 Cutler, Haufler, and Porter, "Private Authority and International Affairs," p. 22.

48 Cutler, "Locating 'Authority' in the Global Political Economy."

49 See A. Claire Cutler, "Critical Reflections on Westphalian Assumptions of International Law and Organization: A Crisis of Legitimacy," *Review of International Studies*, 27 (2) (2001), 133–50.

50 See Cutler, "Globalization, Law, and Transnational Corporations."

51 Fleur Johns, "The Invisibility of the Transnational Corporation: An Analysis of International Law and Legal Theory," *Melbourne University Law Review*, 19 (1994), 893–921.

52 Cutler, "Private Authority in International Trade Relations," p. 299.

53 Walzer, "Liberalism and the Art of Separation."

54 Cutler, Haufler, and Porter, "Contours and Significance of Private Authority," p. 367.

55 See Ronald B. Mitchell, "Sources of Transparency: Information Systems in International Regimes," *International Studies Quarterly*, 42 (1998), 109–30, and his references to the self-reporting activities of private corporations in different substantive areas.

56 See Cutler, "Critical Reflections."

57 William Twining, "Globalization and Legal Theory: Some Local Implications," *Current Legal Problems*, 49 (1996), 7.

58 Ibid., 8–9. See also Boaventura de Sousa Santos, *Toward a New Common Sense: Law, Science and Politics in the Paradigmatic Transition* (New York and London: Routledge, 1995), on the plurality of legal orders operating subnationally, locally, nationally, and transnationally in the world today.

59 See Cutler, "Global Capitalism and Liberal Myths"; and Cutler, "Artifice, Ideology, and Paradox: The Public/Private Distinction in International Law," *Review of International Political Economy*, 4 (2) (1997), 261–85.

60 Cutler, "Private Authority in International Trade Relations," p. 316.

61 See Scheuerman, "Economic Globalization and the Rule of Law."

62 For further development of these trends and the distinction between hard and soft law and for the unifying influence of a global "mercatocracy" or merchant class and a global business culture, see Cutler, "Public Meets Private."

63 Cutler, "Private Authority in International Trade Relations," p. 316.

64 Cox, "Social Forces," p. 87.

Part II

Market authority: globalization and "globaloney"

3   Economic governance in an electronically networked global economy

Stephen J. Kobrin

Geographical space as a source of explanation affects all historical realities, all spatially defined phenomena; states, societies, cultures, and economies.[1]

In the Westphalian state system the basic unit of economic governance is the national market defined, as is the sovereign state, in terms of mutually exclusive geographic jurisdiction.[2] Economic governance – attempts to exert authority over economies and economic actors – is exercised through borders and territorial jurisdiction.

In this chapter I argue that the emerging global world economy compromises the effectiveness of national market-based economic governance. As the minimal spatial extent of product markets grows larger than the geographic scope of the larger national markets, the latter no longer remain viable as basic units in the world economy. As an electronically networked world economy renders economic borders less meaningful, jurisdiction loses significance. As markets are increasingly constructed in cyberspace, control through control over territory becomes problematic.

In contrast, an international or crossborder world economy comprising a system of interconnected, geographically defined, national markets does not necessarily compromise territorial control. Although jurisdictional ambiguity or conflict may make economic governance more difficult, regulation and taxation through territorial national markets remain viable.

Globalization entails a systemic change in the organization of economics (and politics) comparable in scope to the transition from the feudal epoch to the modern or Westphalian system in Europe roughly four hundred years ago. I argue that three related and interwoven characteristics of the emerging global economy are particularly problematic for authority exercised through spatially defined national markets:

1. The scale of technology in many strategic industries (its cost, risk, and complexity) renders the minimum effective market size larger than that of even the largest national markets;

2. Networks are replacing hierarchies and markets as a basic form of economic organization; the diffuse, non-centered, and relational character of networks is not consistent with economic authority exercised through bounded and discrete geographic territory; and

3. The migration of markets to cyberspace (or some combination of physical and virtual space) renders geographic space problematic as a basis for effective economic governance.

As many authors have pointed out, "we have been there and done that" – this is actually the second global economy or second wave of globalization.[3] The first global economy, which dates roughly from 1870 to 1914, has been called "the high-water mark" of an open, integrated international economy and the "golden age" of international economic integration.[4]

Pre-1914 levels of international trade and investment were striking; world trade grew by almost 50 percent per decade from the middle of the nineteenth to the early twentieth century, and international capital investments by 64 percent per decade during the forty years before World War I. By most measures the degree of internationalization of the first global economy compares favorably with that of the current or second. To cite one relative comparison, at their late twentieth-century peak, Japan's capital exports (relative to GDP) were only about half of Great Britain's at the turn of the century.[5]

That being said, there is no question that the current "global" economy differs significantly from that of a century ago. First, it is *broader* in terms of the number of national markets encompassed (albeit to varying degrees) as constituent units. Second, it is *deeper* in terms of the density of interaction, of flows of trade and investment, than it was prior to 1914.

Third, and perhaps most important, the dominant mode of organization of international economic transactions changed significantly in the late twentieth century from the market (trade and portfolio investment) to hierarchy or the internationalization of production through the multinational enterprise (MNE).[6] By the late 1990s, 60,000 transnational corporations with over 500,000 foreign affiliates accounted for about 25 percent of global output. The United Nations Programme on Transnationals concluded that "international production . . . is at the core of the process of globalization."[7]

That still begs the critical question: does *globalization* define a change in degree or kind? Does it represent an extension of the modern international world economy into somewhat unfamiliar territory, or a systemic transformation which entails changes in both quantity and quality, defining new structures and new modes of functioning? Does globalization define a fundamental change in the mode of organization of the world economy?

While there is general agreement that major changes in the scope and organization of international economic activities are taking place, considerable disagreement over their interpretation remains.[8] Some argue that the interrelated economic and technological developments which are emerging as critical components of *globalization* will result in deep structural adjustments, leading to periods of significant change, perhaps epochal in nature.[9] The French author and politician Jean-Marie Guehenno, for example, links emerging global networks with the death of nation-states and of the state structure.[10]

Others claim that all that has ended is what Eric Hobsbawm calls the "age of extremes," the economic dislocations and mass destruction – real or threatened – which have characterized the "short" twentieth century from 1914 to the end of the Cold War in 1991.[11] One implication of this line of argument is that with the end of the "age of extremes" we are now able to return to the open, international world economy of the early twentieth century; that what appears to be dramatic change is actually a return to normalcy. Thus, Alan Blinder, who was then vice-chairman of the US Federal Reserve Board, observed that "a great deal of what we have been witnessing since 1950 is simply getting the world back to the level of integration that had been achieved in 1914."[12]

The underlying issue, however, is not whether the level of and/or rate of growth of either trade and investment or of interdependence are greater in 2000 than they were in 1900. It is whether a qualitative structural change is taking place, and that cannot be demonstrated by quantitative arguments involving crosstemporal comparisons of economic data.[13]

Put differently, is the current *global* world economy merely "more" international, or does it entail a deep change in political-economic structure? If the distinction is to have meaning, it is important to be precise about definitions. *International* is a relatively new word dating from the late eighteenth century;[14] it is a modern concept which was not relevant before the emergence of territorially defined nation-states and national markets. An international economy *links* discrete, mutually exclusive, geographic national markets through crossborder flows of trade and investment.

"The worldwide international economy is one in which the principal entities are nation-states, and involves the process of the growing interconnection between national economies . . . [it] is an aggregate of nationally located functions."[15] An international economy is unambiguously *modern*; it involves relations between sovereign units of the Westphalian state system and hierarchically structured, often vertically integrated, discrete economic actors. It is profoundly *geographic* in that borders of states and markets delineate its constituent components.

The internationalization of production is not necessarily inconsistent with this framework: MNEs are seen by many observers as national firms with a clear center or home country, which engage in international operations and require access to territory to function. At the end of the day, MNEs are international or crossborder entities which *are* of the existing interstate system and are firmly rooted in national jurisdiction.

In contrast *globalization* entails a qualitative transformation of the international world economy. As noted above, the argument is based on three related propositions. First, dramatic increases in the scale of technology in many industries – in its cost, risk, and complexity – have rendered even the largest national markets too small to be meaningful economic units; they are no longer the "principal entities" of the world economy. National markets are *fused* transnationally rather than linked across borders.

Second, the recent explosion of transnational strategic alliances is a manifestation of a fundamental change in the mode of organization of international economic transactions from markets and/or hierarchies (i.e., trade and MNEs) to global networks. Last, and related to the second point, the emerging global economy (and many emerging global political actors) is digitally integrated and entails the migration of markets from geographic space to cyberspace.

My primary interest in this chapter is the impact of globalization of the world economy on economic governance, on national markets and nation-states. I argue that globalization compromises the basic symmetry of political and economic organization, of nation-states and national markets, which is characteristic of much of the twentieth century.

An asymmetry of geographic scope is emerging as economic units (markets) expand in space well beyond the limits of political units (national territories). More important is the emerging asymmetry in mode of organization as interstate politics remains geographically grounded in sovereign territory while major sectors of the world economy (and many significant non-state actors) are organized in terms of non-territorial electronic networks. Geographic space is losing meaning as the basis for the organization of markets. As a result, geographically rooted economic governance has become problematic, and non-state or private actors are increasingly involved in authoritative decision-making.[16]

The next section of this chapter deals with three components of globalization in some considerable detail: the scale of technology; alliances and crossborder networks; and the movement of markets to cyberspace. I then turn to networks as a mode of economic organization and the emergence of a networked global economy. Implications for states and the state system will then be discussed. The chapter concludes with some thoughts about possible futures.

Components of economic globalization

Scale of technology

Markets, as well as economic governance, are typically conceptualized in spatial or geographic terms. In his *Principles*, Marshall quotes Cournot to define a market as "not any particular market place in which things are bought and sold, but the whole of any *region* in which buyers and sellers are in such free intercourse with one another that the prices of the same goods tend to equality easily and quickly."[17]

That raises a pertinent but little considered question: why should markets spread geographically beyond a local area or region? The simplest explanation, and the oldest, is that the supply of some goods is found in one locale and their demand in another: e.g., precious metals, spices, and petroleum. The geographic expansion of markets also allows for a more productive division of labor: "Smithian" gains from specialization, exploitation of differences in resource endowments, and the adaptation of skills.[18]

Last, spreading fixed capital costs over a larger market area can reduce unit costs and produce gains from scale. The application of science and technology to production processes and products toward the end of the nineteenth century provided an irresistible motive for the geographic expansion of markets. Firms found that the need for larger production runs to achieve economies of scale and, later, the demands of competitive research and development budgets mandated expansion of the geographic bounds of markets.

In most transnationally integrated industries, internationalization is driven by scale rather than specialization; a process Kenichi Ohmae characterizes as a dramatic shift from a variable to a fixed-cost environment has occurred.[19] He notes that in a number of critical industries, the scale of production and/or technology has increased to the point at which fixed costs must be amortized over a larger market base than is available in even the largest national markets.

While "Smithian" expansion is consistent with an international world economy, expansion driven by scale, and especially technological scale, may not be. An international world economy is constructed through the mutual interconnection or crossborder integration of national economic spaces. As Manuel Castells notes, a global economy is something different: "it is an economy with the capacity to work as a unit in real time on a planetary basis."[20] An international economy *links* distinct national markets; a global economy *fuses* national markets into a coherent whole.

Furthermore, at this point in time, it is the cost and risk of technology rather than the need for larger production runs that are the primary motivation for the transnational integration of markets. In many strategic industries, international expansion is required to fully amortize the enormous research and development expenses associated with rapidly evolving process and product technology. There are only a few industries (e.g., automobiles and construction equipment) in which the fixed costs of manufacture are the motivation for international market integration, and even there developments such as computer-aided design/manufacture and flexible production are reducing rapidly the number of units needed to fully exploit scale economies.

While the point is difficult to "prove," F. M. Scherer has concluded that in only a very small minority of industries is concentration approaching oligopoly at the *national level* justified by production scale economies in the US market.[21] In a previous study, I found that technological intensity was the primary determinant of the transnational integration of US firms, and that proxies for manufacturing scale were not significant.[22]

On the other hand, there is no question that the cost, risk, and pace of technological development have increased significantly over the past four decades. For example, *constant dollar* research and development expenditures for US industry increased almost five and one-half fold between 1953 and 1990; they increased 150 percent between 1980 and 1990 alone. In fact, with the exception of the early 1970s and the early 1990s, non-Federal government constant dollar R&D expenditures have grown at an annual rate of well over 6 percent over the last four decades.[23] Research and development spending as a percentage of sales for US industry doubled in the sixteen years between 1976 and 1992: from 1.9 to 3.8 percent.[24]

As the extent of a company's research and development effort is mandated by the nature of its technology and competition rather than its size, this rapid growth of spending requires a corresponding expansion of sales – and ultimately, internationalization – if profitability is to be maintained. Put another way, it is impossible to maintain a competitive level of R&D expenditure in industries such as pharmaceuticals, semiconductors, telecommunications, or aerospace based upon sales in even the largest national market. Firms *must* sell very similar products in a number of the larger markets to remain players in the industry. In that sense, the marked increase in the cost, risk, and complexity of technology over the last decades of the twentieth century has fused markets globally rather than linking them internationally, at least in these strategic, technology-intensive industries.

At this point it appears that the global integration of markets by a single firm may no longer be sufficient to offset the huge costs and risks of technological development in a number of strategic industries. The last decade has seen an exponential increase in technology-driven collaborative agreements or strategic alliances among leading multinationals from the major industrial countries.

Strategic alliances

Strategic alliances are relevant for two reasons. First, in many instances they are an indicator that the *scale* of technology – the cost, risk, and complexity of research and development – has grown to the point where it is beyond the reach of even the largest and most global firms. Second, alliances are a manifestation of the emergence of a networked global economy; they represent a change in the *mode* of organization of international economic transactions.

Although comprehensive data on alliances do not exist, virtually every attempt at data-gathering reveals their dramatic growth over the last two decades; one study estimated a 31 percent compound annual growth rate for the number of high-technology alliances over the 1980s.[25] Booz Allen & Hamilton reports that alliance-generated sales among the Fortune 1000 grew from less than 2 percent in 1980 to 19 percent by 1996; they are projected to be 35 percent by 2002.[26]

The vast majority of alliances are triad-based; most studies find that over 90 percent of all agreements are between firms from North America, Europe, and Japan.[27] Alliances also tend to be concentrated in a limited number of industries: typically automobiles and high-technology sectors such as pharmaceuticals, biotechnology, aerospace, information technology, and new materials.[28] A single firm in these industries often enters into very large numbers of alliances: in the last half of the 1990s, IBM formed about 800 alliances, AT&T 400, and Hewlett Packard 300.[29]

The motivations for strategic alliances are complex and varied.[30] One motivation is clearly global market access: the need to compete simultaneously in all major markets, or at least in all the legs of the triad. A second reflects the continued importance of national boundaries: government preferences for "local" firms in industries such as aerospace in which an alliance with a national or regional firm may be a necessary requisite of sales to either the military or a national airline. Third, one can never dismiss an interest in reducing competition as a motive for collaboration.[31]

The most important motivation for alliance formation, however, is the increasing cost, risk, and complexity of technology.[32] Even the world's largest and most international firms can no longer "bet the company" on the next generation of semiconductors or jumbo jets; in many industries the cost of a competitive R&D budget has risen to the point where it is no longer possible to "go it alone." An example is provided by the alliance between IBM, Siemens, and Toshiba to develop a 256-megabyte chip motivated by the need to share an estimated US$ 1 billion in development costs and the large associated risks.[33]

Perhaps more important, technologies have become so complex and rapidly changing that even industry leaders cannot master them internally. An analysis of over 4,000 strategic alliances, in which innovation or an exchange of technology represented at least part of the agreement, concluded that "cooperation has to be understood in the light of attempts made by companies to cope with the complexity and the interrelatedness of different fields of technology and their efforts to gain time and reduce uncertainty in joint undertakings during a period of technological uncertainty. Other motives appear to play a very limited role."[34]

In summary, the evidence strongly suggests that the minimum size of markets needed to support technological development in industries such as aerospace, semiconductors, and pharmaceuticals is now larger than the largest national markets. Furthermore, in some industries single-firm internationalization no longer appears sufficient as even the largest multinationals must cooperate to deal with the cost, risk, and complexity of technology.[35] Alliances represent a transformation of the mode of organization of international economic transactions from hierarchically structured MNEs to networks. This has important implications for the viability of territorially defined national markets and geographically ordered economic governance, which will be discussed in detail below.

Digitalization of the world economy

The world economy is increasingly electronically integrated and digital. Networks, and especially transnational networks, are creatures of the information age held together by information technology.[36] Computers, facsimile machines, high-resolution monitors, and the internet are the "threads" of the global web of the emerging electronically networked world economy.[37]

More important, markets are migrating from geographic space to cyberspace as electronic commerce grows in both the business-to-business and the business-to-consumer spheres. Finally, physical products are becoming digital services, data transmitted electronically over the internet. (The increasing importance of downloaded software or music in the MP3 format provide examples.) We are entering an era in which information in the form of electronic cash will be routinely exchanged for information in the form of a digital book, symphony, photograph, or computer program. In short, we face a dual revolution: the migration of markets from geographic space to cyberspace and the morphing of products from real "atoms" to digital "bits." Both render geographically defined national markets and economic governance rooted in territorial jurisdiction problematic.

Thomas Malone and John Rockart argue that the electronics and information revolution has resulted in an about-turn, making extra-firm coordination cheaper and more efficient once again.[38] Electronic information technology facilitates the integration of geographically dispersed operations and allows networked coordination to replace ownership and hierarchy as a primary mode of control.[39] One result is the emergence of flexible networks replacing production by a single large firm. Hierarchical, vertically integrated transnational firms have "fragmented" into "diverse" networks reintegrated through information technology.[40]

There is widespread agreement that electronic information systems are critical to alliances. Albert Bressand, Catherine Distler, and Kalypso Nicolaidis, for example, argue that electronic networks play a central role in wealth creation as production and transactions merge into complex, information-intensive processes; networks are a manifestation of the blurring of the boundary between the factory and the marketplace.[41] Clarence Brown makes a similar point: as intrafirm integration increasingly depends on electronic information technologies, modern manufacturing enterprises are coming to have a great deal in common with information service firms.[42] He notes that this applies to interfirm links – to subcontractors and customers – and that these linkages are rapidly becoming global in scope.

It is directly relevant that in 1995 *Fortune* combined the Industrial and Service "500," arguing that the new economy has virtually obliterated the distinction between industrial and service business. The article notes the digital revolution has "dematerialized" manufacturing, citing one source claiming that three-fourths of the value added in manufacturing is now information.[43] All firms, regardless of sector, are becoming information processors.

I have discussed the implications for national markets of the migration of markets to cyberspace and the digitalization of products in detail elsewhere.[44] One example will make the point here.

The Indian software industry is a dramatic example of a relatively poor country entering the global economy, or to be more specific a segment of that country. The industry has grown at an annual rate of 50 to 69 percent through the 1990s. It is also export-oriented, with exports in 1998–99 totaling US$ 2.65 billion and estimated at US$ 3.9 billion in 1999–2000.[45]

Between 40 and 50 percent of software is exported directly over satellite or the internet. The vast majority takes the form of services, upgrading systems, installing new programs, and the like. Target markets are often financial services and insurance companies in the United States and Europe. It is quite possible for an Indian programmer in Bangalore to be working directly on a computer in a bank in New York City, installing a new program or upgrading the system.

That raises a question of interest: where did the transaction take place? It is far from clear which "jurisdiction" gets to tax it, or whether it is an export or an import. There is a very real possibility that national markets and territorial jurisdiction are not directly relevant when markets are constructed in cyberspace. Geography and territorial jurisdiction do not map on cyberspace.

A networked world economy

Increasingly, network metaphors are used to describe the emerging world economy: a shift from standardized mass production to flexible production, from vertically integrated, large-scale organizations to disaggregation of the value chain and horizontally networked economic units.[46] In Dunning's terms, hierarchical enterprises are being replaced by alliance capitalism.[47]

The information revolution is a critical factor in the emergence of networks as a mode of organization of the world economy. Global networks are both real and virtual; in fact, many combine elements of both. Thus, Castells argues that international networks of firms and subunits of firms are the basic organizational form of the "informational/global" economy, and that the "actual operating unit becomes the business project, enacted by a network."[48]

Similarly, UNCTAD reports that traditional oligopolies (industries with very concentrated market structures) are being replaced by global knowledge-based network oligopolies.[49] These knowledge-based oligopolies share four interesting characteristics:[50] collaboration aims at generating new knowledge or using or controlling its evolution; they are dynamic, as collaboration focuses on shaping future boundaries of an industry or technological trajectories; they are composed of networks of firms, as alliances form the basic building block of the global oligopoly; and they form across as well as within industries. (Data processing networks which involve the merger of information and communications technology are an example.)

Ford, General Motors, and Chrysler have announced an agreement to move virtually all of their purchasing activity to the internet. Covisint is an online business-to-business electronic commerce network which will handle US$ 80 billion in annual purchasing with more than 30,000 suppliers and, eventually, a US$ 300 billion extended supply chain. As with other business-to-business networks, users will be able to create marketplaces, take part in auctions, and complete purchases "with the click of a mouse."[51] By mid-2001, Covisint had grown to manage transactions which amounted to 13 percent of the "Big Three's" annual procurement.[52]

While global networks such as Covisint are revolutionary, they are but hybrid interim steps toward true informational networks. As products are digitalized – for example software, electronic books, and music – global networks will involve exchanges of information for information, services for various versions of electronic cash that take place entirely in cyberspace.[53]

The emergence of networks as a basic mode of organization of international economic transactions may be of more profound importance than increases in the scale of technology. It is important to conceive of a networked world economy in terms of a complex web of transactions rather than a series of dyadic or triadic cooperative arrangements between firms. A large multinational firm may well be involved in tens if not hundreds of alliances linking various parts of its organization with others. Dicken characterizes these webs as multilateral rather than bilateral, and polygamous rather than monogamous.[54] I now turn to a brief theoretical discussion of networks before discussion of the impact of a networked global economy on economic and political organization.

Network forms of organization

Strategic alliances and electronic networks represent a networked mode of organization of international economic transactions which can be distinguished from both trade (markets) and multinational firms (hierarchies). Although there is general agreement that networks are a basic form of economic organization, a central question, which is pertinent here, is whether "markets, hierarchies, and networks are discrete organizational alternatives employing distinctive control mechanisms or plural forms on a continuum employing, price, authority, and trust simultaneously."[55]

Oliver Williamson includes hybrids or *networks* – "various forms of long-term contracting, reciprocal trading, regulation, franchising, and the like" – with *markets* and *hierarchies* as generic forms of economic organization.[56] He locates hybrids on a continuum between markets and hierarchies, the polar modes of economic organization. Similarly, Wayne Baker argues that most real organizational forms fall between market and hierarchy, and suggests that they are an intermediate or hybrid form of interface.[57]

In a very influential article, however, Walter Powell argues against portraying economic exchange as a continuum with markets and hierarchies at the poles and hybrids in between. Network forms of organization – typified by reciprocal patterns of communication and exchange – represent a distinctive mode of coordinating economic activity and economic organization.[58]

Similarly, an OECD report concludes that networks are a distinctive form of economic organization and the "notion of the continuum fails to capture the complex realities of know-how trading and knowledge exchange in innovation. Networks... represent a type of arrangement with its own specific distinctive features which henceforth must be considered in *its own right*."[59]

Networks have been described as "social units with relatively stable patterns of relationships over time."[60] Networks differ from markets in the assumption of longer-term, sequential transactions, and from hierarchies in the absence of an authoritative control relationship. Networks are a social form of exchange, "more dependent on relationships, mutual interests and reputation... [while] network forms of exchange... entail indefinite, sequential transactions within the context of a general pattern of interaction."[61]

Networks have a number of characteristics that affect the nature of international integration and interdependence. First, they are a form of "collective action" involving cooperative relationships, in which the actors implicitly agree to forego the right to pursue their own interests at the expense of others.[62] Network linkages entail relationships over time rather than individual or "spot" transactions; given longer-term reciprocity, trust becomes critical. Network relationships are inherently or "implicitly" interdependent.[63]

Second, networks do violence to the idea of formal boundaries; vertical, horizontal, and spatial.[64] It becomes difficult if not impossible to define organizational boundaries, to establish where one firm stops and another begins. At best, borders are blurred and ambiguous; more realistically they become conceptually irrelevant.[65]

Last, networks are relational: individual attributes are less important than position in determining organizational power and outcomes. "From a network perspective, variations in the actions of actors (and the success or failure of these actions) can be better explained by knowing the positions of actors relative to others... than by knowing how their attributes differ from one another."[66] Thus power is a function of position in the network. As a corollary, networks have no center.

If networks are significantly different from both markets and hierarchies, trade, multinational firms, and alliances (both virtual and real) represent distinct modes of organization of international economic transactions. Trade involves production by national firms in national markets linked by "arms-length" spot exchanges, typically of raw materials, commodities, and finished goods. MNEs internalize production: the firm's administrative hierarchy becomes the primary mode of organization of the international economy. In the integrated international firm, the exchange of intermediate goods through intra-industry and intrafirm trade becomes increasingly important.

The emergence of global networks signals the replacement of integrated transnational hierarchies by a cooperative and reciprocal organization of economic transactions. The basic unit and venue of production become ambiguous; indeed, there is a real question about the appropriateness of these terms. The most important flows across transnational networks are intangible: knowledge and information.

Although the periods overlap and are approximate, trade was the primary mode of integration of the international economy from the late nineteenth century through the first two post-World War II decades, the internationalization of production predominated through MNEs from the mid-1960s until the mid-1980s, and alliances or networked integration emerged in the late 1980s. Two caveats are important. First, I am not proposing a "stage theory" of international integration, but rather am concerned with changes in the dominant mode over time. Second, reality is complex and messy and there are large sectors of every economy in which production has remained entirely national and "networks" are confined to television and to job-seekers.

Globalization, national markets, and nation-states

I have argued that a global economy differs in kind from the international economy which preceded it in three critical and interrelated respects. First, in many industries the scale of technology has driven the minimum size of markets well beyond that encompassed by even the largest national markets. Second, in many of these same industries, electronically integrated networks are replacing hierarchies as the most important mode of organization of international economic transactions. Last, given the digitalization of the world economy and the emergence of the internet, markets are migrating from geographic space to cyberspace. All of these trends have significant impacts on the Westphalian, territorial organization of economics and politics, and on relationships of authority within them.

In the nineteenth century, all production took place in discrete national markets which were linked through crossborder trade and portfolio investment. Although levels of interdependence were high and policy autonomy constrained, the national market was the basic unit in the international system. As noted above, the very use of the term *international* implies the existence of discrete and meaningful territorially defined national economic (and political) units.

In contrast, at the dawn of the twenty-first century, national markets are losing meaning as *the* discrete units of the world economy, as the scale of technology is *fusing* them into a larger whole. The transition to electronic networks and to cyberspace also affects the structure of the world economy. Networks are inherently interdependent, do violence to all sorts of boundaries, and are constructed relationally, so that the concept of a center may lose meaning.

As Castells so aptly notes, positions in the international division of labor no longer coincide with countries; "they are organized in networks and flows, using the technological infrastructure of the informational economy."[67] In a similar vein, Hirst and Thompson depict national economies being subsumed and rearticulated into the global system, and argue that the international economy is becoming autonomized.[68]

National borders are not irrelevant. Nation-states have differing interests and objectives, and attempt to enforce their will on firms and other governments; national boundaries still "create significant differentials on the global economic surface."[69] The critical point, however, is that globalization implies that the national economy is no longer the unit of economic accounting or the frame of reference for economic strategies.[70]

Globalization may well represent a return to an earlier stage in the evolution of the capitalist world economy. Hobsbawm argues that, in contrast to the past three hundred years when production was local and the world economy was based on territorially defined national economies, the current phase of development is marked by the reemergence of transnational elements. "The national economy is no longer the building block of the world economy, but has a rival in the immediately global market which can be supplied directly by firms capable of organizing their production and distribution in principle without reference to state boundaries."[71]

Authority, sovereignty, and the geographic order

Robert Keohane observes that sovereignty is typically discussed rather than defined.[72] Formal sovereignty is a legal concept implying supremacy within a territory and independence from outside authorities in the exercise of state authority. In contrast, autonomy and effectiveness are political constructs; the former implies that a state can and does make its own decisions with regard to internal and external issues, and the latter is a measure of the extent to which its purposes are achieved.

Internal sovereignty entails legitimation of the state vis-à-vis competing domestic claimants. It conceptualizes the state in the Weberian sense as having an effective monopoly of force over a territory and population, the "undisputed right to determine the framework of rules, regulations, and policies within a given territory and to govern accordingly."[73]

External sovereignty involves the basic principles on which the modern interstate order is based: the division of the political order into fixed, territorially defined, and mutually exclusive enclaves and mutual recognition that each state represents a specific society within an exclusive domain.[74] In fact, Hendrik Spruyt argues that a primary explanation for the spread of sovereign territorial institutions was that respective jurisdictions, and thus limits to authority, could be specified precisely through agreement on fixed borders.[75] In the Westphalian system, states are assumed to be the only legitimate sources of political authority.

In examining the impact of globalization on markets, states, and the state system, one must separate analytically constraints imposed on autonomy, effectiveness, or capacity from impacts on formal sovereignty. Two sets of questions need to be asked. First, are the constraints that globalization imposes on state autonomy qualitatively different from those resulting from the interdependence associated with an international or crossborder world economy? If so, at what point do constraints on state autonomy compromise formal internal sovereignty? Second, will the emergence of an electronically networked global economy compromise external sovereignty and the idea of territoriality itself as a mode of economic and political organization? I believe the second question to be, by far, the more important.

Globalization and autonomy

State autonomy has never been absolute, and decision-making power has always been constrained by international economic transactions; the tradeoff between the efficiency gains from crossborder economic activity and autonomy is far from new. The problem facing governments has always been "how to benefit from international exchange while maintaining as much autonomy as possible."[76]

What is new this time around? Even if one grants that flows of trade and investment are greater in both absolute and relative terms in 2000 than in 1900, and that there is "more" interdependence (however measured), that is still only a quantitative difference. Why should globalization have a qualitatively different impact on state autonomy? Does globalization – taken in terms of the phenomena discussed in this chapter – render a state's ability to exert authority over its economy and over economic actors more problematic?

Participation in an international economy has always presented states with a tradeoff between efficiency and a loss of autonomy, and in many instances governments have chosen to preserve the latter. Without judging their economic merit, in opting for import-substitution policies such as forcing local production of automobiles, policy-makers were willing to trade off higher local costs for automobiles (reduced efficiency) for the promise of a more developed industrial capability and increased future autonomy.

That option is not available in industries such as telecommunications, pharmaceuticals, semiconductors, and aerospace, in which even the largest national markets are too small to support the research and development efforts needed to remain competitive. If transnational markets are an absolute requisite of continued technological innovation, governments face a discrete zero–one decision rather than a continuous, marginal tradeoff. Accepting higher costs (e.g., lower efficiency) for some degree of autonomy is not a realistic possibility; mutual dependence is inevitable, and breaking its bonds implies a degree of withdrawal that few states could tolerate. The choice is to compete transnationally or to forego the next generation of microprocessors, pharmaceuticals, or telecommunications technology entirely.

At a minimum, states must allow their firms to participate in global markets. While in theory governments could participate in the global economy while closing their borders to participation by others, that option is not viable in practice. In these strategic industries at least, independence or autonomy is a very limited option. *State or public authority is compromised.*

At this time in many high-technology industries, participating in the global economy implies participating through alliances and cooperative efforts. As Zacher notes, states "are becoming increasingly *enmeshed* in a network of interdependencies and regulatory and/or collaborative arrangements from which exit is generally not a feasible option."[77]

Alliances and other forms of global networks also constrain states' ability to control economic actors through territorial jurisdiction. At this point in time, the vast majority of MNEs are responsive to their headquarters government; even the most international have a clear center in terms of operations and management. That is not the case for alliances and the emerging knowledge-based networked oligopolies discussed earlier. They are diffuse and often relational: it is far from clear, for example, whether the American, German, or Japanese government could exert substantial regulatory control over the IBM–Siemens–Toshiba alliance to develop chips. Where are strategic alliances "centered"?

In an electronically networked global economy, the borders of national markets, the concept of territoriality itself, and the distinction between the domestic and international economy (or domestic and international policy) become problematic. In *Being Digital*, Nicholas Negroponte makes a distinction between trade in *atoms* and trade in *bits*.[78] Atoms take the form of tangible material which must cross borders physically and can be controlled by political authorities. Bits, on the other hand, are transmitted electronically, typically by satellite, which process renders the borders of national markets virtually meaningless.

If software is imported in the form of disks and manuals, it is subject to border controls, tariffs, and the like. However, if it is transmitted digitally – downloaded from the internet, for example – any sort of control becomes problematic and autonomy is directly constrained. As noted above, the Indian software industry has evolved from sending Indian programmers abroad to work at a client's site (known as "body-shopping") to satellite linkages through which programmers physically situated in India work directly on the client's host computer, wherever in the world it is located.[79] If an Indian programmer located in Bangalore edits a program on a computer in New York, there is no question that economic value has been created. It is far from clear, however, whether the transaction took place in India or the United States and, thus, which jurisdiction gets to tax it or control it. Furthermore, neither government may actually know that the transaction took place.

Susan Strange has argued that states are losing authority, in part to markets and MNEs, and in part to other actors in the international system,[80] and that the authority of governments of all states has weakened as result of technical and financial change and of integration of national economies into one single global market economy. As noted in the introduction to this volume, as the authority of states has weakened, a growing number of other actors have taken on authoritative roles in the international political system. These sources of private authority include amorphous "actors" such as global financial markets, and specific actors such as MNEs, both individually and collectively. They also include the rising number of NGOs and other civil society groups active in international politics.

The question remains, however: at what point do constraints on state autonomy affect formal sovereignty? As Geoffrey Goodwin puts it, the issue is "whether the capacity of states to order their own internal affairs and to conduct their own external policies has been so undermined or eroded as to make the concept of state sovereignty increasingly irrelevant in practice despite its persistence in legal and diplomatic convention."[81] Although this question is not immediately answerable, it is nonetheless critically important.

External sovereignty and territoriality

All forms of political organization occupy geographic space. However, that does not mean that they are *territorial*, systems of rule "predicated on and defined by fixed territorial parameters."[82] The distinguishing characteristic of the modern state is that it is territorial, and that of the modern state system that it organizes geographic space. As James Anderson notes:

Modern states . . . are all territorial in that they explicitly claim, and are based on, particular geographic territories, as distinct from merely occupying geographic space which is true of all social organizations . . . territory is typically continuous and totally enclosed by a clearly demarcated and defended boundary.[83]

What makes the modern state system historically unique is this "differentiation" into "territorially defined, fixed and mutually exclusive enclaves of legitimate dominion."[84] Joseph Camilleri and Jim Falk argue that the first function of the sovereign state was the organization of space and that the spatial qualities of the state are "integral to the notion of sovereignty and international relations theory."[85] As Ronald Deibert notes, what might be called "High Westphalia – a condition of territorial exclusivity and spatial differentiation" is what marks the modern period.[86]

The modern construction of economics is also inherently territorial; the market, national markets, and even the international economy are geographic constructs. As noted above, national markets were created by political authorities in part to *territorialize* economic activity.[87]

In general, regional markets – the European Union is the best example – are motivated by the need to expand the geographic bounds of national markets to increase efficiency in terms of specialization and/or scale. An international economy, then, comprises national or regional economic spaces linked through economic transactions; economic integration is the extension of a market in geographic space.[88] In part, globalization involves "deepening" or closer integration across national, regional, and global geographic spaces.[89]

An argument has been made that, regardless of how international the world economy becomes, at the end of the day all economic activity takes place within national boundaries.[90] The implication is that even the most integrated MNE does not alter the basic geographic structure of the world economy; any given step in the production process or any given economic transaction can be located precisely in geographic space and thus assigned unambiguously to a specific national territorial jurisdiction and national market. While that argument may hold for a modern international economy, it is not necessarily valid in a post-modern, electronically networked global economy.

There is nothing in the nature of markets that demands that they be defined spatially. In part, the spatial definition of markets is a function of the stage of technological development, the need for physical contact between buyers and sellers. In part, it is a result of the path of development of the modern political-economic system. Many of the emerging global networks construct markets in electronic rather than geographic space. The international financial system provides both the best current example and a metaphor for the future.

The world financial market does not comprise linked national markets; in fact, it does not comprise geographic locations at all. It is a network integrated through electronic information systems, hundreds of thousands of electronic monitors in trading rooms all over the world linked together through satellites.[91] It is a system which is no longer nationally centered, "in which national markets, physically separate, function as if they were all in the same place." Global financial integration has been described as "the end of geography."[92]

If a trader in New York presses a key on her computer and buys euros in London, where did the transaction take place? Chase Manhattan Corporation has built a center to process transactions worth trillions of dollars each year in Bournemouth, England, linked by satellite to its offices in New York, Hong Kong, Luxembourg, and Tokyo. Would anyone argue that all of these "transactions" can be located in the United Kingdom?[93]

The concept of geographic space does not apply directly to cyberspace. It is far from clear what jurisdictions and boundaries mean when markets take the form of information systems. One can question whether all economic activity takes place within national boundaries or even whether economic activity can occur in more than one place at the same time. At the end of the day, the real question is whether the spatial concepts of borders, territory, and jurisdiction apply to electronically organized global networks.

The information revolution – the linking of telecommunications and computers – makes the very idea of a market as a geographic construct obsolete; they have become global networks rather than places.[94] John Ruggie suggests that a nonterritorial region is emerging in the world economy, "a decentered yet integrated space-of-flows ... which exists along side the spaces-of-places that we call national economies." He goes on to note that in this nonterritorial region the distinctions between internal and external become problematic.[95]

In summary, the very idea of a national market as an economic (or political) construct appears to have lost meaning in the post-modern world economy. As Peter Dombrowski and Richard Mansbach observe, "Markets are now effectively deterritorialized, and there is a growing incompatibility between the political boundaries of states and the economic boundaries of markets."[96]

Given the emergence of electronic global networks, neither territoriality nor mutually exclusive geographic organization retain relevance. The result has been to strip markets of both geographic and political meaning. The net effect of both is to raise questions about the meaning of sovereignty – at least relative to economies and economic governance – in its external sense of a system ordered in terms of mutually exclusive territoriality.

Sovereignty and modernity cannot be separated. Both entail the unambiguous and mutually exclusive ordering of space; both are profoundly geographic. Camilleri and Falk go so far as to claim that "[s]overeignty, both as an idea and an institution, lies at the heart of the modern and therefore Western experience of space and time."[97]

Both Gianfranco Poggi and Friedrich Kratochwil note a crisis of territoriality. The latter observes that the fact that political systems are territorial and boundary-maintaining, and economic systems are not, affects the very core of the state as a political entity.[98] It is to that asymmetry that I now turn.

Economic and political geography

While one can certainly agree with Miles Kahler that international economic space seldom coincides perfectly with political space, during most of the twentieth century there was a rough symmetry between politics and economics: both nation-states and national markets have been bounded by the same set of unambiguous borders and organized geographically.[99] Nation-states and national markets, however, constitute but one of a number of historical modes of organizing political and economic authority and, in historical terms, relatively short-lived ones at that.[100] It is not unreasonable to argue that the symmetry between states and markets in both geographic scope and mode of organization – which we tend to take as the natural order of things – is characteristic of only a very brief window of time: perhaps the hundred years spanning the late nineteenth to the late twentieth centuries.

Martin Parker distinguishes between post-modern as a historical period and postmodern as a theoretical perspective (he uses the hyphen to
distinguish between the two).[101] Thus, one can meaningfully talk about
a modern or Westphalian political-economic system structured in terms
of unambiguous territorial jurisdiction, or the transition from modern
to post-modern organizations in terms of the disintegration of "Fordist"
vertically integrated hierarchical firms, without assuming a postmodern
epistemology.

At the start of the twenty-first century a post-modern global economy is
situated in a political system which is still grounded, at least conceptually,
in modernity. As noted above, in many of the industries now regarded
as strategic, the minimal market size needed to support a competitive
research and development effort is larger than even the largest national
markets; they are no longer the basic structural unit of the global economy.

Perhaps of more fundamental importance is the fact that most of the
concepts we use to understand international politics are still organized
in terms of territory and borders. Economic activity, on the other hand,
is increasingly organized in terms of electronic networks. The result is
a developing asymmetry of scope and mode of organization between a
modern, territorially based, and geographically organized international
political system comprising nation-states, and an emerging post-modern
world economy where national markets and, indeed, the very concepts
of territoriality and geography are becoming less relevant.

That being said, two caveats are necessary. First, as I will discuss below,
the international political system is also in the midst of traumatic change.
As is discussed elsewhere in this volume, non-state and non-territorial
actors are emerging which wield significant "private" political authority.
Second, neither the international nor the global world economy is all-
encompassing. Many sectors of economic activity are still domestic and
little affected by crossborder transactions; many others remain grounded
in a crossborder or international economy. While the focus of this chapter
is on post-modern as a historical period rather than postmodern as an
epistemology, the simultaneous existence of domestic, international, and
global economies would not be inconsistent with the latter.

Back to the future[102]

Geoffrey de Joinville, a thirteenth-century French medieval lord, acquired
a considerable portion of Ireland through a "strategic alliance." His half-
sister's husband – the uncle of the queen of England – arranged a marriage
with Matilda, granddaughter of Walter de Lacy, Lord of Meath, who

brought substantial Irish lands with her.[103] After his marriage, de Joinville owed simultaneous allegiance to the kings of England and France.

As E. H. Carr argued many years ago, it is difficult for contemporary observers to even imagine a world in which political power is organized on a basis other than territory.[104] However, neither de Joinville's fiefdoms nor the international financial market are modern, geographically based forms of political or economic organization. Political control in one case and economic transactions in the other are organized without regard to mutually exclusive geography or meaningful and discrete borders. To a large extent both pre- and post-modern forms of organization are aterritorial.

Over twenty years ago Hedley Bull argued that the emergence of a modern and secular counterpart of Western Christendom, with its characteristic overlapping authority and multiple loyalties, was within the realm of possibility.[105] The post-modern future may well resemble the medieval past more closely – at least metaphorically – than the more immediate, geographically organized world of national markets and nation-states.

Although medieval "states" occupied geographic space, politics was not organized in terms of unambiguous geography. Political authority took the form of hierarchical personal relationships, often overlapping and intertwined mutual obligations and rights, as de Joinville well illustrates. Borders were diffuse, representing a projection of power rather than a limit of sovereignty. In that context, power and authority could not be based on mutually exclusive geography.

The Middle Ages lacked the singular relationship between authority and territory characteristic of the modern era; geographic location did not determine identity and loyalty. Overlapping and competing political authorities were the norm rather than the exception. At times, the spheres of pope, emperor, prince, and lord were all interwoven and comprised complex aterritorial networks of rival jurisdiction.

Citing other sources, John Ruggie describes the medieval system of rule in terms of a "patchwork" of overlapping and incomplete rights of government which were "inextricably superimposed and tangled." He labels the medieval institutional framework *heteronomous*, connoting a "lattice-like network of authority relations." These overlapping, interwoven, and incomplete systems of authority often resulted in competing claims to the same geographic area.[106]

To assert singular territorial authority, early modern monarchs had to exert primacy over a patchwork of dukedoms, principalities, and other localized authorities as well as transnational institutions such as the papacy and monastic and knightly orders. Until that was accomplished, the concept of an unambiguous relationship between authority and territory was unknown.

Sovereignty – in its modern sense – *is* unambiguous political authority. The underlying idea of the modern political system is exclusive authority over a discrete geographic space, which entails the absence of both domestic competitors and extraterritorial superiors. It implies that the state is the ultimate domestic authority and bows to no external power, be it pope or emperor.[107]

Singular territorially based authority is once more becoming problematic in our emerging post-modern global political economy. States are no longer the sole sources of legitimate authority; in fact we face a world of overlapping and ambiguous "authorities" which may shift as the context changes. As noted above, MNEs and markets are one source of authority in the international system and NGOs and other civil society groups another. There are times when significant international political negotiations have involved these two sets of actors, with states on the sidelines.

An excellent example is the battle over the price of AIDS drugs in Africa and other poor regions in late 2000 and the spring of 2001. After considerable negotiation and pressure from a variety of well-organized groups, the pharmaceutical companies offered to reduce dramatically the price of "AIDS cocktails" in South Africa and a number of other African countries. What is of interest here is that the primary negotiators were the private sector – pharmaceutical multinationals – and NGOs including Doctors Without Borders/Médecins Sans Frontières and a range of AIDS activists. The principal actors were private authorities rather than states.[108]

While the medieval analogy has very obvious limits, the past may well contain applicable lessons for the future. A neat, unambiguous ordering of economic and political authority along geographic lines may no longer be the norm. Borders are diffuse and permeable, compromised by transnational integration and global telecommunications. Relationships are increasingly networked rather than hierarchical with both individuals and organizations enmeshed in complex, polygamous worldwide webs. Multiple and competing loyalties result.

James Rosenau foresees the emergence of a dual system of sovereignty-bound and sovereignty-free actors – or state-centric and multicentric worlds – coexisting together. "The result is a paradigm that neither circumvents nor negates the state-centric model but posits sovereignty-bound and sovereignty-free actors as inhabitants of separate worlds that interact in such a way as to make their coexistence possible."[109]

One of the primary characteristics of modernity is a lack of ambiguity. The international political system is structured in terms of discrete and mutually exclusive geography: disputed border areas aside, every point in geographic space belongs unambiguously to a single nation-state and market. With very few exceptions every individual under the law, including every corporation, is a citizen of a single state. Similarly, the essence of the modern integrated economic organization is a clear hierarchy and a single chain of command: one boss, one company. Every individual, and every transaction, can be located in organizational space.

We may well be at a point of transition comparable to what Ruggie describes as the "most important contextual change in international politics in this millennium: the shift from the medieval to the modern international system."[110] The emergence of an electronically networked global economy may herald an analogous transition to a post-modern political-economic system.

There is, however, a danger in trying to project modern assumptions into a post-modern era. Linearity or unrepeatable time is basic to modernity.[111] We assume that time's arrow is unidirectional and that progress is irreversible; that there is a historic progression from classical to medieval to modern to – perhaps – post-modern. That assumption may be wrong.

The state?

This chapter has argued that globalization will markedly constrain the autonomy and effectiveness of states and, at a minimum, raise serious questions about the meaning of internal and external sovereignty. One point should be clear: I am not claiming that the state will wither away or even be rendered impotent. Rather, I argue that globalization will affect the structure and functioning of both states and the interstate system.

At a minimum, states will be still be responsible for any number of critical functions: for the welfare of their citizens, for basic social and physical infrastructure, and for insuring economic viability, albeit in a very different context. Furthermore, while globalization will transform relatively large number of critical, strategic sectors, it certainly does not affect all sectors, firms, and individuals equally. There will still be firms that function as domestic actors and those that function in a more traditional international or crossborder economy.

There is no question, however, that the meaning of sovereignty will evolve and that the state's role relative to supranational and subnational actors will change. The medieval analogy is useful. It should be clear at this point that I agree with Hirst and Thompson that the political order is becoming more polycentric, with states seen as one level in a very complex system of often overlapping and competing agencies of governance.[112] As discussed elsewhere in this volume, states are no longer the sole source of political authority; private political authorities have emerged and coexist with public authorities in an complex, interwoven, and ambiguous relationship.

There is certainly some recognition of the need for some sort of control at the center. The World Trade Organization (for example) has been given greater adjudication powers than its predecessor (the General Agreement on Tariffs and Trade). Furthermore, regional agreements such as the European Union, the North American Free Trade Agreement (NAFTA), and the Association of South East Asian Nations (ASEAN) appear to be proliferating. The progress of the EU to this point, including the successful adoption of a common currency, has major implications for state sovereignty.

At the same time, there appears to be increasing pressure for devolution of powers downwards to subnational entities, whether they are individual states in federal systems such as the United States or regions within Europe. The situation is complicated further by the rise of nongovernmental organizations (NGOs) as important actors in international politics; one thinks immediately of Greenpeace in environmental politics or Amnesty International in human rights.

The modern system of political and economic organization may well have been an exception. There is no reason to assume that a lack of geographic ambiguity, or even of territoriality itself, is inherent in the human condition.[113] The post-modern era may well resemble the medieval in terms of ambiguity, multiple loyalties, multiple levels of authority, and the coexistence of multiple types of political and economic actors. It is certainly consistent with a post-modern world view to reject the "modernist narrative of progress" and "embrace many simultaneously different and even contradictory accounts of reality."[114]

A medieval lord dealt with allegiances to multiple sovereigns, perhaps an emperor, and the coexistence of secular and sacred authority as the norm. Is there any reason a post-modern person could not deal with subnational, national, regional, international, civil society, and supranational "authorities" simultaneously? Or with multiple and ill-defined allegiances? Or with a system ordered on some basis other than geography?

This chapter has argued that globalization entails the technologically driven expansion of the scope of markets well beyond the limits of even the largest national territories, the replacement of markets and hierarchies by relational networks as the mode of organization of international economic transactions, and the migration of markets to cyberspace. Globalization signifies the emergence of a post-modern world economy that is not consistent with a modern, territorially defined, international political system. While the emerging asymmetry could be resolved by some sort of "world order," that is not likely in the foreseeable future. Modern economic and political actors will have to learn to deal with the ambiguity and uncertainty of the post-modern future.

NOTES

1 Fernand Braudel, *Afterthoughts on Material Civilization and Capitalism* (Baltimore, Md.: Johns Hopkins University Press, 1977), p. 20.
2 This chapter is a revision of "The Architecture of Globalization: State Sovereignty in a Networked Global Economy," ch. 5 in John H. Dunning (ed.), *Governments, Globalization and International Business* (Oxford and New York: Oxford University Press, 1997), pp. 146–71. I would like to thank Mark Casson, John Dunning, Vicki Golich, Ben Gomes-Cassares, John Ikenberry, Robert Keohane, Bruce Kogut, Robert Kudrle, Richard Lipsey, Richard Locke, Tom Malnight, Simon Reich, John Ruggie, Karl Suvant, John Stopford, and Raymond Vernon for comments on previous drafts. The Reginald Jones Center at the Wharton School provided partial support for this research.
3 Richard E. Baldwin and Phillipe Martin, "Two Waves of Globalization: Superficial Similarities, Fundamental Differences," Working Paper 6904 (National Bureau of Economic Research, 1999).
4 Paul R. Krugman, "A Global Economy Is Not the Wave of the Future," *Financial Executive*, March–April 1992, 10–13; John Dunning, *Multinational Enterprises and the Global Economy* (Reading, Mass.: Addison-Wesley, 1993); Paul Streeten, *Interdependence and Integration of the World Economy: The Role of States* (New York: Oxford University Press, 1992), pp. 125–26.
5 Martin Wolf, "Globalization and the State," *Financial Times*, 18 September 1995, 22. Sodersten and Rosecrance, et al., argue that, prior to World War I, international trade was a higher proportion of national income and direct and indirect investment a larger fraction of GNP than at the time they were writing (the mid-1970s). See Bo Sodersten, *International Economics*, 2nd edn. (New York: St. Martin's Press, 1980), and Richard Rosecrance, A. Alexandroff, W. Koehler, J. Kroll, S. Laquer, and J. Stocker, "Whither Interdependence," *International Organization*, 31 (3) (1977), 385–424.
6 In 1998, sales of subsidiaries of MNEs abroad (US$ 11 trillion) substantially exceeded exports of US$ 7 trillion. See United Nations Conference on Trade and Development, *World Investment Report: 1999* (New York and Geneva: United Nations, 1999), p. xix. Furthermore, a significant proportion of what appears to be trade is actually crossborder intrafirm transfers, and sales of subsidiaries of MNEs located outside the home country now substantially exceed the value of goods "traded" internationally. In the mid-1990s, UNCTAD estimates that intrafirm trade accounts for about 35 percent of all international transactions and, for the United States, sales of affiliates exceed crossborder sales of goods and services by a factor of 2.5 to 1: United Nations Conference on Trade and Development, "Trends in Foreign Direct Investment," TD/B/ITNC/2 (Geneva: UNCTAD, 1995).

7 UNCTAD, *World Investment Report: 1999*, pp. xvii, xix. For a dissenting view on the tendency toward the internationalization of production, see David M. Gordon, "The Global Economy: New Edifice or Crumbling Foundations?," *New Left Review*, March–April 1988, 24–65.

8 Peter Dicken, "The Roepke Lecture in Economic Geography. Global–Local Tensions: Firms and States in the Global Space-Economy," *Economic Geography*, 70 (2) (1994), 101–02.

9 Richard G. Lipsey and Cliff Bekar, "A Structuralist View of Technical Change and Economic Growth," *Bell Canada Papers on Economic and Public Policy*, vol. 3 (Kingston, Ont.: John Deutsch Institute, Queen's University, 1995), pp. 9–75. See also Martin Albrow, *The Global Age: State and Society Beyond Modernity* (Stanford: Stanford University Press, 1997).

10 Jean-Marie Guehenno, "Asia May Offer a New Model of Politics," *International Herald Tribune*, 16 May 1994.

11 Eric J. Hobsbawm, *The Age of Extremes: A History of the World, 1914–1991* (New York: Pantheon Books, 1994).

12 *New York Times*, 12 March 1995, E5.

13 Charles-Albert Michalet, "Transnational Corporations and the Changing International Economic System," *Transnational Corporations*, 3 (1) (1994), 6–22.

14 The *Oxford English Dictionary* attributes its first use to Bentham in 1780 in a discussion of international jurisprudence, in which he explicitly states that the word is a new one.

15 Paul Hirst and Graham E. Thompson, "The Problem of Globalization: International Economic Relations, National Economic Management and the Formation of Trading Blocs," *Economy and Society*, 21 (4) (1992), 358–60.

16 See A. Claire Cutler, Virginia Haufler, and Tony Porter (eds.), *Private Authority and International Affairs* (Albany, N.Y.: SUNY Press, 1999).

17 Alfred Marshall, *Principles of Economics*, 8th edn. (London: Macmillan, 1961), pp. 270 and 274 (emphasis added).

18 Smithian growth results from "the creation of commerce and voluntary exchange between two previously disjoint units – be they individuals, villages, regions, countries, or continents": William N. Parker, *Europe, America and the Wider World: Essays on the Economic History of Western Capitalism* (Cambridge: Cambridge University Press, 1984), p. 1. Also see Joel Mokyr, *The Lever of Riches: Technological Creativity and Economic Progress* (New York: Oxford University Press, 1990), pp. 4–6.

19 Kenichi Ohmae, *The Borderless World* (New York: Harper Business, 1990).

20 Manuel Castells, *The Rise of the Network Society* (Malden, Mass.: Blackwell, 1996), p. 93.

21 F. M. Scherer, "Economies of Scale and Industrial Concentration," in Harvey Goldschmid, H. Michael Mann, and J. Fred Weston (eds.), *Industrial Concentration: The New Learning* (Boston: Little Brown and Company, 1974), pp. 16–54.

22 Stephen J. Kobrin, "An Empirical Analysis of the Determinants of Global Integration," *Strategic Management Journal*, 12 (1991), 17–31.

23 J. E. Jankowski, Jr., *National Patterns of R&D Resources*, NSF 92–330 (Washington, D.C.: National Science Foundation, 1992).

24 See Peter Coy, Neil Gross, Silvia Sansoni, and Kevin Tilley, "R&D Scoreboard," *Business Week*, 3378 (27 June 1994), 78–103, and Kelley Holland and Paula Dwyer, "Technobanking Takes Off," *Business Week*, 3399 (18 November 1994), 52–53.

25 See Benjamin Gomes-Casseres, "Computers: Alliances and Industry Evolution," in David B. Yoffee (ed.), *Beyond Free Trade: Firms, Governments and Global Competition* (Boston: Harvard Business School Press, 1993), pp. 79–128; Richard N. Osborn and C. Christopher Baughn, "Forms of Interorganizational Governance for Multinational Alliances," *Academy of Management Journal*, 33 (1990), 503–19; and Vern Terpstra and Bernard L. Simonin, "Strategic Alliances in the Triad: An Exploratory Study," *Journal of International Marketing*, 1 (1993), 4–25, among many others. The LARA/ CEREM data base, for example, of 1,086 agreements involving at least one European partner shows an average of 67 a year in 1980–82, 133 in 1983–85, and 243 in 1986–87: Lynn Krieger Mytelka, "Crisis, Technological Change and the Strategic Alliance," in Mytelka, *Strategic Partnerships: States, Firms and International Competition* (Rutherford, N.J.: Fairleigh-Dickinson University Press, 1991), pp. 10–11.

26 Quoted in Gabor Garai, "Leveraging the Rewards of Strategic Alliances," *Journal of Business Strategy*, 20 (2) (1999), 40–43.

27 United States Congress, Office of Technology Assessment, *Multinationals and the National Interest: Playing by Different Rules*, OTA-ITE-569 (Washington, D.C.: US Government Printing Office, 1993).

28 United States Congress, Office of Technology Assessment, *Multinationals and the US Technology Base*, OTA-ITE-612 (Washington, D.C.: US Government Printing Office, 1994).

29 Garai, "Leveraging the Rewards of Strategic Alliances."

30 Mytelka, *Strategic Partnerships*.

31 Raymond Vernon argues that this is the primary motivation for the current wave of strategic alliances: letter to the author, November 1993.

32 Again, while generalization is difficult, existing data do appear to support technology as the dominant driver of interfirm cooperative agreements. An OECD report, for example, sums evidence from "one of the best data banks" to conclude that R&D cooperation represents the single most important objective of interfirm agreements: Organization for Economic Cooperation and Development, *Technology and the Economy: The Key Relationship* (Paris: OECD, 1992). Similarly, in reviewing a number of empirical studies, Mytelka concludes that knowledge production and sharing is an increasingly important component of strategic partnerships: Mytelka, "Crisis, Technological Change and the Strategic Alliance," p. 9.

33 United Nations Conference on Trade and Development, *World Investment Report: 1993* (New York: United Nations, 1994).

34 John Hagedoorn, "Understanding the Role of Strategic Technology Partnering: Interorganizational Modes of Cooperation and Sectoral Differences," *Strategic Management Journal*, 14 (5) (1993), 378.

35 A caveat is necessary. Although the growth of alliances has been dramatic over the past decade, their presence is not universal. While the data are still

fragmentary, alliances appear to concentrate in industries characterized by technological or capital intensity. It should be noted, however, that these industries (e.g., aerospace, semiconductors, telecommunications, and automobiles) are the most important strategically in terms of national economic competitiveness and security.

36 Stewart R. Clegg, *Modern Organizations* (London: Sage, 1990).

37 Robert B. Reich, *The Work of Nations* (New York: Alfred A. Knopf, 1991).

38 Thomas W. Malone and John F. Rockart, "How Will Information Technology Reshape Organizations? Computers as Coordination Technology," in Stephen Bradley, Jerry A. Hausman, and Richard L. Nolan (eds.), *Globalization, Technology, and Competition: The Fusion of Technology and Computers in the 1990s* (Boston: Harvard Business School Press, 1993), pp. 37–56.

39 Dicken, "Roepke Lecture."

40 Martin Parker, "Post-modern Organizations or Postmodern Theory?," *Organization Studies*, 13 (1) (1992), 9.

41 Albert Bressand, Catherine Distler, and Kalypso Nicolaidis, "Networks at the Heart of the Service Economy," in Bressand and Nicolaidis (eds.), *Strategic Trends in Services* (New York: Ballinger, 1989), pp. 17–33.

42 Clarence J. Brown, "New Concepts for a Changing International Economy," *Washington Quarterly*, 11 (1) (1988), 89–101.

43 Thomas A. Stewart, "A New 500 for the New Economy," *Fortune*, 15 May 1995, 168–78.

44 Stephen J. Kobrin, "You Can't Declare Cyberspace National Territory: Economic Policy Making in the Digital Age," in Don Tapscott, Alex Lowy, and David Ticoll (eds.), *Blueprint to the Digital Economy* (New York: McGraw-Hill, 1998), pp. 355–70.

45 *Financial Times*, 1 December 1999.

46 UNCTAD, *World Investment Report: 1993*; Manuel Castells, "The Informational Economy and the New International Division of Labor," in Martin Carnoy, Castells, Stephen S. Cohen, and Fernando Henrique Cardoso (eds.), *The New Global Economy in the Information Age* (University Park, Penn.: Penn State University Press, 1993), pp. 15–43; Charles-Albert Michalet, "Strategic Partnerships and the Changing Internationalization Process," in Mytelka, *Strategic Partnerships*, pp. 35–50; and *Economist*, "The Global Firm: RIP," 6 February 1993, 69.

47 John H. Dunning, *Globalization, Economic Restructuring and Development: The Sixth Raul Prebish Lecture* (Geneva: UNCTAD, 1994). See also David Harvey, *The Condition of Postmodernity: An Enquiry into the Origins of Cultural Change* (Cambridge, Mass., and Oxford: Blackwell Publishers, 1990), for references to the large and growing literature on this topic.

48 Castells, *Rise of the Network Society*, pp. 191, 165.

49 UNCTAD, *World Investment Report: 1999*, p. 107.

50 These characteristics and much of the discussion is drawn from Lynn Krieger Mytelka and Michel Delapierre, "Strategic Partnerships, Knowledge-Based Networks and the State," in Cutler, Haufler, and Porter, *Private Authority and International Affairs*, pp. 129–49.

51 *Electronic Buyer's News*, 6 December 1999, and *Crain's Detroit Business*, 8 November 1999.
52 Steve Konici, "Covisint Books Impressive Procurement Volume," Informationweek.com, 18 July 2001 (*www.informationweek.com*).
53 Stephen J. Kobrin, "Electronic Cash and the End of National Markets," *Foreign Policy*, 107 (Summer 1997), 65–77.
54 Dicken, "Roepke Lecture."
55 Candace Jones and William S. Hesterly, "A Network Organization: Alternative Governance Form or a Glorified Market?" (presented at the Academy of Management meeting, Atlanta, Ga., August 1993), p. 3. The literature on networks is large and growing. For an introduction and references, see Sumantra Goshal and Christopher A. Bartlett, "The Multinational Corporation as a Strategic Network," *Academy of Management Review*, 15 (1990), 603–25; Raymond Miles and Charles C. Snow, "Organizations: New Concepts for New Norms," *California Management Review*, 27 (3) (1986), 62–73; Nitin Nohria and Robert C. Eccles, *Networks and Organizations: Structure, Form and Action* (Boston: Harvard Business School Press, 1992); and Barry Wellman and S. D. Berkowitz, *Social Structures: A Network Approach* (Cambridge: Cambridge University Press, 1988).
56 Oliver E. Williamson, "Comparative Economic Organization: The Analysis of Discrete Structural Alternatives," *Administrative Science Quarterly*, 36 (1991), 280.
57 Wayne E. Baker, "Market Networks and Corporate Behavior," *American Journal of Sociology*, 96 (3) (1990), 589–625.
58 Powell characterizes the continuum view as quiescent and mechanical, and argues that, by "sticking to the twin pillars of markets and hierarchies, our attention is deflected from a diversity of organizational designs that are neither fish nor fowl, nor some mongrel hybrid, but a distinctly different form": Walter Powell, "Neither Market Nor Hierarchy: Network Forms of Organization," *Research in Organization Behavior*, 12 (1990), 295, 298, 299. Also see J. Carlos Jarillo, "On Strategic Networks," *Strategic Management Journal*, 9 (1988), 31–41, and Hans B. Thorelli, "Networks: Between Markets and Hierarchies," *Strategic Management Journal*, 7 (1986), 37–51.
59 OECD, *Technology and the Economy*, p. 78 (emphasis in original).
60 Noel M Tichy, Michael L. Tushman, and Charles Fombrun, "Social Network Analysis for Organizations," *Academy of Management Review*, 4 (4) (1979), 509.
61 Powell, "Neither Market Nor Hierarchy," 300–01.
62 Ibid.
63 Jarillo, "On Strategic Networks," Miles and Snow, "Organizations," and Thorelli, "Networks."
64 Baker, "Market Networks and Corporate Behavior."
65 Powell, "Neither Market Nor Hierarchy."
66 Nohria and Eccles, *Networks and Organizations*, p. 7. See also Wellman and Berkowitz, *Social Structures*.
67 Castells, *Rise of the Network Society*, p. 147.
68 Hirst and Thompson, "Problem of Globalization."
69 Dicken, "Roepke Lecture," 149.

70 See Castells, "Informational Economy"; W. Michael Blumental, "The World Economy and Technological Change," *Foreign Affairs*, 66 (1988), 529–50; Thomas H. Lee and Proctor P. Reed (eds.), *National Interests in an Age of Global Technology* (Washington, D.C.: National Academy Press, 1991); and Reich, *Work of Nations*.

71 Hobsbawm, *Age of Extremes*, p. 135.

72 Robert O. Keohane, "Sovereignty, Interdependence, and International Institutions," in Linda B. Miller and Michael Joseph Smith (eds.), *Ideas and Ideals: Essays on Politics in Honor of Stanley Hoffman* (Boulder, Colo.: Westview Press, 1993), pp. 91–107.

73 David Held and Anthony McGrew, "Globalization and the Liberal Democratic State," *Government and Opposition*, 28 (2) (1993), 265.

74 John Gerard Ruggie, "Territoriality and Beyond: Problematizing Modernity in International Relations," *International Organization*, 47 (1) (1993), 139–74, and J. Samuel Barkin and Bruce Cronin, "The State and the Nation: Changing Norms and the Rules of Sovereignty in International Relations," *International Organization*, 48 (1) (1994), 107–30. External sovereignty includes the concept of "juristical statehood," that states are organizations recognized by established states as sovereign: Keohane, "Sovereignty, Interdependence, and International Institutions," p. 96.

75 Hendrik Spruyt, *The Sovereign State and Its Competitors* (Princeton, N.J.: Princeton University Press, 1994).

76 Robert O. Keohane and Joseph S. Nye, *Power and Interdependence*, 2nd edn. (Glenview, Ill.: Scott Foresman and Company, 1989), p. 248.

77 Mark Zacher, "The Decaying Pillars of the Westphalian Temple: Implications for International Order and Governance," in James N. Rosenau and Ernst-Otto Czempiel (eds.), *Governance Without Government: Order and Change in World Politics* (Cambridge: Cambridge University Press, 1992), p. 60 (emphasis in original).

78 Nicholas Negroponte, *Being Digital*, 1st edn. (New York: Knopf, 1995).

79 S. K. Pandit, "Wired to the Rest of the World," *Financial Times*, 10 January 1995, 12.

80 Susan Strange, *The Retreat of the State: The Diffusion of Power in the World Economy* (Cambridge: Cambridge University Press, 1996).

81 Geoffrey L. Goodwin, "The Erosion of External Sovereignty?," in Ghita Ionescu (ed.), *Between Sovereignty and Integration* (New York: John Wiley and Sons, 1974), p. 101.

82 Spruyt, *Sovereign State and Its Competitors*, p. 35.

83 James Anderson, "Nationalism and Geography," in Anderson (ed.), *The Rise of the Modern State* (Brighton, UK: Harvester Press, 1986), p. 117. See also Hedley Bull, *The Anarchical Society: A Study of Order in World Politics* (New York: Columbia University Press, 1977), and Gianfranco Poggi, *The State: Its Nature, Development and Prospects* (Stanford: Stanford University Press, 1990), among a large number of other authors discussing this subject.

84 Ruggie, "Territoriality and Beyond," 151.

85 Joseph Camilleri and Jim Falk, *The End of Sovereignty?* (Cheltenham, UK: Edward Elgar, 1992), p. 238. Similarly, Krasner argues that the "central

characteristic" of the sovereignty regime is exclusive control over a given territory: Stephen D. Krasner, "Westphalia and All That," in Judith Goldstein and Robert O. Keohane (eds.), *Ideas and Foreign Policy: Beliefs, Institutions, and Political Change* (Ithaca, N.Y., and London: Cornell University Press, 1993), p. 259.

86 Ronald Deibert, "Harold Innis and the Empire of Speed," *Review of International Studies*, 25 (1999), 287.

87 As Braudel notes, their development was far from spontaneous: "The national market was a form of coherence imposed by both political ambitions . . . and by the capitalist tensions created by trade . . . a political space transformed by the state into a coherent and unified economic space . . . a large-scale economy, territorialized so to speak, and sufficiently coherent for governments to be able to shape and maneuver it to some extent": Braudel, *Afterthoughts*, p. 99, and Braudel, *The Perspective of the World Civilization and Capitalism: 15th–18th Century*, vol. III (New York: Perennial Library, Harper and Row, 1986), pp. 277, 294.

88 Richard N. Cooper, *Economic Policy in an Interdependent World* (Cambridge, Mass.: MIT Press, 1986).

89 UNCTAD, *World Investment Report: 1993*, p. 118.

90 Ibid., p. 119.

91 Walter B. Wriston, *The Twilight of Sovereignty* (New York: Charles Scribners and Sons, 1992).

92 John M. Stopford and Susan Strange, *Rival States, Rival Firms: Competition for World Market Shares* (Cambridge: Cambridge University Press, 1991), p. 40, and Richard O'Brien, *Global Financial Integration: The End of Geography* (London: Pinter, 1992).

93 Holland and Dwyer, "Technobanking Takes Off," 52–53.

94 Joseph S. Nye, Jr., *Bound to Lead: The Changing Nature of American Power* (New York: Basic Books, 1990).

95 Ruggie, "Territoriality and Beyond," 172. See also Manuel Castells and Jeffrey Henderson, "Techno-economic Restructuring, Socio-political Processes and Spatial Transformation: A Global Perspective," in Henderson and Castells (eds.), *Global Restructuring and Territorial Development* (London: Sage Publishers, 1987), pp. 1–117.

96 Peter Dombrowski and Richard Mansbach, "From Sovereign States to Sovereign Markets?" (working paper, Department of Political Science, Iowa State University, 1998), p. 4.

97 Camilleri and Falk, *End of Sovereignty?*, p. 11. Similarly, Ruggie argues that the concept of sovereignty is no more than the "doctrinal counterpart of the application of single-point perspectival forms to the spatial organization of politics": Ruggie, "Territoriality and Beyond," 159.

98 Poggi, *The State*, and Friedrich Kratochwil, "Of Systems, Boundaries, and Territoriality: An Inquiry into the Formation of the State System," *World Politics*, 39 (1) (1986), 27–52.

99 Miles Kahler, *International Institutions and the Political-Economy of Integration* (Washington, D.C.: Brookings Institution, 1995), p. 1.

100 Paul Kennedy, *Preparing for the Twenty-first Century* (New York: Random House, 1993), and Ruggie, "Territoriality and Beyond."

101 Martin Parker, "Post-modern Organizations or Postmodern Theory?"
102 See Stephen J. Kobrin, "Neo-Medievalism and the Post-Modern World Economy" *Journal of International Affairs*, 51 (2) (Spring 1998), 361–87, for an article-length discussion of this theme. Parts of this section are taken from that article.
103 Robert Bartlett, *The Making of Europe* (Princeton: Princeton University Press, 1993).
104 E. H. Carr, *The Twenty Years' Crisis, 1919–1939* (New York: Harper and Row Publishers, 1964 [1946]), p. 229.
105 Bull, *Anarchical Society*.
106 John Gerard Ruggie, "Continuity and Transformation in World Politics: Toward a Neorealist Synthesis," *World Politics*, 35 (2) (January 1983), 274.
107 Spruyt, *Sovereign State and Its Competitors*.
108 Mark Schoofs and Michael Waldhotz, "New Regimen: AIDS-Drug Price War Breaks Out in Africa," *Wall Street Journal*, 7 March 2001.
109 James Rosenau, *Turbulence in World Politics* (Princeton, N.J.: Princeton University Press, 1990), p. 247.
110 Ruggie, "Continuity and Transformation in the World Polity," 273.
111 Camilleri and Falk, *End of Sovereignty?*
112 Hirst and Thompson, "Problem of Globalization."
113 Ruggie notes at least three ways in which systems of rule have differed from the modern territorial state. First, they need not be territorial at all; second, they need not be territorially fixed; and third, they may not entail mutual exclusion: "Territoriality and Beyond," 49.
114 Camilleri and Falk, *End of Sovereignty?*, p. 52.

4   Global finance, political authority, and the problem of legitimation

Louis W. Pauly

The exercise of political authority through market mechanisms is not a new phenomenon. The question of the extent to which such authority at the global level becomes "privatized" in the contemporary era is, however, a novel and important one. This chapter seeks to advance debate on that question by offering an interpretation of recent developments in international financial markets.

Power and authority in integrating markets

Mainstream economists now routinely express their puzzlement at the rise and rapid expansion of "anti-globalization" protest movements around the world. If the protestors would only learn some basic economics and a little Ricardian trade theory, we often hear, they would realize that the costs of international interdependence and even deepening integration are overwhelmed by the benefits. It is, however, becoming very hard to believe that simple ignorance is driving a spreading reaction to global change. Mass demonstrations sweeping through relatively prosperous cities like Seattle, Washington, D.C., Quebec City, and Genoa in the early years of the twenty-first century reflected broad agenda-defining coalitions among a variety of not necessarily convergent interests. But they also suggested something deeper. Certainly protestors commonly claimed that corporate power and vested interests were usurping public space and dictating the agenda for public policy, that elected governments actually charged with making policy were becoming powerless, and that an ideology of free market individualism was eroding social cohesion around the world. At the systemic level, their concerns seemed to center on what we might call the constitution of international political authority. Who makes the rules at the systemic level? Whose interests are most effectively served? Who pays the price? The word "globalization" itself led to such questions.

In his contribution to this book, Stephen Kobrin introduces empirical material suggestive of the appropriateness, even urgency, of such questions. The neomedieval metaphor he proposes neatly engages the core issues of accountability, responsibility, and legitimacy at a time when economic and political power appears to be dispersing. With the same issues in mind, this chapter introduces a contrasting position.

I take contemporary international financial markets as my principal empirical point of reference. Since Kobrin focuses on the globalization of production, this choice partly explains the difference in our views. I am more generally skeptical, however, about the inevitable erosion of the authority of the modern state in the face of global economic change. At the risk of a degree of exaggeration, for present purposes our two positions may therefore be read as opposing arguments in a now well-established debate. Beyond clarifying the contours of that debate within the framework of this book, my objective in this brief essay is to indicate some important points of reference for the next stage in its deepening. The challenge, taken up most directly herein by Saskia Sassen and Claire Cutler, is to craft useful tools for a more fundamental analysis of the transformation of political authority as global economic integration proceeds. The editors advance that cause by proposing and explicating a conceptual category they call market authority.

My thesis may be summarized as follows. In a world in which financial regulatory power is dispersing and no particular national authority is truly dominant, crossborder financial markets ultimately rest today not on private authority but on interdependent public authorities and, increasingly, on the delegated public authority of international political institutions. When we speak of the authority of the market in other than an ultimate sense, we appropriately mix private and public categories. The fact that actual governments routinely obfuscate their final authority in financial markets is no accident. Blurring the boundary lines between public and private, indeed, is part of an intentional effort to render opaque political responsibility for the wrenching adjustments entailed in late capitalist development. Understanding that intentionality, its history, and the deeper reasons behind it can provide a useful starting point for assessing such policies as those aimed at managing systemic risk or at redistributing adjustment burdens.[1] It can also help to explain the mandates and missions of international financial institutions, like the International Monetary Fund and the World Bank, which are taken by protestors and supporters alike to symbolize a globalizing economic order. Finally, it can contribute to grounding scholarly efforts aimed at developing richer theoretical propositions regarding the fundamental nature of authoritative transformation in that order.

The "globalization" of finance

During the last quarter of the twentieth century, short-term capital flows across the borders of advanced industrial countries expanded at a staggering pace.[2] Even more striking than the rising volumes tracked in every magazine or journal article on the subject was the underlying normative shift witnessed during that period of time. Indeed, the relative ease with which such flows could occur represented a distinct reversal of the general set of national policy preferences evident during the years immediately following World War II. By some measures, the scale of international capital movements was only recovering levels evident in the pre-World War I period. In recent years, nevertheless, the explosive growth, global reach, and speed of contemporary capital movements (short-term as well as long-term) came widely to be seen as the harbinger of a new era. Promising to some, and threatening to others, "global finance" became a short-hand term to evoke the ideas of an integrated world economy and a more deeply inequitable one.

In the wake of regional financial catastrophes in the late 1990s, it is increasingly understood that the economic expansion potentially facilitated by international financial markets comes with new risks for governments, societies, and individuals. Two sets of concerns lay behind associated policy debates in the early years of the succeeding decade. The first highlights the challenge of simultaneously harnessing the power of open markets to accelerate economic development and growth while limiting the political constraints and social costs linked to that openness. The underlying dilemma is one of political legitimacy.[3] The second brings to the fore the difficulty of limiting the possibility of financial market failures (or managing them effectively when they occur) when the power of private actors is enhanced and the authority to regulate them is dispersed. In each case, the political tensions are obvious. They are also not fully resolvable, given the deeper structure of the international political economy at the dawn of the twenty-first century. In such a world, the logic of markets suggests globalism, while the logic of politics remains deeply marked by distinctly national identities. Heraclitus said that we can never step into the same stream twice, but the international financial flows we are now seeing certainly bear a distinct resemblance to those witnessed a century ago.[4]

The cause of freer trade won renewed rhetorical support after the cataclysm beginning in 1914 abruptly halted the first age of "global" finance, which was really mainly a trans-Atlantic phenomenon. Rhetoric was translated into successful policy only after an even greater catastrophe ended in 1945. The interdependent international economic order deliberately built in its aftermath by the victorious allies (minus the Soviet Union and China) mainly through the restoration and expansion of world trade was to be underpinned by a system of stable exchange rates. The United States and its allies designed the "Bretton Woods" system in 1944 to avoid both the perceived rigidities of the nineteenth-century gold standard and the undisciplined currency manipulations commonly deemed to have contributed to the depth and duration of the Great Depression.

During the following decades, the explicit policy preference for freer trade came ever more widely to be supplemented by official efforts to reduce impediments to foreign direct investment. The vast postwar expansion in trade (in both goods and services) and in crossborder investment in plant and equipment had far-reaching effects. One of them – currency convertibility in the current and/or capital accounts of national payments balances – cannot be separated from that broader policy movement toward more liberal trade and investment regimes.

Production, trade, and investment must be financed. If resulting financial claims are freely convertible across national currencies, liquid balances in governmental, corporate, or personal accounts can be used for a broad range of purposes. In advanced economies, in fact, there exists an historical tendency for purely financial operations to grow at a rate far exceeding tangible business requirements. Much of this growth reflects speculation, which can either stabilize or destabilize other economic variables. In practical terms, it has proven impossible to draw a clear and unassailable dividing line between the use of convertible financial claims, on the one hand, prudently to hedge business risks and, on the other, purely to gamble. To many observers, therefore, the economic history of the latter decades of the twentieth century has been decisively marked by crossborder markets for short-term capital taking on a life of their own entirely disconnected from real political economies where goods, services, and new technologies are produced. The truth is more complicated.

Throughout the post-World War II period, albeit at different paces and with occasional backsliding, the United States, Canada, and a number of European states deliberately reduced direct controls and taxes on financial transactions, loosened longstanding regulatory restrictions on financial intermediaries, permitted the expansion of lightly regulated "offshore" financial markets, and oversaw the introduction of new technologies that sped up capital movements and stimulated the development of innovative financial products.[5] In the 1970s, Japan cautiously joined the trend.[6] Throughout the 1980s and 1990s, many newly industrializing countries followed.

Again, though, relatively open financial markets were not altogether new in world politics. Conditions approximating today's "global finance" existed before 1914 among the most advanced economies and their dependencies. The extremities of war and economic depression succeeded in disrupting a system of economic adjustment that accommodated, even necessitated, international capital flows. In theory, if not always in practice, the behavioral norms embedded in the international monetary system prescribed relatively passive domestic policy responses to external economic changes. In fact, stability in that system proved episodic.

Among other shifts in the tectonic plates of world politics, the tumultuous era beginning in 1914 witnessed the gradual rise of the modern democratic nation-state, the citizens of which came to expect that institution to ensure not only their military security, but also their increasingly broadly defined economic security. Those expectations defined the terrain upon which the Bretton Woods consensus evolved in practice. The contemporary reconstruction of "global" capital markets is intimately linked to the disruption of that consensus in the 1970s and the dawn of a new era of flexible exchange rates. As the twenty-first century opened, however, it was not yet evident that the expectations of citizens concerning the responsibilities of democratic nation-states had substantively changed. Much rhetoric to the contrary notwithstanding, national welfare states continued to exist even as their financing now confronted the reality of more open capital markets. The true historical novelty of that development was to combine the policy preferences supporting those markets with the acceptance of political responsibility by states for the total security of their citizens.

Often abstracting from the fact that governments can let their exchange rates float, economic commentators, prominent bankers, and conservative politicians thereafter frequently underscored the internal "discipline" on autonomous state action implied by international capital mobility. If that discipline implied cutting back the welfare states of the post-World War II era, they asserted, then it had to be done. Many of their opponents on the left may have disliked such a conclusion, but they intuitively understood its logic. A mounting body of popular literature written both by conservatives and radicals, indeed, envisaged the consolidation of a new global order, the borderless order of advanced capitalism.

Whether they embraced it or loathed it, such a vision tended to be evoked in the language of inevitability. Enjoining governments to yield to signals emanating from the "global market," this language implied that a profound shift in policy-making authority was necessarily taking place, a shift away from the national level. Proponents typically extolled the surrender of the retrograde idea of "sovereignty" to the rational economic logic of markets beyond national control. Opponents might not have appreciated such a conclusion, but their own research often bolstered the notion that transnational coalitions beyond the nation-state increasingly exercised determinative influence over a widening range of economic and social policies.[7]

National political authority and international institutions

The concept of sovereignty in international relations has always been contested.[8] Its association over time with the institution of the state, moreover, is linked with a number of material and normative transformations.[9] But conflating that concept with the notion of policy autonomy, as is commonly done, blurs an important distinction. In a financially integrating world, a turning away from deeper intimacy by legally sovereign states or by the collectivity of states remains entirely conceivable, if increasingly costly. Indeed, some did turn away as severe debt crises confronted them in the 1980s and 1990s, only to return to more liberal policy stances after the crises dissipated.

In practical terms, to be sure, most states now confront tighter economic constraints – or clearer policy tradeoffs – as a consequence of a freer potential flow of capital across their borders. The erosion of their absolute freedom to pursue internally generated policies is the flipside of the opportunities for accelerated growth (beyond that capable of being financed by domestic savings) presented by that same flow of capital. Again, the phenomenon itself is not new, and it has boded neither well nor ill for the legal principle of sovereignty. Instead, what is new is the widespread perception that all states, all societies, and all social groups are now similarly affected by the forces of global integration. The historical record belies such a perception, which blurs important distinctions between and within states. Underneath much of the overt discourse on vanishing sovereignty and the inexorable logic of efficient markets, it seems, there lies a covert discourse on power, hierarchy, and legitimacy, or, in other words, on political authority.

Exchange rate regimes tell us a great deal about the internal choices states make when they seek to harness the benefits of economic openness without incurring unacceptable costs. The sum of those choices during the past few decades laid the foundation for contemporary crossborder financial markets. Those markets do not reflect economic happenstance. They are the consequences of a political project tied directly to the domestic priorities and external strategies of leading states. Open capital markets increase the range of external policy choices for those states.

Within them, such markets expand opportunities for powerful firms and a widening group of citizens. Through those markets, in turn, the priorities and normative preferences of those states, those firms, and those citizens are projected onto other states. The "silent revolution" of economic liberalization sweeping through much of the developing world in the latter years of the twentieth century was intimately related both to the material implications of that projection and to a convergent ideological transformation.[10]

Nevertheless, simple conclusions in this regard remain unsatisfying. Even if it is shrinking, there remains room for national variation in response to the opportunities and constraints presented by more open capital markets. By their "private" nature, moreover, such markets obscure distributive issues. Indeed, this is arguably the principal reason why their existence correlates so closely with democratic governing systems. Some will win, some will lose, dominant market participants will increasingly define standards for others, but the political blame for such outcomes will be diffused. As the twentieth century came to a close, nonetheless, a series of financial crises reminded everyone that those markets could not and did not manage themselves. Throughout the preceding five decades, it was precisely in this kind of environment that certain new kinds of international institutions were designed, institutions promising feasible management, not inevitable integration. The problem of systemic legitimation needs to be addressed in just such a context.

The legitimacy of a globalizing economy

Following World War II, the victorious states, minus the Soviet Union, attempted to craft a new world order. John Ikenberry is quite right in asserting that the initial dream of a global market at the center of that order was never practicable. Anne Marie Burley and John Ruggie, moreover, quite plausibly argue that the dream was originally cast in terms of the modified liberalism of the New Deal.[11] Certainly after 1947, however, the real order combined a military alliance, national economic development, a managed trading system, and an underlying assumption that markets could and would eventually emulate the structure of American markets. More open capital markets on the US model followed two decades later.

It cannot, however, be said that states ever made stark and irrevocable decisions to favor financial openness above all other economic objectives. They simply adjusted a widening range of internal policies first to accommodate and then to promote potentially more mobile international capital flows. Simultaneously, and not by coincidence, they also shaped or reshaped the mandates of international organizations like the

International Monetary Fund (IMF), the World Bank, the Bank for International Settlements (BIS), the Organization for Economic Cooperation and Development (OECD), and less formal groupings like the G-8, the Financial Stability Forum, and *ad hoc* task forces on various monetary and financial issues.

The architects of the original Bretton Woods system imagined a rule-based form of international cooperation. An explicit legal agreement among them specified their duty to collaborate through one particular multilateral organization – the IMF. The original Articles of Agreement of the IMF specified certain rules to guide the exchange rate policies of members and gave the organization the power both to sanction justified changes in exchange rates and to provide temporary financing in cases where such changes were not required. Governments did not formally have to coordinate their internal monetary and fiscal policies in order to keep their exchange rates stable. The rigor of exchange rate rules, it was hoped, would automatically promote necessary adjustments in internal policies.

In practice, the rules of the game were often honored in the breach and the IMF was frequently marginalized. When the system worked, it actually depended upon a low degree of international capital mobility and upon the willingness of the United States to keep its import markets open and its domestic price level stable, thereby providing to its trading partners an adequate supply of liquidity at a reliable price. In any event, technical innovation and policy liberalization in leading currency markets, as well as the financial implications of rapidly rising foreign direct investment, eventually combined to make it ever more difficult to control short-term capital movements. At the same time, inflationary macroeconomic policies in the United States eventually rendered the country an unreliable monetary anchor. It remained absolutely clear, however, that an integrating world economy required adequately firm political foundations. Since they could be provided only by public authority, and no single public authority appeared able or willing, a continuation of the post-war experiment seemed thereafter to depend upon reliable collaboration among various public authorities.

Since the 1970s, stabilizing key exchange rates by way of concerted action or negotiated policy coordination has occasionally been tried. But the major powers have most often relied on the assumption that exchange rates would stabilize in the long run if anti-inflationary macroeconomic polices were pursued independently. In short, they became convinced that internal self-discipline, now modestly reinforced by formal surveillance procedures within international organizations like the IMF and the OECD, would have salubrious external effects. Such a shared consensus was logically required if a new order in which international capital mobility had *de facto* priority was not to prove politically disruptive or patently illegitimate.

To be sure, many states continued to rely on various measures to influence the inflow or outflow of short-term capital. In the wake of disruptive bouts of capital flight in a number of countries, for example, such measures would sometimes be acquiesced in by other states and by the IMF. But that approval, whether formal or tacit, was almost always conditional on an understanding that new capital controls would be temporary. The reluctance of states unambiguously to embrace what we might call "the capital mobility norm," their handling of periodic emergencies in international capital markets in an *ad hoc* manner, and their preference not to designate clearly an international organizational overseer for truly integrated capital markets nevertheless suggests deeper concerns. Continuing controversies on all of these points revolve around traditional issues of power and authority. The legitimacy of a new order tending in the direction of global financial integration remains in question. More fundamentally, the struggle suggests that the architects of such an order cannot easily calibrate emergent market facts with persistent political realities.

One doesn't need to be an extremist to sense the dimensions of the problem. One only needs to observe market and governmental reactions to the financial crises that characterize any order that relies on private markets. Such markets may be efficient in the long run, but they have always been prone to bouts of mass hysteria in the short run. Since 1945, prompted by periodic emergencies, advanced industrial states regularly engaged in efforts to manage that proclivity. In an interdependent financial order, crises with potentially devastating systemic effects can begin in all but the poorest countries.

From Mexico in 1982 and 1995 to Russia, East Asia, and Latin America in the late 1990s, many national disasters threatened to become catastrophes for the system. But who was truly responsible for the necessary bailouts and for their sometimes perverse effects? Who would actually be held responsible if the panicked reaction to financial turbulence in one country began to bring down large commercial and investment banks and bank-managed investment funds around the world? "No one," a number of practitioners and analysts now say, for the authority to manage global finance has dispersed into the supranational ether or has been privatized.[12] This is a dubious response. Despite the screen of accountability always implied in regimes aiming to advance public policy agendas through the indirect means of private markets, actual crises ever since the end of the

Bretton Woods regime continued to suggest that national governments would be blamed and that they would respond.

The desire to avoid such an end game in the new world of international capital mobility provides the driving force behind persistent multilateral and regional efforts to clarify, strengthen, and rationalize the mandates of international financial institutions. The same dynamic reinforces internal pressures within many states to move toward "independent" central banks. In the best case, technocratic agencies promise to promote adequate standards of financial regulation and supervision around the world, design functional programs for crisis avoidance and crisis management, and provide mechanisms for states credibly to collaborate with one another for mutual benefit. (Such specific issues constitute key items on the contemporary policy agenda now commonly labeled "constructing a new financial architecture.")[13] In the worst case, such agencies can take on the role of scapegoats, thus serving as a buffer in the political crises that would inevitably follow any systemic financial catastrophe. What technocratic agencies have difficulty addressing, however, are basic questions of social justice. Not only are standards across diverse societies themselves still diverse, but those agencies are charged with helping to manage a system in which the mobility of capital is not matched by the mobility of people.

Justice and legitimate political authority are inextricably linked. At its core, therefore, that system reflects the fact that the governments of states cannot shift ultimate political authority, to the level of governance suggested by the term "global finance." Perhaps they do not yet need to do so, because the term exaggerates the reality of international financial integration at the dawn of a new century.[14] Surely, however, the vast majority of their citizens do not yet want them to do so. Only in Western Europe, within the restricted context of a regional economic experiment still shaped by the legacy of the most horrendous war in world history, was a shift in power and authority beyond the national level in sight. And, even there, the fundamental construction of an ultimate locus of authority remained highly controversial.[15] Elsewhere in the industrial world, intensifying interdependence remained the order of the day as the citizens of still national states sought the benefits of international capital mobility without paying the ultimate political costs implied by true integration. To them, continuing turbulence in so-called emerging markets seemed like a distant roll of thunder. Their perennial hope was that the storm would, at best, gradually dissipate or, at worst, remain far away. There was no evidence, however, that they had resigned themselves to simply weathering such a storm if it ever did threaten them directly. On the contrary, experience suggested that, at the core of the system, duly constituted political authorities stood ready to respond decisively. They appeared to understand intuitively that markets were a tool of policy, not a substitute for it.[16]

Implications

By way of conclusion, let me make one policy-related observation and one analytical implication for the principal issue explored in this book. It follows from my last point that the calls of right-wing commentators to abolish agencies like the IMF rest on a fundamental, and unrealistic, assumption: that capital mobility and flexible exchange rate regimes will conduce to national and global stability because states will not abuse the macroeconomic policy autonomy they thereby gain. And even if certain governments do threaten to abuse that autonomy, the problem can effectively be handled by domestic monetary rules and central bank independence. A less optimistic position seems more plausible.

At base, free market enthusiasts contend that IMF-like agencies create moral hazard. My own view is that moral hazard is unavoidable when democratic welfare states are driven by overwhelming domestic pressures and interests to temper the vagaries of financial markets. All that can be done is to displace that hazard from the domestic arena to the international arena or vice versa. In bad times, the fundamental role of crisis manager must be filled if markets are not to disintegrate. In good times, a less ambitious but still useful role exists for an overseer of the process of interdependent adjustment to economic change.

With the resurrection of integrating financial markets in the contemporary period, an institution like the IMF becomes more, not less, important: not because of the economics, but because of the politics. If the IMF were abolished, a new agency capable of doing similar things, especially in an emergency, would have to be created: unless, of course, the US Treasury, the German Finance Ministry, the Japanese Ministry of Finance, or other public authorities did the job directly. To imagine that the role could in fact be left unfilled and that everything would be just fine is an effort worthy of Voltaire's Dr. Pangloss.

What role, precisely? Ask Robert Rubin, then US treasury secretary, or Bill McDonough of the Federal Reserve Bank of New York in 1998 when the Long Term Capital Management hedge fund threatened to set the clock back to 1929. Ask US central bank governor Alan Greenspan in the early 1990s when US money center banks were dangerously undercapitalized and international losses could have pushed several over the brink. Ask Jacques de Larosière, managing director of the IMF in 1982 when

Mexico declared a debt moratorium.[17] In such situations, it is always easy to say, "Let the market work." But it is politically unthinkable actually to do it. "The market," in this case the post-1970s experiment in global financial integration, is itself an unfinished political project of the advanced industrial states. Stabilizing that market is an unavoidable aspect of that experiment, and it involves two dimensions: managing systemic risk and ensuring that modicum of symmetry in adjustment burdens required to sustain the logic of interdependence.

The term "symmetry" is used in this policy arena as a rough synonym for fairness among creditors and debtors. Consideration of it recalls the central idea behind this book. As the concept of market authority proposed herein is developed in the future, the material outlined in this chapter suggests its historical contingency. It also reminds us of the irreducible expectation of justice that the claim of authority entails.

The authority to stabilize globalizing financial markets has an ultimate quality to it, a quality invisible when those markets function reasonably well. There is no reason why it cannot be delegated for a time to the private sector, and there are very good reasons having to do with political accountability why such delegation might even become commonplace. Self-regulatory organizations, as oxymoronic as the term sounds, are nothing new in the broader international economy. The International Chamber of Commerce, for example, has for a century now promoted voluntary codes of conduct in this or that area of business activity. In the financial arena, recent examples of such delegation include private sector efforts to provide some common international structure for markets in financial derivatives and for international payments.

When such efforts accomplish their goals, catastrophes are avoided, few notice, and public officials willingly recede into the shadows. But when such efforts fail, or threaten to fail, the overarching issue of social justice returns to counterbalance ideological demands for ruthless efficiency. One of two things then happens. Agents of legitimate public authority reassert their ultimate regulatory power, or, if they truly cannot, markets collapse.[18]

The latter possibility has, ever since 1929, concentrated the minds of financial regulators at the core of the global economy. The desire to avoid it correlates with determination simultaneously to obfuscate their authority and to preserve their ultimate room for maneuver. In integrating crossborder financial markets, at least, the private element in market authority might just be too obvious. It certainly calls out for more extended theorization.

Mainstream theories in international political economy, sometimes labeled "liberal internationalist," need to engage more deeply the kinds of structural theories suggested by Saskia Sassen, Claire Cutler, and the editors of this volume.[19] A plausible insight, however, does provide that mainstream with a promising starting point for future debate. The fragility of globalizing financial markets, occasionally glimpsed, and the evolving mandates of the international financial institutions now intimately linked to them draw attention to the fact that the public authorities lying beneath their surface seem now to require a high degree of cooperation among themselves if their ultimate regulatory power is not to prove illusory. If such cooperation fails, mainstream theories of international political economy suggest that the rise of fully privatized and self-sustaining markets of global scale would be a highly unlikely outcome. Future development of the concept of market authority in the era of globalization does not end here, but it could productively begin by taking such a position clearly into account.

NOTES

1 By bounding my analysis empirically, I do not preclude the possibility that the essential legitimation of private power can be construed differently, especially against the backdrop of broader conceptions of social space and political rule and their evolution over time. Some of the sociological work cited by my colleagues in this book, or of students of international regimes commonly referred to as strong cognitivists or strong constructivists, relatedly underlines the essential malleability of political identity over long historical periods. For useful surveys, see, for example, George M. Thomas, et al. (eds.), *Institutional Structure: Constituting State, Society and the Individual* (Newbury Park, Cal.: Sage, 1987); and Andreas Hasenclever, Peter Mayer, and Volker Rittberger, *Theories of International Regimes* (Cambridge: Cambridge University Press, 1997), ch. 5.
2 Some of the following develops material introduced in my "Capital Mobility and the New Global Order," in Richard Stubbs and Geoffrey Underhill (eds.), *Political Economy and the Changing World Order*, 2nd edn. (Oxford and New York: Oxford University Press, 2000), pp. 119–28.
3 For background, see Geoffrey Underhill, "Keeping Governments out of Politics: Transnational Securities Markets, Regulatory Cooperation, and Political Legitimacy," *Review of International Studies*, 21 (3) (1995), 251–78; Louis W. Pauly, "Capital Mobility, State Autonomy, and Political Legitimacy," *Journal of International Affairs*, 48 (2) (Winter 1995), 369–88; and Ian Hurd, "Legitimacy and Authority in International Politics," *International Organization*, 53 (2) (Spring 1999), 379–408.
4 See Craig N. Murphy, *International Organization and Industrial Change: Global Governance Since 1850* (New York: Oxford University Press, 1994); Louis W. Pauly, *Who Elected the Bankers? Surveillance and Control in the World Economy* (Ithaca, N.Y.: Cornell University Press, 1997); and Ralph Bryant, *Turbulent Waters: Cross-Border Finance and International Governance* (Washington, D.C.: Brookings Institution, forthcoming).

5 See Eric Helleiner, *States and the Reemergence of Global Finance* (Ithaca, N.Y.: Cornell University Press, 1994).

6 Henry Laurence takes the case forward into the 1990s in *Money Rules: The New Politics of Finance in Britain and Japan* (Ithaca, N.Y.: Cornell University Press, 2001).

7 See, for example, Robert O'Brien, Anne Marie Goetz, Jan Aart Scholte, and Marc Williams (eds.), *Contesting Global Governance: Multilateral Economic Institutions and Global Social Movements* (Cambridge: Cambridge University Press, 2000).

8 See Stephen D. Krasner, *Sovereignty: Organized Hypocrisy* (Princeton, N.J.: Princeton University Press, 1999).

9 See Thomas J. Biersteker and Cynthia Weber (eds.), *State Sovereignty as a Social Construct* (Cambridge: Cambridge University Press, 1996); and Rodney Bruce Hall, *National Collective Identity: Social Constructs and International Systems* (New York: Columbia University Press, 1999).

10 See James Boughton, *Silent Revolution: The International Monetary Fund, 1979–1989* (Washington, D.C.: International Monetary Fund, 2001).

11 G. John Ikenberry, "Rethinking the Origins of American Hegemony," *Political Science Quarterly*, 104 (3) (1989), 375–400; Ikenberry, *After Victory* (Princeton, N.J.: Princeton University Press, 2000); Anne-Marie Burley, "Regulating the World: Multilateralism, International Law, and the Projection of the New Deal Regulatory State," in John G. Ruggie (ed.), *Multilateralism Matters* (New York: Columbia University Press, 1993), pp. 125–56; and Ruggie, *Winning the Peace* (New York: Columbia University Press, 1996).

12 See, for example, Susan Strange, *Mad Money* (Ann Arbor, Mich.: University of Michigan Press, 1998). Jerry Cohen's 1998 book seems to move in a similar direction when he diagnoses a "new geography of power" in international monetary affairs. But one must separate out his comments on the supply side of money from the demand side. On the demand side, he sees a profound blurring of the nature of monetary power in many states. On the supply side, however, he depicts more conventionally a movement from a unitary monetary order to a tripolar or multipolar order – all entirely based upon traditional public authority. See Benjamin J. Cohen, *The Geography of Money* (Ithaca, N.Y.: Cornell University Press, 1998).

13 See, for example, Barry Eichengreen, *Toward a New International Financial Architecture* (Washington, D.C.: Institute for International Economics, 1999); Council on Foreign Relations Independent Task Force, *Safeguarding Prosperity in a Global Financial System* (Washington, D.C.: Institute for International Economics, 1999); Morris Goldstein, "Strengthening the International Financial Architecture: Where Do We Stand?," Working Paper 00–8 (Washington, D.C.: Institute for International Economics, 2000).

14 See Bryant, *Turbulent Waters*.

15 For a recent treatment of the underlying theoretical and policy issues involved, see Michael Th. Greven and Louis W. Pauly (eds.), *Democracy Beyond the State? The European Dilemma and the Emerging Global Order* (Lanham, Md., and Toronto, Ont.: Rowman & Littlefield Publishers and University of Toronto Press, 2000).

16 For development of this point in a related context, see Paul N. Doremus, William W. Keller, Louis W. Pauly, and Simon Reich, *The Myth of the Global Corporation* (Princeton, N.J.: Princeton University Press, 1998).

17 Highly relevant here is Stanley Fischer, "On the Need for an International Lender of Last Resort," *Essays in International Economics*, No. 220 (International Economics Section, Department of Economics, Princeton University, Princeton, N.J., November 2000).

18 Recall here Weber's classic understanding of political legitimacy as the belief that the authority to issue commands – to compel obedience – is matched by perceptions of an obligation to comply among the recipients of those commands.

19 Liberal internationalist theories within IPE are well reviewed and critiqued in Robert Gilpin, *Global Political Economy* (Princeton, N.J.: Princeton University Press, 2001).

5   The state and globalization

Saskia Sassen

This chapter attempts to recover the ways in which the state participates in governing the global economy in a context increasingly dominated by deregulation, privatization, and the growing authority of non-state actors.[1] A key organizing proposition, derived from my previous work on global cities,[2] is the embeddedness of much of globalization in national territory, that is to say, in a geographic terrain that has been encased in an elaborate set of national laws and administrative capacities. The embeddedness of the global requires at least a partial lifting of these national encasements, and hence signals a necessary participation by the state, even when it concerns the state's own withdrawal from regulating the economy.

The question becomes one of understanding the specific type of authority/power this participation might entail for the state or, more precisely, for the particular state institutions involved. Does the weight of private, often foreign, interests in this specific work of the state become constitutive of that authority and indeed produce a hybrid that is neither fully private nor fully public? My argument is that, indeed, we are seeing the incipient formation of a type of authority and state practice that entail a partial denationalizing of what had been constructed historically as national.[3] This conceptualization introduces a twist into the analysis of private authority because it seeks to detect the presence of private agendas inside the state, that is, inside a domain represented as public. However, it differs from an older scholarly tradition on the captured state which focused on cooptation of states by private actors, because it emphasizes the privatization of norm-making capacities and the enactment of these norms in the public domain.

The purpose here is, then, to understand and specify a particular aspect of globalization and the state which is lost in what are typically rather dualized accounts of this relation; in such accounts, the spheres of influence of respectively the national and the global, or of state and non-state actors, are seen as distinct and mutually exclusive. While it may indeed be the case that most components of each of these are separate and mutually exclusive, there is a specific set of conditions or components that does not fit in this dual structure. Key among these are some components of the work of ministries of finance, central banks, and the increasingly specialized technical regulatory agencies, such as those concerned with finance, telecommunications, and competition policy. In this regard, then, my position is not comfortably subsumed under the proposition that nothing has much changed in terms of state power, nor under the proposition of the declining significance of the state.

An important methodological assumption here is that focusing on economic globalization can help us disentangle some of these issues precisely because, in strengthening the legitimacy of claims by foreign investors and firms, it adds to and renders visible the work of accommodating their rights and contracts in what remain basically national economies. However, these dynamics can also be present when privatization and deregulation concern native firms and investors, even though in much of the world privatization and deregulation have been constituted through the entry of foreign investors and firms.

In the first section I will introduce a number of conceptual issues about the denationalizing of specific forms of state authority which arise out of the at least partial location of global processes in national institutional orders. The second and third sections will discuss key features of this locational and institutional embeddedness of the global economy. And the final section will sketch out the particular substance and conditionality of this new mode of authority which, though housed or located in national state capacities and institutions, is not national in the way we had come to understand this feature of states over the last century. The empirical focus for much of the examination is confined to states under the so-called rule of law, and especially the United States.

Embeddedness and denationalization

A number of scholars have addressed various dimensions of this participation by the state. For some, it shows that globalization is made possible by states, and that, hence, not much has changed for states and the interstate system; the present era is merely a continuation of a long history of changes that have not altered the fundamental fact of state primacy.[4] There is today also a growing literature which interprets deregulation and privatization as the incorporation by the state of its own shrinking role;[5] in its most formalized version this position emphasizes the state's constitutionalizing of its own diminished role. In this literature economic globalization is not confined to capital crossing geographic borders as is captured in measures of international investment and trade, but is in fact conceptualized as a politico-economic system. And there is, finally, a growing literature, represented by various chapters in this book, that emphasizes the relocation of national public governance functions to private actors within both national and transnational domains.

The focus developed in this chapter adds yet another dimension to this growing and diverse scholarship by emphasizing that state participation is producing a denationalizing of particular components of state authority which remain, nonetheless, inside the state. As states participate in the implementation of the global economic system they have, in many cases, undergone significant transformations. The accommodation of the interests of foreign firms and investors entails a negotiation. At the heart of this negotiation is the development inside national states – through legislative acts, court rulings, executive orders – of the mechanisms necessary for the reconstitution of certain components of national capital into "global capital," and necessary to accommodate new types of rights/entitlements for foreign capital in what are still national territories in principle under the exclusive authority of their states.[6] The mode of this negotiation in the current phase has tended in a direction that I describe as a denationalizing of several highly specialized national institutional orders.

These particular transformations inside the state are partial and incipient but strategic. For instance, such transformations can weaken or alter the organizational architecture for the implementation of international law insofar as the latter depends on the institutional apparatus of national states. Further, they have also created the conditions whereby some parts of national states actually gain relative power[7] as a result of that participation in the development of a global economy. As particular components of national states become the institutional home for the operation of some of the dynamics that are central to globalization, they undergo change that is difficult to register or name. This is one instantiation of what I call a process of incipient denationalization – that is, of specific components of national states that function as such institutional homes.

This partial, often highly specialized, or at least particularized, denationalization can also take place in domains other than that of economic globalization, notably the more recent developments in the human rights regime that allow national courts to sue foreign firms and dictators, or that grant undocumented immigrants certain rights. Denationalization is, thus, multivalent: it endogenizes global agendas of many different types of actors, not only corporate firms and fiancial markets, but also human rights objectives. In this chapter I will confine myself to economic globalization.

The question for research then becomes: what is actually "national" in some of the institutional components of states linked to the implementation and regulation of economic globalization? The hypothesis here is that some components of national institutions, even though formally national, are not national in the sense in which we have constructed the meaning of that term over the past hundred years.

One of the roles of the state vis-à-vis today's global economy has been to negotiate the intersection of national law and foreign actors – whether firms, markets, or supranational organizations. This raises a question as to whether there are particular conditions that make execution of this role in the current phase distinctive and unlike what it may have been in earlier phases of the world economy. We have, on the one hand, the existence of an enormously elaborate body of law developed mostly over the past hundred years, which secures the exclusive territorial authority of national states to an extent not seen in earlier centuries, and, on the other, the considerable institutionalizing, especially in the 1990s, of the "rights" of non-national firms, the deregulation of crossborder transactions, and the growing influence/power of some of the supranational organizations. If securing these rights, options, and powers entailed an even partial relinquishing of components of state authority as constructed over the past century, then we can posit that this sets up the conditions for a necessary engagement by national states in the process of globalization.

We need to understand more about the nature of this engagement than is represented by concepts such as deregulation. It is becoming clear that the role of the state in the process of deregulation involves the production of new types of regulations, legislative items, court decisions[8] – in brief, the production of a whole series of new "legalities."[9] The background condition here is that the state remains as the ultimate guarantor of the "rights" of global capital, i.e., the protector of contracts and property rights, and, more generally, a major legitimator of claims.[10] In this regard the state can be seen as incorporating the global project of its own shrinking role in regulating economic transactions[11] and giving it operational effectiveness and legitimacy.[12] The state here can be conceived of as representing a technical administrative capacity which cannot be replicated at this time by any other institutional arrangement; although not in all cases,[13] this is a capacity backed by military power, with global power in the case of some states. The objective for foreign firms and investors is to enjoy, transnationally, the protections traditionally exercised by the state in the national realm of the economy for national firms, notably guaranteeing property rights and contracts. How this gets done may involve a range of options. To some extent this work of guaranteeing is becoming privatized, as is signaled by the growth of international commercial arbitration,[14] and by key elements of the new privatized institutional order for governing the global economy.[15]

It is in fact some states, particularly the United States and the UK, that are producing the design for these new legalities, i.e., items derived from Anglo-American commercial law and accounting standards, and are hence imposing these on other states given the interdependencies at the heart of the current phase of globalization. This creates and imposes a set of specific constraints on the other participating states.[16] Legislative items, executive orders, adherence to new technical standards, and so on will have to be produced through the particular institutional and political structures of each of these states. In terms of research and theorization, this is a vast uncharted terrain: it would mean examining how that production takes place and gets legitimated in different countries. This signals the possibility of crossnational variations (which then would need to be established, measured, interpreted). The emergent, often imposed consensus in the community of states to further globalization is not merely a political decision: it entails specific types of work by a large number of distinct state institutions in each of these countries. Clearly, the role of the state will vary significantly depending on the power it may have both internally and internationally.

The US government as the hegemonic power of this period has led/ forced other states to adopt these obligations toward global capital. And, in so doing, it has contributed to strengthening the forces that can challenge or destabilize what have historically been constructed as state powers.[17] In my reading this holds both for the United States and for other countries. One way in which this becomes evident is in the fact that, while the state continues to play a crucial, though no longer exclusive, role in the production of legality around new forms of economic activity, at least some of this production of legalities is increasingly feeding the power of a new emerging structure marked by denationalization or privatization of some of its components.

A crucial part of the argument is the fact of the institutional and locational embeddedness of globalization. Specifying this embeddedness has two purposes. One is to provide the empirical specification underlying my assertion that the state is engaged, which in turn feeds the proposition about the denationalizing of particular state functions and capacities. The second purpose is to signal that, given this embeddedness, the range of ways in which the state can be involved is far broader than what it is today, when it is largely confined to furthering economic globalization. Conceivably state involvement could address a whole series of global issues, including the democratic deficit in the multilateral system governing globalization.[18]

The locational and institutional embeddedness of the global economy

Some of the key features of economic globalization allow for a broader range of forms of state participation than is generally recognized in analyses of the declining significance of the state. There are at least two distinct issues here. One is that the current condition, marked by the ascendance of private authority, is but one possible mode of several in which the state could be articulated. The other is that this current condition still leaves room for new forms of participation by the state as well as new forms of crossborder state collaboration in the governing of the global economy.[19] Among these are forms of state participation aimed at recognizing the legitimacy of claims for greater social justice and democratic accountability in the global economy, although both would require administrative and legal innovations.[20] The effort here is then not so much to show the enormous power and authority amassed by global markets and firms, but rather to detect the particular ways in which the power and authority of the state does and could shape and reshape those particular forms of private economic power.

There are three features of the global economy I want to emphasize here. First, the geography of economic globalization is strategic rather than all-encompassing, and this is especially so when it comes to the managing, coordinating, servicing, and financing of global economic operations. The fact that it is strategic is significant for a discussion about the possibilities of regulating and governing the global economy. Second, the center of gravity of many of the transactions that we refer to in an aggregate fashion as the global economy lies in the North Atlantic region, a fact which also facilitates the development and implementation of convergent regulatory frameworks and technical standards, and enables a convergence around "Western" standards. If the geography of globalization were a diffuse condition at the planetary scale, and one involving equally powerful countries and regions with a much broader range of differences than those evident in the North Atlantic, the question of its regulation might well be radically different. Third, the strategic geography of globalization is partly embedded in national territories, i.e., global cities and Silicon Valleys. The combination of these three characteristics suggests that states may have more options to participate in governing the global economy than much of the focus on the loss of regulatory authority allows us to recognize.

There are sites in this strategic geography where the density of economic transactions and the intensity of regulatory efforts come together in complex, often novel configurations. Two of these are the focus of this section. They are foreign direct investment, which mostly consists of crossborder mergers and acquisitions, and the global capital market, undoubtedly the dominant force in the global economy today. Along with trade, they are at the heart of the structural changes constitutive of globalization and the efforts to regulate it. These two processes also make evident the enormous weight of the North Atlantic region in the global economy.

Both foreign direct investment and the global capital market bring up specific organizational and regulatory issues.[21] There is an enormous increase in the complexity of management, coordination, servicing, and financing for firms operating worldwide networks of factories, service outlets, and/or offices, and for firms operating in crossborder financial markets. For reasons I discuss later, this has brought about a sharp growth in control and command functions, and their concentration in a crossborder network of major financial and business centers. This in turn contributes to the formation of a strategic geography for the management of globalization. Nowhere is this as evident as in the structure of the global capital market and the network of financial centers within which it is located. Elsewhere I examine this institutional order as the site of a new type of private authority.[22]

Each of these also is at the heart of a variety of regulatory initiatives. The growth of foreign direct investment has brought with it a renewed concern with questions of extraterritoriality and competition policy, including the regulation of crossborder mergers. The growth of the global capital market has brought with it specific efforts to develop the elements of an architecture for its governance: international securities regulation, new international standards for accounting and financial reporting, various European Union provisions. Each has tended to be ensconced in fairly distinct regulatory frameworks: foreign direct investment in antitrust law, and global finance in national regulatory frameworks for banking and finance.[23]

Further, while this strategic geography of globalization is partly embedded in national territories, this does not necessarily entail that existing national regulatory frameworks can regulate those functions. Regulatory functions have shifted increasingly toward a set of emerging or newly invigorated crossborder regulatory networks and the development of a whole array of standards to organize world trade and global finance. Specialized, often semi-autonomous regulatory agencies, and the specialized crossborder networks they are forming, are taking over functions once enclosed in national legal frameworks, and standards are replacing rules in international law. The question for research and theory is whether this mode of regulation is sufficient, and whether state participation may not emerge again as a more significant factor for the ultimate workability of some of these new regulatory regimes.

Finally, the empirical patterns of foreign direct investment and global finance show to what extent their centers of gravity lie in the North Atlantic region. The northern trans-Atlantic economic system (specifically the links among the European Union, the United States, and Canada) represents the major concentration of processes of economic globalization in the world today. This holds whether one looks at foreign direct investment flows generally, at crossborder mergers and acquisitions in particular, at overall financial flows, or at the new strategic alliances among financial centers. At the turn of the millennium this region accounts for two-thirds of worldwide stock market capitalization, 60 percent of inward foreign investment stock and 76 percent of outward stock, 60 percent of worldwide sales in mergers and acquisitions, and 80 percent of purchases in M&As. There are other major regions in the global economy: Japan, South East Asia, Latin America. But except for some of the absolute levels of capital resources in Japan, they are dwarfed by the size of the northern trans-Atlantic system.

This heavy concentration in the volume and value of crossborder transactions raises a number of questions. One concerns its features, the extent to which there are interdependence and (in that sense) the elements of a crossborder economic system. The weight of these trans-Atlantic links needs to be considered against the weight of established zones of influence for each of the major powers – particularly, the rest of the western hemisphere in the case of the United States, and Africa and Central and Eastern Europe for the European Union.

If there is considerable interdependence in the northern trans-Atlantic system, then the question of regulation and governance is likely to be of a different sort than if globalization for each of these major regions has meant in practice strengthening their ties and presence in their respective zones of influence. The United States and individual EU members have long had often intense economic transactions with their zones of influence. Some of these have been reinvigorated in the new economic policy context of opening to foreign investment, privatization, and trade and financial deregulation.

In my reading of the evidence, both the relations of the North Atlantic powers with their respective zones of influence and the relations within the system have changed. We are seeing the consolidation of a transnational economy that has its center of gravity in the North Atlantic system both in terms of the intensity and value of transactions, and in terms of the emerging system of rules and standards. This system is articulated with a growing network of sites for investment, trade, and financial transactions in the rest of the world. It is through this incorporation in a hierarchical global network, which has its center in the North Atlantic, that the relations with their zones of influence is now constituted. Thus, while the United States is still a dominant force in Latin America, several European countries have become major investors there, on a scale far surpassing past trends. And while several European Union countries have become leaders in investment in Central and Eastern Europe, US firms are playing a role they have never before played.

What we are seeing today is a new grid of economic transactions superimposed on the old geoeconomic patterns. The latter persist to variable extents, but they are increasingly submerged under this new crossborder grid which amounts to a new, though partial geoeconomics. In my own research I have found that these new configurations are particularly evident in the organization of global finance and, to a lesser extent, in direct foreign investment, especially crossborder mergers and acquisitions.

The fact of systemic conditions in the new geoeconomics is significant for the question of regulation. The orders of magnitude and the intensity of transactions in the North Atlantic system facilitate the formation of standards even in the context of what are, relatively speaking, strong differences between the United States and continental Europe in their legal, accounting, antitrust, and other rules. It is clear that even though these two regions have more in common with each other than with much of the rest of the world, their differences matter when it comes to the creation of crossborder standards. The fact of shared Western standards and norms, however, in combination with enormous economic weight has facilitated the circulation and imposition of US and European standards and rules on transactions involving firms from other parts of the world. There is a sort of globalization of Western standards. Much has been said about the dominance of US standards and rules, but European standards are also evident, for instance in the new antitrust rules being developed in Central and Eastern Europe.

Worldwide networks and central command functions

There are, clearly, strong dispersal trends contained in the patterns of foreign investment and capital flows generally: the offshoring of factories, the expansion of global networks of affiliates and subsidiaries, the formation of global financial markets with a growing number of participating countries. What is excluded from this account is the other half of the story. This worldwide geographic dispersal of factories and service outlets takes place as part of highly integrated corporate structures with strong tendencies toward concentration in control and profit appropriation. The

North Atlantic system is the site for most of the strategic management and coordination functions of the new global economic system.

Elsewhere I have shown that, when the geographic dispersal of factories, offices, and service outlets through crossborder investment takes place as part of such integrated corporate systems, there is also a growth in central functions; we can see a parallel trend with financial firms and markets.[24] One hypothesis this suggests is that the more globalized firms become, the more their central functions grow – in importance, in complexity, in number of transactions.[25] The specific forms assumed by globalization over the last decade have created particular organizational requirements. The emergence of global markets for finance and specialized services, the growth of investment as a major type of international transaction – all have contributed to the expansion in command functions and in the demand for specialized services for firms.[26]

We can make this more concrete by considering some of the staggering figures involved in this worldwide dispersal, and imagining what it entails in terms of coordination and management for parent headquarters, such as the fact that by the late 1990s there were almost half a million foreign affiliates of firms worldwide, most of them belonging to firms from North America and Western Europe.[27] There has been a greater growth in foreign sales through affiliates than through direct exports: the foreign sales through affiliates were US$ 11 trillion in 1999 and through worldwide exports of goods and services US$ 8 trillion. This has of course also fed the intrafirm share of so-called free crossborder trade. The data on foreign direct investment show clearly that the United States and the EU are the major receiving and sending areas in the world. Finally, the transnationality index of the largest transnational firms shows that many of the major firms from these two regions have over half of their assets, sales, and workforces outside their home countries.[28] Together these types of evidence provide a fairly comprehensive picture of this combination of dispersal and the growth of central functions.

The globalization of a firm's operations brings with it a massive task of coordination and management. Much of this has been going on for a long time but has accelerated over the decades. Further, this dispersal does not proceed under a single organizational form – rather, behind these general figures lie many different organizational forms, hierarchies of control, degrees of autonomy. The globally integrated network of financial centers is yet another form of this combination of dispersal and the growing complexity of central management and coordination.

Of importance to the analysis here is the dynamic that connects the dispersal of economic activities with the growth of central functions. In terms of sovereignty and globalization, this means that an interpretation of the impact of globalization as creating a space economy that extends beyond the regulatory capacity of a single state is only half the story; the other half is that these central functions are disproprotionately concentrated in the national territories of the highly developed countries.

By central functions I do not only mean top-level headquarters; I am referring to all the top-level financial, legal, accounting, managerial, executive, and planning functions necessary to run a corporate organization operating in more than one country, and increasingly in several countries. These central functions are partly embedded in headquarters, but also in good part in what has been called the corporate services complex, that is, the network of financial, legal, accounting, and advertising firms that handle the complexities of operating in more than one national legal system, national accounting system, advertising culture, etc., and do so under conditions of rapid innovations in all these fields. Such services have become so specialized and complex that headquarters increasingly buy them from specialized firms rather than producing them in-house. These agglomerations of firms producing central functions for the management and coordination of global economic systems are disproportionately concentrated in the highly developed countries – particularly, though not exclusively, in the kinds of cities I call global cities. Such concentrations of functions represent a strategic factor in the organization of the global economy.

One argument I am making here is that it is important to unbundle analytically the fact of strategic functions for the global economy or for global operation, and the overall corporate economy of a country. These global control and command functions are partly embedded in national corporate structures but also constitute a distinct corporate subsector. This subsector can be conceived of as part of a network that connects global cities across the globe.[29] For the purposes of certain kinds of inquiry this distinction may not matter; for the purposes of understanding the global economy, it does. And it seems to me that this distinction also matters for questions of regulation, notably regulation of crossborder activities.

If the strategic central functions – both those produced in corporate headquarters and those produced in the specialized corporate services sector – are located in a network of major financial and business centers, the question of regulating what amounts to a key part of the global economy is not the same as if the strategic management and coordination functions were as distributed geographically as are the factories, service outlets, and affiliates. However, regulation of these activities is evolving along lines of greater specialization and crossborder capabilities than most current state-centric national systems can comfortably accommodate today.

Another instance today of this negotiation between a transnational process or dynamic and a national territory is that of the global financial markets. The orders of magnitude have risen sharply, as illustrated by the US$ 68 trillion in the 1999 value of internationally traded derivatives, a major component of the global economy. These transactions are partly embedded in telecommunications systems that make possible the instantaneous transmission of money/information around the globe. Much attention has gone to these capacities for instantaneous transmission. But the other half of the story is the extent to which the global financial markets are located in particular cities, especially though not exclusively in the highly developed countries; indeed, the degrees of concentration are unexpectedly high.

Stock markets worldwide have become globally integrated. In addition to deregulation in the 1980s in all the major European and North American markets, the late 1980s and early 1990s saw the addition of such markets as Buenos Aires, Sao Paulo, Bangkok, Taipei, etc. The integration of a growing number of stock markets has contributed to raise the capital that can be mobilized through stock markets. Worldwide market value reached over US$ 30 trillion in 2000. This globally integrated stock market, which makes possible the circulation of publicly listed shares around the globe in seconds, is embedded in a grid of very material, physical, strategic places – that is, cities belonging to national territories.

A crucial issue for understanding the question of regulation and the role of the state in the global capital market is the ongoing embeddedness of this market in these networks of financial centers operating within national states; these are not offshore markets. The North Atlantic system contains an enormous share of the global capital market through its sharp concentration of leading financial centers.[30] Further, as the system expands through the incorporation of additional centers into this network – from Eastern Europe, Latin America, etc. – the question of regulation also pivots on the existence of dominant standards and rules, i.e. those produced by the economies of the North Atlantic.

In my reading, studies that emphasize deregulation and liberalization do not sufficiently recognize an important feature, one which matters for the analysis here: the global financial system has reached levels of complexity that require the existence of a crossborder network of financial centers to service the operations of global capital. Each actual financial center represents a massive and highly specialized concentration of resources and talent; and the network of these centers constitutes the operational architecture for the global capital market.

Denationalized state agendas

The representation of economic globalization coming out of the two pre-ceding sections is quite different from many of the standard accounts. For the purposes of this section it is especially two of the features of glob-alization as discussed above that matter. One of these is that the global economy needs to be produced, reproduced, serviced, financed. It can-not be taken simply as a given, such as the fact of more interdependence, or merely as a function of the power of multinational corporations and financial markets. There is a vast array of highly specialized functions that need to be ensured. These have become so specialized that they can no longer be contained in corporate headquarters functions. Global cities are strategic sites for the production of these specialized functions to run and coordinate the global economy. Inevitably located in national territo-ries, these cities are the organizational and institutional location for some of the major dynamics of denationalization. While such processes of de-nationalization – for instance, certain aspects of financial and investment deregulation – are institutional and not geographic, the geographic loca-tion of many of the strategic institutions – financial markets and financial services firms – means these processes are embedded geographically.

The second feature, partly connected to the first, is that the global economy to a large extent materializes in national territories. Its topogra-phy is one that moves between digital space and national territories. This requires a particular set of negotiations which have the effect of leaving the geographic boundaries of the national state's territory unaltered, but do transform the institutional encasements of that geographic fact, that is, the state's territorial jurisdiction or, more abstractly, exclusive territo-riality.

Precisely because global processes need to be coordinated and serviced and because many of these functions materialize to a large extent in na-tional territories, national states have had to become deeply involved in the implementation of the global economic system. In this process states have experienced transformations of various aspects of their institutional structure. This signals that the global economy and the national state are not mutually exclusive domains. Globalization leaves national territory basically unaltered but is having pronounced effects on the exclusive ter-ritoriality of the national state – that is, its effects are not on territory as such but on the institutional encasements of the geographic fact of national territory. But alongside and, in my reading, distinct from this diminished territorial authority of the state, there is the denationalizing of specific state agendas. The work of states in producing part of the technical and legal infrastructure for economic globalization has involved both a change in the exclusivity of state authority and in the composition of the work of states. Economic globalization entails a set of practices that destabilize another set of practices, i.e., some of the practices that came to constitute national state sovereignty.

Implementing today's global economic system in the context of national territorial sovereignty required multiple policy, analytic, and narrative negotiations. These negotiations have typically been summarized or coded as "deregulation." There is much more going on in these negotiations than the concept "deregulation" captures. The encounter of a global actor – firm or market – with one or another instantiation of the national state can be thought of as a new frontier. It is not merely a dividing line between the national economy and the global economy. It is a zone of politico-economic interactions that produce new institutional forms and alter some of the old ones. Nor is it just a matter of reducing regulations. For instance, in many countries, the necessity for autonomous central banks in the current global economic system has required a thickening of regulations in order to delink central banks from the influence of the executive branch of government and from deeply "national" political agendas.

Central banks illustrate this well. These are national institutions, concerned with national matters. Yet over the last decade they have become the institutional home within the national state for monetary policies that are necessary to further the development of a global capital market and indeed, more generally, a global economic system. The new conditionality of the global economic system – the requirements that need to be met for a country to become integrated into the global capital market – contains as one key element the autonomy of central banks.[31] This facilitates the task of instituting a certain kind of monetary policy, e.g., one privileging low inflation over job growth even when a president may have preferred it the other way around, particularly at reelection time. While securing central bank autonomy has certainly eliminated a lot of corruption, it has also been the vehicle for one set of accommodations on the part of national states to the requirements of the global capital market. A parallel analysis can be made of ministries of finance (known as the Treasury in the United States and the UK) which have had to impose certain kinds of fiscal policies as part of the new conditionalities of economic globalization.

There is a set of strategic dynamics and institutional transformations at work here. They may incorporate a small number of state agencies and units within departments, a small number of legislative initiatives and of executive orders, and yet have the power to institute a new normativity at the heart of the state; this is especially so because these strategic sectors are operating in complex interactions with private, transnational, powerful actors. Much of the institutional apparatus of the state remains basically unchanged; the inertia of bureaucratic organizations, which creates its own version of path dependence, makes an enormous contribution to continuity.

In my current research on the United States, I am extricating from what has been constructed as "US legislative history" a whole series of legislative items and executive orders that can be read as accommodations on the part of the national state and as its active participation in producing the conditions for economic globalization. This is a history of microinterventions, often minute transformations in the regulatory or legal frameworks that facilitated the extension of particular crossborder operations of US firms. This is clearly not a new history, neither for the United States nor for other Western former imperial powers (e.g., the "concessions" to trading companies under British, Dutch, and other colonial regimes). Yet, I argue, we can identify a new phase, one which has very specific instantiations of this broader feature.[32]

Among the first of these new measures in the United States, and perhaps among the best-known, are the tariff items passed to facilitate the internationalization of manufacturing, which exempted firms from import duties on the value added of reimported components assembled or manufactured in offshore plants. I date this microhistory of legislative and executive interventions to the late 1960s, with a full crystallization of various measures facilitating the global operations of US firms and the globalization of markets in the 1980s, and work continuing vigorously in the 1990s. The Foreign Investment Act of 1976, the implementation of International Banking Facilities in 1981, the various deregulations and liberalizations of the financial sector in the 1980s, and so on – these are but the best-known landmarks in this microhistory.

Further, the new types of crossborder collaborations among specialized government agencies concerned with a growing range of issues emerging from the globalization of capital markets and the new trade order are yet another aspect of this participation by the state in the implementation of a global economic system. A good example is the heightened interaction in the past three or four years among competition policy regulators from a large number of countries. This is a period of renewed concern about competition policy because economic globalization puts pressure on governments to work toward convergence given the crosscountry diversity of competition laws or enforcement practices. This convergence around specific competition policy issues can coexist with ongoing, often enormous differences among these countries when it comes to laws and regulations about those components of their economies that do not intersect with globalization. There are multiple other instances of this highly specialized type of convergence: regulatory issues concerning telecommunications, finance, the Internet, etc. It is, then, a very partial type of convergence among regulators of different countries who often begin to share more with each other than they do with colleagues in their home bureaucracies.

What is of particular concern here is that today we see a sharp increase in the work of establishing convergence.[33] We can clearly identify a new phase in the past ten years. In some of these sectors there has long been an often elementary convergence, or at least coordination, of standards. For instance, central bankers have long interacted with each other across borders, but today we see an intensification in these transactions, which becomes necessary in the effort to develop and extend a global capital market. The increase of crossborder trade has brought with it a sharpened need for convergence in standards, as is evident in the vast proliferation of International Organization for Standardization (ISO) items. Another example is the institutional and legal framework necessary for the operation of the crossborder commodity chains identified by Gereffi.[34]

One outcome of these various trends is the emergence of a strategic field of operations that represents a partial disembedding of specific state operations from the broader institutional world of the state that had been geared exclusively to national agendas. It is a field of crossborder transactions among government agencies and business sectors aimed at addressing the new conditions produced and demanded by economic globalization. In positing this I am rejecting the prevalent notion in much of the literature on globalization that the realm of the national and the realm of the global are two mutually exclusive zones. My argument is rather that globalization is partly endogenous to the national, and is in this regard produced through a dynamic of denationalizing what had been constructed as the national.[35]

It is also a field of particular types of transactions: they are strategic, cut across borders, and entail specific interactions with private actors. These transactions do not entail the state as such, as in international treaties, but rather consist of the operations and policies of specific subcomponents of the state – for instance, legislative initiatives, specialized technical regulatory agencies, or some of the agendas pursued by central banks. These are transactions that cut across borders in that they concern the standards and regulations imposed on firms and markets operating globally,[36] and hence produce a certain convergence at the level of national regulations and law in the creation of the requisite conditions for globalization. The result is a mix of new or strengthened forms of private authority and partly denationalized state authority, such as the instituting of private interests into state normativity.[37]

Conclusion

The chapters in this volume show us the repositioning of the state in a broader field of power partly constituted through the formation of a new private institutional order linked to the global economy, but also through the growing importance of a variety of other institutional orders, from the new roles of the international network of NGOs to the international human rights regime. In this chapter the focus is not on that private institutional order but rather on the ways in which the state participates in the implementation of a global economic system. The focus is particularly on modes of participation that have the effect of transforming certain features of the state, including ways that are often not evident. The aim was to map an intermediate zone where private authority and state authority meet and produce a third type of authority. This is an intermediate institutional zone in need of conceptualization and empirical specification. This chapter begins to map some of its features.

Economic globalization has emerged as a key dynamic in the formation of a transnational system of power which lies in good part outside the formal interstate system. One instance of this is the relocation of national public governance functions to transnational private arenas, much of the focus in this volume. But I argue that it also lies, to a far higher degree than is usually recognized, inside particular components of national states. This second feature can be recognized in the work done by legislatures, courts, and various agencies in the executive to produce the mechanisms necessary to accommodate the rights of global capital in what are still national territories under the exclusive control of their states. Rather than interpreting this as signaling that not much has changed, or as a capturing of the state by private interests, I interpret this as a denationalizing of what had been constructed in national terms.

The much examined decrease in state regulatory capacities resulting from some of the basic policies associated with economic globalization is a far more differentiated process than notions of an overall decline in the significance of the state suggest. And it entails a more transformative dynamic inside the state than the notion of a simple loss of power suggests. There are significant policy implications to this type of reading. Up to now much of the work of the state has concerned the claims made by powerful economic actors. I would like to posit the possibility of new types of state authority, including the possibility of forms going well beyond the current modes of state action. In principle, such new modes could also involve elements of a new politics of accountability vis-à-vis global actors rather than the current orientation of state work toward furthering the rights and guarantees of global capital. The enabling condition is, precisely, the institutional and locational embeddedness of the global economy, at least partly, in national institutional orders and territories.

NOTES

1 This chapter is part of my larger multiyear research project to be published as *Denationalization: Economy and Polity in a Global Digital Age* (under contract with Princeton University Press, September 2003).

2 Saskia Sassen, *The Global City: New York, London, Tokyo* (Princeton, N.J.: Princeton University Press, 2001, 2nd edn. [1991]).

3 Sassen, *Denationalization.*

4 Steven D. Krasner, *Sovereignty: Organized Hypocrisy* (Princeton, N.J.: Princeton University Press, 1999).

5 Leo Panitch, "Rethinking the Role of the State in an Era of Globalization," in James Mittelman (ed.), *Globalization: Critical Reflections. International Political Economy Yearbook*, vol. 9 (Boulder, Colo.: Lynne Rienner, 1996), pp. 83–113; Stephen Gill, "Globalization, Democratization, and the Politics of Indifference," in the same volume, pp. 205–28; and Mittelman, *The Globalization Syndrome: Transformation and Resistance* (Princeton, N.J.: Princeton University Press, 2000).

6 Two very different bodies of scholarship which develop lines of analysis that can help in capturing some of these conditions are represented by the work of Rosenau, particularly his examination of the domestic "frontier" inside the national state, and by the work of Walker problematizing the distinction inside/outside in international relations theory. See James N. Rosenau, *Along the Domestic–Foreign Frontier: Exploring Governance in a Turbulent World* (Cambridge: Cambridge University Press, 1997), and R. B. J. Walker, *Inside/Outside: International Relations as Political Theory* (Cambridge: Cambridge University Press, 1993).

7 Saskia Sassen, *Losing Control? Sovereignty in an Age of Globalization*, 1995 Columbia University Leonard Hastings Schoff Memorial Lectures (New York: Columbia University Press, 1996), chs. 1 and 2.

8 Sol Picciotto, *International Business Taxation: A Study in the Internationalization of Business Regulation* (London: Weidenfeld and Nicolson, 1992); P. G. Cerny, *The Changing Architecture of Politics* (London: Sage, 1990); and Panitch, "Rethinking the Role of the State."

9 I use this term to distinguish this production from "law" or "jurisprudence": Sassen, *Losing Control?*, ch. 1.

10 While well known, it is worth remembering that this guarantee of the rights of capital is embedded in a certain type of state, a certain conception of the rights of capital, and a certain type of international legal regime: it is largely embedded in the state of the most developed and most powerful countries in the world, in Western notions of contract and property rights, and in new legal regimes aimed at furthering economic globalization, e.g., the push to get countries to support copyright law.

11 Gill, "Globalization, Democratization," and Panitch, "Rethinking the Role of the State."

12 Sassen, *Losing Control?*, chs. 1 and 2, and Sassen, *Denationalization*.

13 See Williams, "Transnational Organized Crime and the State," this volume.

14 Yves Dezalay and Bryant Garth, *Dealing in Virtue: International Commercial Arbitration and the Construction of a Transnational Legal Order* (Chicago and London: University of Chicago Press, 1996).

15 See also Cutler, "Private Regimes and Interfirm Cooperation," this volume.

16 This dominance assumes many forms and does not affect only poorer and weaker countries. France, for instance, ranks among the top providers of information services and industrial engineering services in Europe, and has a strong, though not outstanding, position in financial and insurance services. But it has found itself at an increasing disadvantage in legal and accounting services because Anglo-American law and standards dominate in international transactions. Anglo-American firms with offices in Paris do the servicing of the legal needs of firms, whether French or foreign, operating out of France (Sassen, *Global City*). Similarly, Anglo-American law is increasingly dominant in international commercial arbitration, an institution grounded in continental, particularly French and Swiss, traditions of jurisprudence (Dezalay and Garth, *Dealing in Virtue*).

17 See, in this regard, Giovanni Arrighi, *The Long Twentieth Century: Money, Power, and the Origins of Our Times* (London: Verso, 1994); Diana E. Davis (ed.), "Chaos and Governance," *Political Power and Social Theory*, 13, Part IV: Scholarly Controversy (Stamford, Conn.: JAI Press, 1999).

18 Elsewhere (*Denationalization*) I examine how these dynamics also position citizens (still largely confined to national state institutions for the full execution of their rights) vis-à-vis these types of global struggles. My argument is that state participation creates an enabling environment not only for global corporate capital but also for those seeking to subject the latter to greater accountability and public scrutiny. But unlike what has happened with global corporate capital, the necessary legal and administrative instruments and regimes have not been developed. The tradeoffs and the resources that can be mobilized are quite different in the case of citizens seeking to globalize their capacities for governing compared to those of global capital seeking to form regimes that enable and protect it.

19 Alfred C. Aman, Jr., "The Globalizing State: A Future-Oriented Perspective on the Public/Private Distinction, Federalism, and Democracy," *Vanderbilt Journal of Transnational Law*, 31 (4) (1998), 769–870.

20 I examine these two issues in greater detail in Sassen, *Denationalization*.

21 For a detailed examination of these two aspects, see Sassen, *Global City*, chs. 4, 5, and 7.

22 Sassen, *Losing Control?*, ch. 2.

23 It is quite possible that globalization may have the effect of blurring the boundaries between these two regulatory worlds.

24 Sassen, *Global City*.

25 This process of corporate integration should not be confused with vertical integration as conventionally defined. See also Gary Gereffi, "Global Production Systems and Third World Development," in Barbara Stallings (ed.), *Global Change, Regional Response: The New International Context of Development*

(New York: Cambridge University Press, 1995), pp. 100–42, on commodity chains, and Michael Porter, *The Competitive Advantage of States* (New York: Free Press, 1990), on value-added chains, two constructs that also illustrate the difference between corporate integration at a world scale and vertical integration as conventionally defined.

26 A central proposition here, developed at length in my work (*Global City*), is that we cannot take the existence of a global economic system as a given, but rather need to examine the particular ways in which the conditions for economic globalization are produced. This requires examining not only communication capacities and the power of multinationals, but also the infrastructure of facilities and work processes necessary for the implementation of global economic systems, including the production of those inputs that constitute the capability for global control and the infrastructure of jobs involved in this production. The emphasis shifts to the *practice* of global control: the work of producing and reproducing the organization and management of a global production system and a global marketplace for finance, both under conditions of economic concentration. The recovery of place and production also implies that global processes can be studied in great empirical detail.

27 Affilliates are but one form of operating overseas and hence their number underrepresents the dispersal of a firm's operations. There are today multiple forms, ranging from new temporary partnerships to older types of subcontracting and contracting.

28 This index is an average based on ratios of the share that foreign sales, assets, and employment represent in a firm's total of each. If we consider the world's top 100 transnational corporations (TNCs) in 1997, the EU had 48 of these firms and the United States 28; many of the remaining were from Japan. Thus together the EU and the United States accounted for over two-thirds of the world's 100 largest TNCs. The United States, the UK, France, Germany, and Japan together accounted for 3/4 of these 100 firms in 1997; this has been roughly so since 1990. The average transnationality index for the EU is 56.7 percent compared to 38.5 percent for the United States (but 79.2 for Canada). Most of the US and EU TNCs in this top 100 list have very high levels of foreign assets as a percentage of total assets: for instance, 98 percent for Seagram, 97 percent for Thomson, 96 percent for Asea Brown Boveri, 91 percent for Bayer, 91 percent for Nestlé, 85 percent for Michelin, 85 percent for Unilever, 79 percent for Hoechst, 77 percent for Philips Electronics, 71 percent for Ericsson, 69 percent for Ferruzi/Montedison, 68 percent for Coca-Cola, 67 percent for Rhône-Poulenc, 62 percent for Elf Aquitaine, 59 percent for BMW, 58 percent for Exxon, 55 percent for McDonald's, 55 percent for Volkswagen Group, 51 percent for IBM, 45 percent for Renault, 43 percent for Siemens, and so on. The share of foreign in total employment is often even higher. (See Organization for Economic Cooperation and Development, *Transborder Data Flow Contracts in the Wider Framework Mechanisms for Privacy Protection in Global Networks* [Paris: OECD, 2000], for the full listing.)

29 In this sense, global cities are different from the old capitals of erstwhile empires, in that they are a function of crossborder networks rather than simply the most powerful city of an empire. There is, in my conceptualization, no

such entity as a single global city as there could be a single capital of an empire; the category global city makes sense only as a component of a global network of strategic sites. The corporate subsector which contains the global control and command functions is partly both embedded in, and constitutive of this network.

30 Two major developments that can alter some of the features of the present configuration are the growth of electronic trading and the growth of the eurozone. The creation of an enormous consolidated capital market in the eurozone raises serious questions about the feasibility of maintaining the current pattern with as many international financial centers as there are member countries; some of these markets may lose top international functions and get repositioned in complex and hierarchical divisions of labor. Second, electronic trading is leading to a distinct shift toward setting up strategic alliances among major financial centers, producing a combination of a crossborder digital market embedded in a set of specific city-based financial markets. I have examined this at greater length in Sassen, *Global City*, chs. 4, 5, and 7.

31 While we take this autonomy for granted in the United States or in most EU countries (though not all – thus France's central bank is still not considered as quite autonomous from the executive), in many countries the head of state or local oligarchies have long had undue influence on central banks. Incidentally, this influence has not necessarily always worked to the disadvantage of the disadvantaged, as is evident for instance in monetary policies that promoted employment by letting inflation rise.

32 I am trying to distinguish current forms from older notions of the state as a tool of capital, comprador bourgeoisies, or neocolonialism. Further, there are important parallels in this research with scholarship focused on the work of the state in producing the distinction between private and public law (see Cutler, "Private Regimes and Interfirm Cooperation," in this volume), and with scholarship on the work of the state in setting up the various legal and administrative frameworks that gave the modern state its shape.

33 I use the term convergence for expediency. In the larger project I posit that conceptualizing these outcomes as convergence is actually problematic and often incorrect. Rather than a dynamic whereby individual states wind up converging, what is at work is a global dynamic that gets filtered through the specifics of each "participating" state. Hence my central research concern is not so much the outcome, "convergence," but the work of producing this outcome.

34 Gereffi, "Global Production Systems."

35 Further, insofar as it is partly embedded in national settings, e.g., global cities, the state has had to re-regulate specific aspects of its authority over national territory.

36 An important point, which is usually disregarded in much general commentary about the global economy, is that a firm can participate in the latter even if it operates inside a single country: the key is whether it participates in a market or a transaction that is part of the global "system." My concern in this regard has been to show that there is considerable institutional development of that which is called the global economy – it is not simply a matter of goods or money

crossing borders. For a firm's operations to be part of the global economy, they need to be encased in this institutional framework. If they are not, they may constitute an informal crossborder transaction or part of the new transnational criminal economy. A simplified illustration of the point that the distinctiveness of participating in the global economy does not necessarily lie in the fact of crossing borders is, for example, a US-based firm (whether US or non-US) that invests in a non-US firm listed on the New York stock market. The point here is that there is a regime – a set of conditions and legalities – that governs the listing of foreign firms on a stock market that has been incorporated in the global system and that governs the conditions under which the investor can acquire stock in that firm. I see the key, determining issue to be whether the firms and investors involved are operating under the umbrella of this regime. This umbrella is partly constituted through national institutions and partly, perhaps increasingly so, through the new privatized institutional framework I discuss later. What comes together in this example in my reading are some of the specifications I summarize in the global city model and in the notion of denationalization. On the other hand, the following would not be an instance of firms operating in the global economic system, even though it entails actual physical crossing of borders: two individuals residing in different countries making a deal informally for one of them to bring items, also informally – without following regulations, including WTO regulations – for the second individual to sell in the second country, with both individuals using informal accounting and trust systems to guarantee enforcement of the conditions of the agreement. This is an extreme contrast; there are many cases that are more ambiguous than this.

37 As I indicated earlier, I conceptualize denationalization as multivalent. Thus, in the case of human rights, matters which had been considered the prerogative of states – security and protection of its citizens – are universalized and in that sense denationalized (see Sassen, *Denationalization*).

Part III

Moral authority: global civil society and transnational religious movements

6   "Regulation for the rest of us?" Global civil society and the privatization of transnational regulation

Ronnie D. Lipschutz and Cathleen Fogel

Introduction

The protests that took place in Seattle during the November 1999 meeting of the World Trade Organization (WTO), and which have occurred periodically since then, illustrate a growing public demand for greater transparency, representation, and regulation under conditions of globalization.[1] While much rhetoric was expended condemning the WTO for its intrusions on national sovereignty, the alternatives proposed by the groups marching in the streets were less clear. Inasmuch as a return to the prosperity and political conditions of the 1960s is not on the cards, and a return to the anarchic and "beggar-thy-neighbor" circumstances of the 1930s is manifestly undesirable, what constitutes a politically viable response to the negative impacts of globalization? Or, to put the question another way, how can "regulation for the rest of us" be achieved?

We argue here that, in the interests of economic competitiveness and growth, nation-states have yielded a substantial amount of their domestic regulatory authority to transnational regimes and organizations, such as the WTO, the International Monetary Fund, and various other international regimes and institutions.[2] While globalization is much discussed in terms of the mobility of capital and production, and much feared and opposed for its disruptive impacts on labor and social organization more generally, the question of regulation, per se, has not been much considered.[3] Nonetheless, a critical set of problems arising from contemporary globalization are the social, economic and environmental externalities that are not being addressed within the existing international system of regulatory conventions and regimes.[4] As seen in developing country responses to President Bill Clinton's speech at the Seattle WTO ministerial meeting, suggestions that such regulation might be in order and proposals to extend regulation to include transnational social, environmental, and similar problems are strongly opposed by governmental authorities and corporate officials. They seem generally to find international law to be acceptable if it involves trade or monetary matters, but inappropriate if it addresses "non-economic" issues.[5] This issue of regulation at the global level is not, however, one that will disappear even with economic growth, and it is only likely to become more pressing in the future as a result of the further global expansion of capitalism.[6]

For much of the post-World War II period, such international regulation as there was emerged from intergovernmental negotiations, which led to the signing and ratification of agreements and treaties by individual states and the creation of "international regimes."[7] There were few, if any, other channels available for the development of formal international laws and rules. While non-state social actors were permitted access to and influence within a number of intergovernmental institutions such as the UN Economic and Social Commission (ECOSOC), for the most part there were serious restrictions in terms of what they could say or do in these forums. In recent years, such restrictions have lessened, albeit only in selected settings, such as the yearly meetings of the parties to the UN Framework Convention on Climate Change. Even there, opportunities for direct participation in debates and decisions remain limited.

At the same time, regulatory patterns have become much more complicated and diffuse. As Steven Vogel has noted, there has been some decrease in certain forms of national regulation, but these have been replaced, in many cases, by international rules.[8] For example, in the financial sector, international regulation of various types of economic practices and transactions has been put in place in order to ensure the overall stability of the global economy.[9] In a number of instances, the rulings of the World Trade Organization have trumped national law, and the dispute resolution system of the Trade-Related Intellectual Property Rights (TRIPS) convention of the WTO, in particular, appears to have real teeth. But these regulatory trends are limited in scope, and there is no global welfare state to play a role corresponding to that of national governments in ensuring some degree of fairness, representation, and transparency in how laws and rules are promulgated.[10] The notion that ratification by national legislatures suffices for public involvement in global regulatory policy remains more or less the standard line.

The past fifteen years or so have, nonetheless, begun to see a challenge to this state of affairs. While participation in international public affairs by socially based, non-state actors is not new,[11] it appears that the current scope of non-profit, non-governmental activity at all political levels far exceeds that found in the historical record. Not only have social actors become more involved in many international meetings and institutions, and in transnational networks and alliances of various types. They have also become instrumental in the establishment of a growing number of semi-public and private "transnational regimes" intended to regulate negative environmental and social externalities that have, so far, not been addressed through public international conventions and laws. Social groups have come to fulfill a variety of normative and functional roles, ranging from observers of elections, to advisors to UN projects around the world, to writers and implementers of rules and regulations in a range of global forums. Many of these organizations are also taking upon themselves functional responsibility for seeing that regulations – both national and international – are adhered to by both public and private actors.[12] As one observer of these efforts has noted, for example,

Private organizations have recently established numerous programs aimed at improving the environmental performance of industry. Many of the new programs seek to define and enforce standards for environmental management, and to make it difficult for producers not to participate in them. They claim, explicitly and implicitly, to promote the public interest. They take on functions generally performed by government regulatory programs, and may change or even displace such programs. Private environmental regulatory programs thus have the potential to significantly reshape domestic and international policy institutions by changing the locus, dynamics, and substance of policy making.[13]

In concert with the arguments laid out by the editors of this volume, there are at least two frameworks through which such regulation can be viewed. The first is an instrumental approach: globalization imposes costs on certain groups that cannot be recouped without some degree of intervention into markets that will redistribute benefits. This, however, leads to conflicts over efficiencies in the new international division of labor, which cannot be easily resolved. The second is an approach that rests on what the editors call "moral authority," in this instance, mechanisms to introduce social justice into international institutions and practices. Because states, by and large, shy away from considering issues of justice, moral authority is being introduced through mostly private campaigns and projects.

In this chapter, we examine and analyze these institutional developments, with a particular focus on the activities of non-governmental organizations and "global civil society" (for the purposes of this chapter, we exclude businesses and corporations from our analysis).[14] The first part of the chapter discusses the changing global regulatory environment and some of its causes. The second section examines what we call the "new global division of regulatory labor" and the role of global civil society in this process. In the third part, we address the modalities through which such regulatory arrangements are being established and describe briefly several civil society-based regulatory regimes. We conclude with a few cautionary observations.

Several preliminary notes: throughout this chapter, we use the term "globalization" to denote a material, an ideological, and a cognitive process.[15] Globalization is *material* in the sense that it involves the movement of capital, technology, goods, and, to a limited degree, labor to areas with high returns on investment, without regard to the social or political impacts on either the communities and people to which it moves or to those left behind. Globalization is *ideological* in the sense that such movement is rationalized in the name of "efficiency, competition, and profit." And globalization is *cognitive* in the sense that it fosters social innovation and reorganization in existing institutions, composed of real, live people, without regard to the consequences for them. In all three regards, although globalization opens numerous political opportunities for social movements and other forms of political organization and action, a not uncommon result is disruption to existing forms of beliefs, values, and behaviors. Finally, *regulation* includes not only public laws governing practices, both permitted and forbidden, but also private arrangements as well as socially emergent norms, principles, and customs.

Whither global regulation?

In spite of repeated forecasts of the "end of the nation-state,"[16] there is little question that the state will remain an important actor in world politics for some time to come. For the foreseeable future, and in many parts of the world, the strong, industrialized state as a political institution will maintain much of its capabilities, its material and discursive powers, and its domination of the political imaginary.[17] Acknowledging the continuing importance of the state is not, however, the same as saying it will continue to be the same institution or remain as central to world politics as it has been for the past sixty or three hundred years. Indeed, there are major transformations underway in the state as a political institution. States are decentralizing, deregulating, and liberalizing in order to provide more attractive economic environments for financial capital and, as governments proceed along this path, the domestic safety nets provided by the welfare state are being dismantled.[18] That safety net, it should be noted, includes not only policies for health and safety, environmental protection, public education, and so on, but also standard sets of rules that "level the economic playing field" and ensure the sanctity of contracts within countries. These are especially important to both citizens and capital. For the former, it ensures that all parts of a country will, in theory, hew to similar political and social rules and standards while, for the latter, it reduces transaction costs, increases economies of scale, and allows business and exchange to take place under conditions of relative certainty and stability.

Globalization has destabilized this pattern. Nowadays, the greatest profits are to be found in the high-tech and information industries, in transnational finance and investment, and in flexible and niche production and accumulation. This means looking beyond national borders for ways in which to deploy capital, technology, and design, and to gain access to factors of production, in order to maximize returns on investment and secure entry to foreign markets. The fact that different countries have different regulatory standards and factor costs is an advantage to capital, for it allows production in low-cost locations for export to high-cost ones. At the same time, however, one obstacle to capital mobility and broader economic growth is the transaction and other costs that result from compliance with more than 100 sets of national regulations (not to mention other costs that might arise in the course of "doing business" with local authorities). From the perspective of global capital, it is preferable to deal with single sets of rules that apply to *all* countries, as is increasingly the case within the European Union[19] and among the members of international regimes.[20]

But is this counter to our argument about "deregulation"? Not at all. To be sure, globalization of production and capital has been accompanied by liberalization and, at the rhetorical level, at least, a commitment to the deregulation of markets. But therein lies a central paradox of our times: a self-regulating market system is, as Karl Polanyi put it more than fifty years ago in *The Great Transformation* (1944/1957), a "stark utopia"; indeed, markets *require* rules in order to function in an orderly fashion.[21] Thus, while "deregulation" is the mantra repeated endlessly in virtually all national capitals and by all international capitalists, it is *domestic* deregulation that capitals and capitalists desire, not the wholesale elimination of *all* rules. Selective deregulation at home may create a lower-cost environment in which to produce, but uncontrolled deregulation everywhere creates uncertainty and economic instability. Hence, international regulation is relied on increasingly for keeping the global economic system together and working. Note well that this does *not* include transnational social regulation. In addition to reducing transaction costs to capital of 190 different sets of national laws, such regulatory harmonization is also intended to "eliminate politics" from certain conflictual issue areas by shifting regulatory authority out of the domestic sphere and into the international one. There, representative national and subnational institutions lack power and any ability to intervene, thereby trumping the "two-level game" problem.[22] While there is no gainsaying that some interstate regimes do serve essential regulatory functions, others simply remain a means for dominant countries to protect their own parochial interests.

As we noted above, the spread of production, trade, and markets has changed the playing field in certain ways that interstate regimes do not address. One set of problems is the negative social, economic, and environmental impacts that cannot be eliminated by nation-states acting either unilaterally or in small, exclusive groups.[23] The literatures on collective action and on international relations propose that elimination of such problems requires cooperation among states, leading to the creation of interstate regimes. Such agreements, however, comprise only a part of the full repertoire of institutional mechanisms for dealing with what are, from the neoclassical perspective, externalities. At the same time that regimes are being constructed for the purpose of dealing with externalities, they are also serving the cause of regulatory harmonization so that no country will, in principle, be disadvantaged with respect to another. This, however, leads to a second difficulty: such harmonization may not be very rigorous, or it may even make illegal domestic regulation that is intended to protect environmental resources and to maintain standards, as has been seen in some of the WTO's recent rulings made through the dispute resolution mechanism.

Efforts to extend international regulation to environmental and social standards at high levels are, as noted earlier, strongly opposed by many government authorities, corporate officials, and prominent academics, especially in the United States. These individuals generally find supranational rules to be acceptable if they involve barter, banking, budget deficits, or borrowing, but inappropriate if environmental protection, human rights, labor standards, or distributive justice are involved. And, they argue, it introduces "politics" into matters that should be addressed through efficient markets. For example, neoliberal economists tend to regard low working standards as a crucial element of a particular country's comparative advantage within the international division of labor. The specific levels at which standards are set and followed is, according to the conventional argument, a function of a state's "cultural preferences." Any attempt to legislate or alter these preferences would, it is claimed, constitute an unwarranted intrusion into national sovereignty and result in inefficient, politicized outcomes.

The contradiction embedded in this stance is, of course, that a state wishing to maximize its comparative advantage, whether in labor, raw materials, or environmental protection, would set such standards at a very low level, whatever its actual "cultural preferences" might be. In other words, the requirements of effective and efficient participation in the international division of labor mandate that developing countries, many of which are in competition with each other to acquire and retain foreign investment, minimize the costs of those factors in which they hold a comparative advantage. This means that a so-called preference for low social and environmental standards is imposed exogenously and is not a "cultural preference" as is often claimed.

One consequence of this approach is that international regulatory harmonization does not so much eliminate politics from contentious issue areas as privilege the political desires and goals of transnational capital and corporations. By limiting debates to small groups of national representatives and company executives, and "letting the market do it," many of the most influential international regulatory arrangements – especially economic ones – have become both opaque and non-democratic as well as quite limited in scope.[24] And, with a few exceptions, where transnational social regulations *have* been promulgated, the direction of harmonization has been more in the direction of the "lowest common denominator." Absent popular initiatives and efforts to counter such tendencies, the trend in the future is likely to be toward greater privatization of regulation and less democracy and accountability around the world. This latter point is of considerable concern, but it is not the specific focus of this chapter. Rather, our focus is on the nature of activist responses to the limited and relatively closed nature of most interstate regulatory arrangements, and to the growing number of transnational regulatory initiatives that have appeared in recent years and that are not organized directly through nation-states or managed by state-directed international organizations. It is to this "new division of regulatory labor" that we now turn.

The new global division of regulatory labor

International regulation has not always been as public an affair as it is today (and James Scott argues that, even today, much regulation is customary rather than public).[25] Historically, major social activities within societies were governed by customs, laws, and contracts among and between individuals and groups, often but not always with the approval or support of the state.[26] For example, medieval guilds formulated strict rules governing membership and practice; this form of self-regulation has been carried over into the present in the medical and legal professions (which, nevertheless, are permitted to regulate only through explicit authorization by local, provincial, and national governments). Maritime law is an arena where there has long been and continues to be a considerable amount of private regulation.[27] Another example can be found in common pool resource systems, such as those described by Elinor Ostrom and others.[28] The trend toward public regulation was, as Craig Murphy has documented, a consequence of the growing marketization and industrialization of society as well as of growth in long-distance trade.[29] With bonds of social trust dissolved in the acids of economic exchange, *caveat emptor* and "know thy neighbor" were no longer sufficient guides against fraudulent practices and dangerous products. The welfare state represented the apotheosis of public regulation and, although there has been a strong rhetorical commitment in liberal democracies to deregulation since about 1980, it is not so clear that this has actually come about.[30]

In any event, after World War II, most regulation remained national and state-sanctioned. There were certain sectors in which international public regulation was instituted, as in the control of the spread of nuclear weapons, the allocation of radio and television frequencies and geosynchronous satellite slots, and so on.[31] There were, as well, private organizations that certified the quality and performance of other private organizations, such as the Better Business Bureau, *Good Housekeeping*, and the Consumers' Union in the United States. In a few cases, national regulatory systems were "internationalized" and adopted as the basis for regimes. For example, the safety rules of the US Federal Aviation Administration have been generally adopted by all national aviation authorities, although they are not always rigorously followed. Finally, the tradition of semi-private (e.g., International Red Cross) and private (e.g., CARE) voluntary organizations providing assistance internationally is one that never disappeared completely, even during World War II. Domestic public regulation also had the effect of limiting entry into markets and professions (a story told by Frank Norris in *MacTeague*, a novel about the professionalization of dentistry, and its consequences, during the late nineteenth century), and international regulation has had much the same effect in areas such as nuclear weapons development and agricultural trade.

Today, this state monopoly over regulation is well past its twentieth-century apogee. The "fluidization" of regulatory space is a feature arising from globalization, the declining authority of the state, and the growing tendency of individuals and organizations to act outside traditional rules and frameworks.[32] One consequence of the change in the locus of regulation from the state to other arenas is that, although the state remains the most visible actor in *international relations*, the *jurisdictional authority* monopolized by states during the past fifty years or so is spreading throughout an emergent, multilevel, and, for the moment, very diffuse arrangement of globalizing governance that has certain features that we might associate with a world government, but that lacks numerous features of such a system.

Theda Skocpol argues that political community and the regulation of activities that follow – even in a federal state – are not limited to discrete levels of government:

On the one hand, states may be viewed as organizations through which official collectivities may pursue collective goals, realizing them more or less effectively given available state resources in relation to social settings. On the other hand, states may be viewed more macroscopically as configurations of organizations and action that influence the meanings and methods of politics for all groups and classes in society.[33]

Skocpol offers here a conception of the state that is, perhaps, too broad in encompassing society, but her point is an important one. The state is more than just its constitution, agencies, rules, and roles. It is embedded, as well, in a system of governance the operation of which rests on more than statist institutions. From this view, state and civil society can be seen as being mutually constitutive and, where the state engages in *government*, civil society often plays a role in *governance*. James Rosenau describes governance as

a more encompassing phenomenon than government. It embraces governmental institutions, but it also subsumes informal, non-governmental mechanisms whereby those persons and organizations within its purview move ahead, satisfy their needs, and fulfill their wants . . . Governance is thus a system of rule that is as dependent on intersubjective meanings as on formally sanctioned constitutions . . . or regulatory mechanisms in a sphere of activity which function effectively even though they are not endowed with formal authority.[34]

When we examine trends in transnational regulation, what is striking, especially in terms of relationships between social actors and institutionalized mechanisms of government, as well as capital and international regimes, is the growth of institutions of governance at and across *all* levels of analysis, from the local to the global.[35] Subsumed within this system of globalized governance are institutionalized regulatory arrangements, such as interstate regimes and less formalized systems of norms, rules, and procedures that pattern behavior without the presence of written constitutions or material power. This system is not a "state," as we commonly understand the term, but it is state-like, in Skocpol's second sense. Nor, lacking legislative institutions, is it particularly representative, transparent, or democratic.

But in the emerging, multilevel patterns of political action, based on states and international institutions as well as transnational alliances, coalitions, communication, and networking among social movements and non-governmental organizations, we can see indications of the diffusion of global regulatory governance beyond national and interstate institutions. Within this system, "local" management and regulation are as important to coordination within and among local, national, and global political "hierarchies," regions, and countries as the international management manifested in traditional regimes and international organizations. We see the transfer of *functional responsibility and authority* downward to the regional and local levels as well as upward to the global level. All of this is taking place, moreover, with the full connivance of national governments, aided and abetted by a wide variety of other institutions and actors.

In this globalizing "heteronomy," regulatory authority is distributed increasingly among many centers of action, often focused on very specific issue areas and problems. This authority is developing, in part, because specific social actors are taking over responsibilities no one else wants and, in part, because of expertise acquired through global networks of knowledge and practice. The redistribution of authority is generating a form of globalized functional differentiation (rather than world federalism), inasmuch as different regulatory authorities, both governmental and social, are dealing with specific applied problems – environmental, human rights-based, social – rather than a comprehensive range of generalized ones, as the state has done during the decades past. Moreover, because these problems are embedded within a global economic system, local regulatory functionalism reaches beyond localities into and through the global system.[36] Note that this concept is not the same as the functionalism of Mitrany[37] or the neofunctionalism of Haas.[38] Whereas those theories envisioned political *integration* as the outcome of international functional coordination, it is much more likely that this type of functionalism will operate at multiple levels, contributing perhaps to political fragmentation without necessarily fostering political integration, as such.

To a growing degree, moreover, regulatory functions are coming to be located at that level of social organization at which the appropriate combination of "local" and "global" knowledges comes together. This level may be global, regional, or local, although many of the new regulatory authorities will be based in the latter two. It is in this context that what we call "global civil society" acquires its importance. Elsewhere, Lipschutz has argued that global civil society represents a structure of actors and networks within which new regulatory authorities and arrangements emerge.[39] As conventionally understood, civil society includes those political, cultural, and social organizations of modern societies that have not been established or mandated by the state or created as part of the institutionalized political system of the state (e.g., political parties), but are nevertheless engaged in a variety of political activities that are imbricated with institutionalized politics. Globalizing the concept extends this arrangement into the transnational arena, where it constitutes a proto-society composed of local, national, and global institutions, corporations, and non-governmental organizations. Global civil society can be understood, therefore, as shorthand for the growth in neofunctional authority resulting from a "proliferation" of political actors beyond the state.

Civil society associations, understood in the broadest sense, fulfill multiple roles and, although the balance within individual groups between altruism and self-interest can vary greatly, some of both can be found in all of them. Indeed, many associations that fall into this category go beyond collective self-interest to active pursuit of the collective political goods. Furthermore, although civil society might be considered by some to be a liberal bourgeois fetish, it cannot be denied that most of the world's richer and more powerful states are both liberal and bourgeois. For better or worse, therefore, ideology informs practice, and vice versa. What is, perhaps, more important for our purposes is that the state and those organizations in civil society engaged in regulatory functions are neither independent nor autonomous of each other. A state, whether liberal or not, relies on some version of civil society for its legitimacy. Conversely, a civil society cannot thrive without the legitimacy bestowed on it by the state, whether or not its government is democratic. It is in this context that the "privatization" of regulatory authority and the possible need to counter certain restricted forms of rule-making should be contemplated. Those forms of global regulation that serve the narrow self-interests of certain actors will be legitimated through the international state-like processes that pass for global governance. Without some sort of countervailing movement to open up these projects to scrutiny and public participation, the results are likely to be even more undemocratic than is currently the case.

Emerging forms of global regulation

While regulation is generally thought of in terms of rules stipulating standards for permitted and forbidden behaviors and practices, mandated by legislatures, promulgated by some administrative agencies, monitored and enforced by others, and affirmed by the judicial organs of the state, the newly emerging forms of global private regulation are much more diverse.[40] The extension of private regulatory authority and reach away from the state can be categorized along two dimensions: (1) organizational form and sector (public or private); and (2) regulatory tools applied (command and control or market-based). Table 1 summarizes the resulting categories and provides some examples. The "real world" is not, of course, quite so simple. If we look at the range of actors involved in the "privatization" of regulatory activities, we find that they run the gamut from wholly public to wholly private, including more conventional interstate organizations that have begun to "bring in" non-state actors, to

Table 1: *Institutional arenas of global regulation*

	Political	Economic
Public	*Interstate regimes* World Trade Organization International Labour Organization	*Activist regimes* Burma boycotts International Tobacco Control
Private	*Transnational regimes* Fatal Transactions (war diamonds) International Land Mines Convention	*Market regimes* Anti-sweatshop movement ISO-14000

corporate associations and social movement service providers that have little or nothing to do with public political authorities.

Among the many emerging global regulatory projects are the following:

Labor conditions in the apparel industry: For the moment, there are no international regimes, outside the largely unenforced conventions of the International Labour Organization, that explicitly address labor conditions in the apparel industry, a good portion of which is characterized by "sweatshop" conditions. The growth in substandard workplaces is thought to be driven by free trade and wage competition, which has led many American apparel companies to contract with underregulated overseas manufacturers.[41] Existing trade agreements do not address labor issues and countries that are signatories to the General Agreement on Tariffs and Trade (GATT) and the WTO are not permitted to restrict imports on the basis of the conditions of their manufacture. Over the past ten years, a number of grassroots organizations have emerged to lobby, educate, and challenge US apparel manufacturers to improve working conditions and wages in domestic and foreign shops. These groups have achieved a small number of successes, but they have been challenged by the Fair Labor Association, a coalition of corporations and NGOs organized by the White House to formulate voluntary codes of conduct for apparel production.[42]

Controlling international trade in small arms: The International Action Network on Small Arms (IANSA) is a global network of organizations seeking to reduce both demand and supply of light weapons, through a variety of tactics and strategies, including education, information-sharing, development of culturally appropriate "message strategies," and international regulation. IANSA was established in 1998 and has been consciously modeled on the coalition that was instrumental in the promulgation of the International Land Mines Convention. IANSA is a very new project, and it is likely to be strongly resisted because of the vast and growing global market in small arms and light weapons. Indeed, at a July 2001 United Nations conference on the problem, the United States was adamantly opposed to such international regulation.

The global reporting initiative: This project has been established by the Coalition for Environmentally Responsible Economies (CERES) and "incorporates the active participation of corporations, non-governmental organizations (NGOs), international organizations/UN agencies, consultants, accountancy organizations, business associations, universities, and other stakeholders from around the world." The objective is to "promote international harmonization in the reporting of relevant and credible corporate environmental, social and economic performance information to enhance responsible decision-making."[43]

The global toxics initiative: The World Wildlife Fund has begun a project to "end the production, release and use of chemicals that are endocrine disruptors, bioaccumulative or persistent within one generation by no later than 2020." This is taking place in concert with interstate negotiations to control a range of biologically dangerous chemicals, which resulted recently in the UN Convention on Persistent Organic Pollutants.[44]

Table 2 lists a number of civil society based regulatory initiatives.

One issue area in which this range of regulatory projects is especially evident is in the environmental arena and, in particular, efforts to institutionalize sustainable forestry on a transnational scale. In the area of forestry practices, regulation through conventional international regimes has been limited, although several agreements, such as the Forestry Principles offered at the UN Conference on Environment and Development (the "Earth Summit") in 1992, remain on the agenda and might yet be revived.[45] Here we find four basic organizational forms.

1. *Public agreements and conventions*, which are primarily interstate and intergovernmental regimes or organizations that seek harmonization of international standards, as have appeared in connection with the Kyoto Protocol to the UN Framework Convention on Climate Change, the International Tropical Timber Organization (*www.itto.or.jp/Index.html*), and the International Centre for Forestry Research (*www.cgiar.org/CIFOR/*). The resulting regulations are expected to be legislated domestically, where they will apply to both public and private actors.

Table 2: *Civil society-based regulatory campaigns*

Issue area	Sample of activist regulatory campaigns
AIDS/HIV	Global Strategies for HIV Prevention
Anti-big dams	International Rivers Network; World Commission on Large Dams
Anti-GMO	Campaign to Ban Genetically Engineered Foods; Genetic-ID
Child soldiers	Coalition to Stop the Use of Child Soldiers
Climate	Climate Action Network
Corporate accountability	As You Sow; Business for Social Responsibility
Diamonds	Fatal Transactions International Diamond Campaign
Forestry	Forest Stewardship Council; Forest Products Certification
Indigenous rights	Survival International; International Indian Treaty Council
Labor	Campaign for Labor Rights; Maquiladora Health and Safety Network
Land mines	International Campaign to Ban Land Mines
Organic food	Organic Consumers Organization; IFOAM; Pure Food Campaign
Small arms trade	International Action Network on Small Arms
Species diversity	TRAFFIC; Conservation International
Tobacco	International Tobacco Control Network; Tobacco Free Initiative
Toxics	WWF Global Toxics Initiative; Center for Ethics and Toxics
Trade monitoring	Global Trade Watch; Ethical Trading Initiative
Women's rights	Amnesty International Campaign for Women's Human Rights

2. *Quasi non-governmental organizations* (quangos) are organizations with public, semi-public, and/or private memberships, charged with state-authorized functions, such as the International Organization for Standardization (*www.iso.ch/*). Members of international quangos usually include representatives of both public authorities and private actors.

3. *Semi-private initiatives* involve organizations that are either non-governmental organizations or coalitions (Rainforest Alliance; *www.rainforest-alliance.org/*) or include NGOs, social groups, and corporate representatives (Forest Stewardship Council; *www.fscoax.org/principal.htm*). Regulations are voluntary and intended to apply to corporate activities, in either public or private realms, but are not subject to state vetting or rejection. At least one such group offers certification to private producers.

4. *Private initiatives* involve organizations that are either corporate associations (Initiative zur Föderung nachhaltiger, or IFW) or individual

companies (Scientific Certification Systems; *www.scs1.com/forests. html*). Regulations are voluntary and meant to apply only to members (IFW) or to specific industrial sectors (as in forestry standards), or producers may hire auditors to provide certification.

Putting these two dimensions together suggests the potential for a wide range of approaches to issues. Table 3 lists a number of the international regulatory arrangements and initiatives underway with respect to sustainable forestry practices. Although this listing is not comprehensive, and some of the examples defy simple categorization, they illustrate the broad range of organizational forms and methods.

Forms of regulatory tools

As the discussion and tables suggest, the process of global regulatory privatization is being achieved through a growing reliance on markets and market-based strategies as mechanisms to foster compliance. As progress in the formulation of conventions and protocols has slowed and state and corporate resistance has grown – something especially evident in the environmental issue area – there has also developed a general trend toward greater reliance on markets. The out-of-court settlement in 1999 over working conditions in Saipan, between a number of apparel manufacturers and the Union of Needletrades, Industrial and Textile Employees, Global Exchange, the Asian Law Caucus of San Francisco, and Sweatshop Watch of Oakland, demonstrates that this trend toward market-based regulatory instruments is appearing in other social welfare and justice issue areas, as well.

Historically, the regulation of economic practices has been treated separately from environmental and social practices. In using the term "economic practices," we refer specifically to transactions that take place in a regulated market setting, in which rules are meant to ensure the observance of contracts, the probity of sellers, and the quality of goods and services. We use the term "environmental and social practices" to refer to those activities associated with the production and consumption of material goods, which lead to pollution of air and water, toxics production, health impacts, labor standards, etc., and which have been regulated by rules meant to reduce such externalities. While there has always been a significant economic element in regulation of externalities as defined here, until the 1980s rules were motivated more strongly by ecological, health, and safety concerns. During the 1970s, a growing debate over the costs of regulation led to the growing use of cost–benefit analysis, a practice formally institutionalized during the 1980s. This led, in turn, to a search for more "cost-effective" regulatory strategies that appeared

Table 3: *Global initiatives in regulation of sustainable forestry*

Name	Type	Membership	Objective
Center for International Forestry Research (CIFOR)	Quango	Countries, but also NGOs, universities, etc.	To improve the scientific basis for ensuring the balanced management of forests and forest lands; to develop policies and technologies for sustainable use and management of forest goods and services.
Forest Stewardship Council (FSC)	Semi-private (civil society groups)	Environmental NGOs and NGOs, wood products buyers, and certifiers in three assemblies	To establish internationally recognized principles and criteria of forest management as a basis for accrediting regional certifiers
Initiative zur Föderung nachhaltiger Waldbewirtschaftung (IFW)	Private group	German timber trade unions, importers, and processors	Dual process of certification whereby nationally accredited bodies within timber-exporting nations would certify that producers have met high standards of forest management for European labeling
Intergovernmental Working Group on Global Forests (IWGF)	Public	Nine countries	To develop a scientifically based framework of criteria and indicators for the conservation, management, and sustainable development of boreal and temperate forests
International Tropical Timber Organization	Public	Producer and consumer countries (timber trade, international organizations, NGOs present as observers)	To provide an international reference document upon which more detailed national standards could be developed to guide sustainable management of natural tropical forests

Name	Type	Membership	Description
ISO 14001	Quango	National standards bodies	ISO series 14000 template proposed for development of sustainable forestry standard; rejected but under study
Kyoto Protocol	Public	Signatory countries	To establish terms and conditions to meet provisions of Kyoto Protocol regarding management of forests and their role as carbon sinks
Rainforest Action Network	Semi-private (NGO)	Individual members and allied NGOs in other countries	To protect the rainforests and support the rights of their inhabitants through education, grassroots organizing, and non-violent direct action
Scientific Certification Systems	Private firm in Oakland, CA	No membership; producers are certified	"Forest Conservation Program" to evaluate forest management against objective and regionally appropriate principles of sustainable forestry
SGS Forestry	Private firm in Oxford, UK	No membership; producers are certified	"Carbon Offset Verification Service" assesses, surveys, monitors, and certifies project development and management
Smart Wood (Rainforest Alliance, RA)	Semi-private (civil society groups)	No membership; NGO certifies timber producers	Operations certified as Smart Wood sources according to the extent to which they adhere to RA's Generic Guidelines for Assessing Natural Forest Management

Source: Bryan Evans, "Technical and Scientific Elements of Forest Management Certification Programs," paper prepared for the conference on Economic, Social and Political Issues in Certification of Forest Management, University of Pertanian, Malaysia, 12–16 May 1996, at *www.forestry.ubc.ca/concert/evans.html*; CIFOR web site, at *www.cgiar.org/CIFOR/general/about.html*; SGS Forestry Brochure SGS2118/0597.

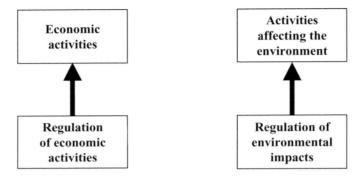

Figure 1: The conventional relationship between function and regulation

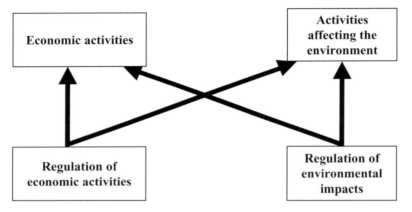

Figure 2: The changing relationship between function and regulation

to involve less political intervention. Figure 1 illustrates in a very simple fashion the relationship between economic practices and environmental externalities.

Over the past decade or so, for both ideological and cost reasons, this pattern has begun to change, as shown in figure 2. Market-based mechanisms, such as tradable pollution permits and independent certification, are replacing or supplementing command and control methods as part of an effort to, in this example, manage environmental impacts.[46] The market-based approach has the supposed virtue of increasing the efficiency with which financial resources are used, but it is also driven by the ability of the rich to purchase rights to pollute from the poor, which could result in a transfer of financial resources from the former to the latter, thereby allowing the poor to pay the costs of environmental improvement for themselves. But there might be undesirable consequences from this, as well, because if market-based auctions and sales operate as suggested by neoclassical economics, they may have the effect of pricing poor countries completely out of the market to pollute and still leave them with insufficient funds to purchase newer environmentally friendly technologies and goods.

What is interesting, in any event, is that, parallel to the growing trend of using economic techniques to regulate environmental practices, there has also developed a trend toward utilizing environmental controls to regulate economic activities (as in the inclusion of environmental concerns in trade agreements). Producers absorb the costs (or pass them on to consumers) of internalizing environmental externalities by adhering or subscribing to a set of regulated behaviors and practices that, when vetted by the appropriate authority, certify them as "environmentally friendly." These regulations are expected to appeal to consumers who, looking for the appropriate certifying mark, will prefer environmentally friendly goods to unfriendly ones. While the change in behavior is motivated by economic concerns, the form of the regulation is not, in itself, market-based; rather, these rules are somewhat akin to a moral code that fosters an environmental "civic virtue," hoping that a shift in consumer demand for such goods will lead to a commensurate shift in supply, thereby fostering "green markets."

We can say, therefore, that such regulatory initiatives are motivated by three somewhat different incentives, which we label normative, functional, and instrumental (for lack of a better term). *Normative* incentives have to do with notions about justice, equity, indigenous rights, biocentrism, and so on. *Functional* incentives have to do with development and implementation of protection and conservation programs. And *instrumental* incentives have to do with the profits and "good works" resulting from certification or approval. Thus, considering the initiatives described in table 3, the Rainforest Action Network appears to be motivated primarily by normative incentives; the Forest Stewardship Council by functional incentives; Scientific Certification Systems by instrumental incentives.

In recent years, the tool that has come into the greatest use by private regulators is certification of both national and private practices. In the environmental area, this is accomplished through what is called "eco-labeling."[47] An eco-label is a claim placed on a product, having to do with its production or performance, that is intended to enhance the item's social or market value by conveying its environmentally advantageous elements. Such a label is intended to make the product more attractive to the environmentally conscious consumer.[48] Three categories of eco-labels are widely recognized: *first-*, *second-*, and *third-party.*[49]

First-party labeling, the most common and simplistic approach, entails producer claims about a product, such as "recyclable," "ozone-friendly," "non-toxic," or "biodegradable." In the absence of a mechanism for verifying these claims, the only guarantee that the product performs accordingly is the producer's reputation.

Second-party labeling is conducted by industry-related entities, such as trade associations, which establish guidelines or criteria for making such environmental claims. Once the standards are met or the guidelines followed, an industry-approved label is placed on the product stating or verifying the product's environmentally friendly qualities. In this instance, corporate members of the certifying organization will seek to ensure the label's value, and to mandate its use, so that no single producer will have an advantage over any other.

Third-party, or independent, labeling is performed by either a governmental agency, a non-profit group, a for-profit company, or an organization representing some combination of these three. As with the second-party type, third-party eco-labeling programs set guidelines that products must meet in order to use their label. They may also conduct audits in order to ensure compliance with the guidelines. As the name implies, third-party organizations are not affiliated with the products they label. The Forest Stewardship Council is engaged in third-party independent labeling and auditing, whereas the International Organization for Standardization provides second-party labeling based on a company's program for compliance with the ISO's own environmental standards.[50]

There appears to be a growing demand for such regulation, although the size of the market remains small and its future uncertain. For example, the total area of sustainably certified forests is certainly less than 1 percent of global forests. At the same time, however, corporations engaged in the production of material goods have no inherent interest in environmental protection, with two exceptions. First, a failure to reduce externalities may increase variable costs from fines and lost business, which requires the kind of policing that ISO 14000 does not address and that many corporations are loath to accept. Second, having a "green" reputation could increase corporate profits. Purchasing rights to pollute, as opposed to reducing pollution, may be efficient in aggregate but, in an open-bid market setting, the ceiling to the cost of such permits may be quite high even as there is little favorable publicity to be gained from admitting that one continues to pollute. A producer who voluntarily controls externalities, and engages in virtuous behavior, can advertise such practices and, with luck, grab a little extra market share. It might even be possible to charge a premium for green certification, for which high-income consumers will (it is hoped) gladly pay. So, there is available here both a moral and a market opportunity. Corporations can do well by doing good, while certifiers can do good by doing well.

Understandably, some are wary of getting into the business of peddling environmental morality as such, even if there might be money to be made from it. For one thing, there is a great deal of sensitivity to "political intervention" into corporate behaviors (although this does not prevent some governments from intervening in other countries' behaviors). For another, there is the argument, made by Bhagwati[51] and others, that such moralities are culturally ethnocentric, and that it is not "fair" for all countries to be forced to hew to the same standards of environmental quality (an argument, made by Larry Summers in his famous memo about the dearth of pollution in poor countries,[52] which seems somewhat hollow, in view of the alacrity with which economic standards are accepted by culturally different countries). Finally, some attempts to devise international regulatory standards that directly affect economic practices have come under intense lobbying and log-rolling pressures, as in the case of the Kyoto Protocol to the UN Framework Convention on Climate Change. Nonetheless, there is a growing corporate good behavior "movement" that believes certification is both moral and good for the bottom line.[53]

The ultimate question remains unanswered: can action through the market provide the incentives for the maintenance and enforcement of the kind of private self-regulation described here? Producers will be attracted to such approaches only if environmentally conscious consumers choose their environmentally friendly certified products. But setting the premium for such products at the "correct" level is no easy task. Moreover, it is one thing to tack a 10 percent green surcharge on a piece of furniture that may cost between US$ 100 and US$ 1,000; it is quite another to charge an extra 10 percent on a US$ 20,000 remodeling job or a US$ 300,000 house. Over the past fifty years, industrial societies have been built on the premise that lower prices enhance purchasing power and maximize individual satisfaction; it will not be so easy to convince consumers that they will be better off if they exercise environmental virtue in the marketplace. The invisible hand notwithstanding, self-interest rarely offers a stable foundation for moral action.

Conclusions

In this chapter, we have presented several linked arguments. First, we proposed that the processes associated with globalization, including domestic deregulation, have fostered a demand for global regulation of social and environmental externalities. This is similar to the "double movement" first described by Karl Polanyi, although, in this instance, the movement against self-regulating markets is taking place at both the domestic and transnational levels rather than at the behest of governments.[54] Second, given structural restrictions on national reregulation in the social sector, and the growing tendency for interstate organizations to yield to the demands of capital as well as the fragmentation of political authority around the world, there are a growing number of actors taking on the task of imposing or campaigning for new regulatory standards. Many of these actors belong to what we call "global civil society." Even though many of these actors are semi-public or private, their activities are not focused on narrowly defined private interests but, rather, address issues having to do with a global common good. The range of frameworks within which new regulations are being formulated is quite broad but, as a whole, they can also be seen as part of an emerging structure of global governance. To be sure, such frameworks are rife with contradictions, antagonisms, and problems, and serious questions regarding representation and democratization have not, so far, been addressed.[55]

In the terms proposed by the editors of this volume, and contributors to it, is the emergence of privatized social regulation, on balance, to be regarded positively or negatively? One's answer to this question depends largely on whether one believes that such regulation should fall within the purview of markets or politics. Rules are necessary for the stability of markets and credibility within them, but legitimacy is of equal importance. If those engaged in exchange in markets do not feel they are getting a fair deal, or those observing the working of markets believe that externalized costs are excessively high, the legitimacy of markets will be impaired to the detriment of the economy as a whole. Regulation through privatized market mechanisms can establish such legitimacy only if the rules are observed by *everyone* engaged in a particular market, and this requires either self-discipline or external enforcement. Vested interests are unlikely to be able to accomplish this in an effective and convincing fashion.

However one regards contemporary political practices, there is, at least, some notion, however residual, of concern for the public good. This is a good that extends beyond the boundaries of specific markets to include even those who lack the resources and voice to participate in privatized social regulation. To be sure, some private efforts, such as the Forestry Stewardship Council, do try to include all stakeholders in decision-making, yet there are many others that make no such effort and ask the public to trust in their good faith. The private good is deemed to be equivalent to the public good – a highly questionable proposition. We do not mean to dismiss entirely the potential of private authority and private regulation; we only caution that it might not, in the long run, turn out to be quite the panacea it appears to be today.

NOTES

1 Ronnie D. Lipschutz, "From Local Knowledge and Practice to Global Governance," in M. Hewson and T. J. Sinclair (eds.), *Approaches to Global Governance Theory* (Albany, N.Y.: SUNY Press, 1999), pp. 259–83.
2 Susan Strange, *The Retreat of the State: The Diffusion of Power in the World Economy* (Cambridge: Cambridge University Press, 1996).
3 D. Vogel, *Trading Up: Consumer and Environmental Regulation in a Global Economy* (Cambridge, Mass.: Harvard University Press, 1995); S. K. Vogel, *Freer Markets, More Rules: Regulatory Reform in Advanced Industrial Countries* (Ithaca, N.Y.: Cornell University Press, 1996); J. Braithwaite and P. Drahos, *Global Business Regulation* (Cambridge: Cambridge University Press, 2000).
4 Richard Falk, *On Humane Governance* (University Park, Penn.: Penn State University Press, 1995), and Falk, *Predatory Globalization: A Critique* (Cambridge: Polity Press, 1999).
5 Jagdish Bhagwati, "Trade and the Environment: The False Conflict?," in D. Zaelke, P. Orbuch, and R. F. Houseman (eds.), *Trade and the Environment: Law, Economics, and Policy* (Washington, D.C.: Island Press, 1993), pp. 159–90.
6 Ronnie D. Lipschutz, *After Authority: War, Peace and Global Politics in the 21st Century* (Albany, N.Y.: SUNY Press, 2000).
7 Stephen D. Krasner (ed.), *International Regimes* (Ithaca, N.Y.: Cornell University Press, 1983).
8 S. K. Vogel, *Freer Markets, More Rules.*
9 E. M. Graham, *Global Corporations and National Governments* (Washington, D.C.: Institute for International Economics, 1996), and Louis Pauly, *Who Elected the Bankers? Surveillance and Control in the World Economy* (Ithaca, N.Y.: Cornell University Press, 1997).
10 Ramesh Mishra, *Globalization and the Welfare State* (Cheltenham, UK: Edward Elgar, 1999).
11 Craig N. Murphy, *International Organization and Industrial Change: Global Governance Since 1850* (New York: Oxford University Press, 1994).
12 T. Princen and M. Finger (eds.), *Environmental NGOs in World Politics* (London: Routledge, 1994); Ronnie D. Lipschutz, with Judith Mayer, *Global Civil Society and Global Environmental Governance* (Albany, N.Y.: SUNY Press, 1996); Lipschutz, "Reconstructing World Politics: The Emergence of Global Civil Society," in Jeremy Larkins and Rick Fawn (eds.), *International Society After the Cold War* (London: Macmillan, 1996), pp. 101–31; P. Wapner, *Environmental Activism and World Civic Politics* (Albany, N.Y.: SUNY Press, 1996); J. Smith, C. Chatfield, and R. Pagnucco (eds.), *Transnational Social Movements and Global Politics: Solidarity Beyond the State* (Syracuse, N.Y.: Syracuse University Press, 1997); Margaret Keck and Kathryn Sikkink, *Activists Across Borders: Advocacy Networks in International Politics* (Ithaca, N.Y.: Cornell

University Press, 1998); and D. Korten, *Globalizing Civil Society: Reclaiming Our Right to Power* (New York: Seven Stories Press, 1998).

13 Errol E. Meidinger, "'Private' Environmental Regulation, Human Rights, and Community," *Buffalo Environmental Law Journal*, 2000, *www.ublaw. buffalo.edu/ fas/meidinger/hrec.pdf*, viewed on 11 May 2000.

14 For a discussion of corporate "civil society," see Virginia Haufler, *Public Role for the Private Sector: Industry Self-Regulation in a Global Economy* (Washington, D.C.: Carnegie Endowment for International Peace, 2001); Ronnie D. Lipschutz, "Doing Well by Doing Good? Transnational Regulatory Campaigns, Social Activism, and Impacts on State Sovereignty," in John Montgomery and Nathan Glazer (eds.), *Challenges to Sovereignty: How Governments Respond* (New Brunswick, N.J.: Transaction, 2002), pp. 291–320.

15 Manuel Castells, *The Rise of the Network Society* (Malden, Mass.: Blackwell, 1996), and Lipschutz, *After Authority*.

16 Kenichi Ohmae, *The End of the Nation-State* (New York: Free Press, 1995).

17 Lipschutz, *After Authority*.

18 Mishra, *Globalization and the Welfare State*.

19 D. Vogel, *Trading Up*.

20 Graham, *Global Corporations and National Governments*.

21 Karl Polanyi, *The Great Transformation* (Boston: Beacon Press, 1957 [1944]); W. R. Mead, "Trains, Planes, and Automobiles: The End of the Postmodern Moment," *World Policy Journal*, 12 (4) (Winter 1995/96), 13–32; and J. Attali, "The Crash of Western Civilization: The Limits of Market and Democracy," *Foreign Policy*, 107 (Summer 1997), 54–63.

22 P. B. Evans, H. Jacobson, and R. Putnam (eds.), *Double-Edged Diplomacy: International Bargaining and Domestic Politics* (Berkeley: University of California Press, 1993).

23 Lipschutz with Mayer, *Global Civil Society*, chs. 2 and 3.

24 For a summary view of this point from the domestic perspective, see I. M. Young, *Justice and the Politics of Difference* (Princeton, N.J.: Princeton University Press, 1990), ch. 3.

25 J. Scott, *Seeing Like a State* (New Haven: Yale University Press, 1998), ch. 1.

26 Braithwaite and Drahos, *Global Business Regulation*.

27 A. Claire Cutler, "Artifice, Ideology, and Paradox: The Public/Private Distinction in International Law," *Review of International Political Economy*, 4 (2) (1997), 261–85.

28 E. Ostrom, *Governing the Commons: The Evolution of Institutions for Collective Action* (Cambridge: Cambridge University Press, 1990); D. W. Bromley (ed.), *Making the Commons Work* (San Francisco: ICS Press, 1992).

29 Murphy, *International Organization*.

30 S. K. Vogel, *Freer Markets, More Rules*.

31 *International Organization*, P. Haas (ed.), Special Issue: Knowledge, Power, and International Policy Coordination, 46 (1) (1992).

32 James N. Rosenau, *Along the Domestic–Foreign Frontier: Exploring Governance in a Turbulent World* (Cambridge: Cambridge University Press, 1997).

33 Theda Skocpol, "Bringing the State Back In: Strategies of Analysis in Current Research," in P. B. Evans, D. Reuschemeyer, and Theda Skocpol

(eds.), *Bringing the State Back In* (Cambridge: Cambridge University Press, 1985), pp. 3–37.

34 James N. Rosenau, "Governance, Order, and Change in World Politics," in Rosenau and Ernst-Otto Czempiel (eds.), *Governance Without Government: Order and Change in World Politics* (Cambridge: Cambridge University Press, 1992), pp. 4–5.

35 J. Leatherman, R. Pagnucco, and J. Smith, "International Institutions and Transnational Social Movement Organizations: Transforming Sovereignty, Anarchy, and Global Governance," Working Paper 5:WP3, Kroc Institute for International Peace Studies, University of Notre Dame, August 1994; and J. Smith, Chatfield and Pagnucco, *Transnational Social Movements*.

36 One example of this is the growing environmental justice movement, which is becoming globalized and addressing not only the local disposition of toxic wastes but their export and disposal in other places around the world; see, e.g., A. Szaz, *Ecopopulism* (Minneapolis: University of Minnesota Press, 1994), and Jennifer Clapp, *Toxic Exports: The Transfer of Hazardous Wastes and Technologies from Rich to Poor Countries* (Ithaca, N.Y.: Cornell University Press, 2001).

37 D. Mitrany, *A Working Peace System* (Chicago: Quadrangle Books, 1966).

38 Ernst Haas, *Beyond the Nation-State* (Stanford: Stanford University Press, 1964).

39 Lipschutz with Mayer, *Global Civil Society*.

40 A. Claire Cutler, Virginia Haufler, and T. Porter (eds.), *Private Authority and International Affairs* (Albany, N.Y.: SUNY Press, 1999).

41 E. Bonacich and R. Appelbaum, *Behind the Label: Inequality in the Los Angeles Apparel Industry* (Berkeley: University of California Press, 2000).

42 Lipschutz, "Doing Well by Doing Good?"

43 See *www.globalreporting.org/AboutGRI.htm*.

44 See *www.worldwildlife.org/toxics/globaltoxics/index.htm*.

45 Ronnie D. Lipschutz, "Why Is There No International Forestry Law? An Examination of International Forestry Regulation, Both Public and Private," *UCLA Journal of Environmental Law and Policy*, 19 (1) (2000/01), 155–82.

46 Note that a permit system does not entirely eliminate command and control rules. Some cap must be set on pollution, either as a total for each individual consumer of permits or as a total for the system as a whole, in which individual consumers can then buy and sell permits.

47 See the Environmental Labeling Toolbox of the International Institute for Sustainable Development for further information about eco-labeling, at *iisd1.iisd.ca/business/envirolabeling.htm*.

48 Anil Markandya, "Eco-labeling: An Introduction and Review," in Simonetta Zarrilli, Veena Jha, and Rene Vossenaar (eds.), *Eco-labeling and International Trade* (New York: St. Martin's Press, 1997), pp. 1–20; and S. Bass and M. Simula, "Independent Certification/Verification of Forest Management," background paper for the World Bank/WWF Alliance Workshop, Washington, D.C., 9–10 November 1999 *www.esd.worldbank.org/wwf/sim-bass.doc*; viewed on 11 May 2000.

49 D. J. Caldwell, "Ecolabeling and the Regulatory Framework: A Survey of Domestic and International Fora," prepared for the Consumer's Choice Council,

Washington, D.C. (discussion draft), 30 October 1998, *www.consumerscouncil. org/ccc/*; viewed on 11 May 2000.

50 J. Cascio, G. Woodside, and P. Mitchell, *ISO 14000 Guide: The New International Environmental Management Standards* (New York: McGraw-Hill, 1996).

51 Bhagwati, "Trade and the Environment."

52 Summers, now the president of Harvard University, was chief economist at the World Bank in 1991 when he wrote a memo asking "shouldn't the World Bank be encouraging *more* migration of the dirty industries to the LDCs [less developed countries] ... I think the economic logic behind dumping a load of toxic waste in the lowest wage country is impeccable and we should face up to that ... I've always thought that underpopulated countries in Africa are vastly underpolluted; their air quality is vastly inefficiently low compared to Los Angeles or Mexico City." Summers later disavowed the memo ("New Treasury Secretary famous words as World Bank Chief," Russell Mokhiber and Robert Weissman, n.d., at *aidc.org.za/archives/usts_wb.html*; viewed on 5 April 2002.

53 E.g., United Kingdom, Foreign and Commonwealth Office, *Global Citizenship: Business and Society in a Changing World* (London: Foreign and Commonwealth Office, 2001).

54 Polanyi, *Great Transformation*. See also Stephen Gill, "Structural Change and the Global Political Economy: Globalizing Elites and the Emerging World Order," in Yoshikazu Sakamoto (ed.), *Global Transformation: Challenges to the State System* (Tokyo: United Nations University Press, 1994), pp. 169–99.

55 Lipschutz, "Doing Well by Doing Good?"

7   The global dimensions of religious terrorism

Mark Juergensmeyer

During the Cold War, America's prime enemy was the vast Soviet empire. Ten years after the fall of that empire, America's most wanted enemy was a single person – Osama bin Laden – a man without a state. Shunned by his native Saudi Arabia, bin Laden encamped in various places, most often in Afghanistan, where even the Taliban have found him to be a difficult guest. But he did not represent them or any other state, not even a rogue regime.

Bin Laden is not, however, a complete anomaly. He symbolizes a variety of movements of religious activism that despise the symbols of secular power in a global age, and he is a significant authority figure within a transnational network that encompasses a certain segment of these disgruntled activists. In America's anguish after the savage aerial assaults on the World Trade Center and the Pentagon on 11 September 2001, a critical question was how to retaliate: who or what should be attacked? Clearly bin Laden was implicated, as he was in the previous assault on the World Trade Center in 1993 and the bombing of American embassies in Africa in 1998, but an appropriate response to these attacks was the subject of a great deal of debate both within and outside American diplomatic circles. In attempting to defeat bin Laden, no one in the US administration was under the illusion that they could defeat terrorism everywhere, nor banish all of bin Laden's own brand of Islamic extremism. Though the United States wanted to punish those states that harbored terrorists, its policy-makers were keenly aware that they were confronting a new kind of enemy: one that was not a nation-state but an emerging transnational force.

The maddening thing about this new enemy was that it could not easily be located: it did not operate under a single command. For one thing, the religious activists who targeted the United States represented different strands of religion – various branches within the Hindu, Sikh, Buddhist, Christian, Jewish, and Muslim faiths – and their goals are diverse. Some aim to create a specific religious state. Others, like bin Laden, have no interest in establishing a single alternative government, but operate on a broader, transnational scale. They oppose what they believe to be sinister forces at work in an American-led transnational economy, one allied with the satellite transmission of secular popular culture.

The spectacular assault on the twin towers of the World Trade Center and the Pentagon, therefore, was the work of guerilla antiglobalists. These targets were symbols of globalization as well as of American strength. The paradox, however, is that to accomplish this assault they had to create their own transnational network. They formed a kind of shadow alternative globalism of their own.

What both religious nationalism and guerilla antiglobalism have in common is their reliance on bases of authority that in secular societies are not perceived as public. These new movements of transnational private authority, such as bin Laden's al Qaeda network, are based on pillars of power that are in fact quite old: religion and extra-legal violence. Indeed, the two are related. Religious ideology provides ethical justifications for violence, thereby providing a moral base for assaulting what Max Weber described as essential for the public authority of the state – a monopoly on the moral sanction for killing. At the same time, violence – especially violence performed in unpredictable and frightening acts of terrorism – empowers religion. In the wake of the World Trade Center assault, bin Laden basked in the stature suddenly attributed to him as America's greatest enemy. Acts of violence have given religious activists a credibility they otherwise would not have had.

Terrorism and religion

Around the world religious terrorism at the turn of the twenty-first century became a way of life. The French dealt with subway bombs planted by Algerian Islamic activists; the British with exploding trucks and buses ignited by groups on both sides in the dispute in Northern Ireland; the Japanese with nerve gas placed in Tokyo subways by members of a Hindu–Buddhist sect. In India, residents of Delhi experienced car bombings by both Sikh and Kashmiri Muslim separatists; in Sri Lanka whole sections of the city of Colombo were destroyed both by Tamil Hindu and Sinhalese Buddhist militants; Egyptians lived with militant Islamic attacks in coffee-houses and on river boats; Algerians lost whole villages to savage attacks perpetrated allegedly by supporters of the Islamic Salvation Front; and Israelis and Palestinians confronted the deadly deeds of extremists from both the Jewish and Muslim sides.

Religious violence has appeared in virtually every part of the world, and in association with every major religious tradition. In the United States most acts of terrorism have been related to Christian militia and racist religious movements: the 1999 attacks on a Jewish day-care center in Los Angeles and ethnic assaults in Illinois and Indiana, abortion clinic bombings in Alabama and Georgia in 1997, the bomb blast at the Olympics in Atlanta in 1996, and the tragic destruction of the federal building at Oklahoma City in 1995. These incidents, the 1993 assault on the World Trade Center, and the spectacular attacks on 11 September 2001 have brought Americans into the same uneasy location occupied by many in the rest of the world: confronting religious violence as a political reality. But what is the political point of such violent demonstrations of power?

To search for answers to this and other questions relating to the emergence of religious terrorism at this moment of history, I have gone to the sources. In a series of case studies, including Hamas suicide bombings, Jewish militancy in Israel, the Tokyo subway nerve gas attack, and abortion clinic bombings in the United States, I interviewed a number of religious activists and their supporters.[1] The point was to try to penetrate into their view of the world, and to look for commonalities in the thinking of violent religious activists across cultural boundaries.

One of these conversations was with Mahmud Abouhalima, convicted for his role in the 1993 bombing of the World Trade Center. When I talked with him he was serving a life sentence at the Federal Penitentiary at Lompoc, California. He was open to discussing a wide range of topics regarding the relationship between religion and politics but, since he was hoping to appeal his conviction, he was wary about getting into the specifics of his own case. He did, however, discuss the bombing of the Oklahoma City federal building and the trials of Terry Nichols and Timothy McVeigh. In trying to help me understand why someone would choose a government building – and hundreds of innocent workers and bystanders who happened to be at the wrong place at the wrong time – Abouhalima told me that it was done "for a very, very specific reason." Abouhalima added that "they wanted to reach the government with the message that we are not tolerating the way that you are dealing with our citizens."[2] It was a message, he said, that normal life was intolerable, and that someone other than the government had the power to act in a dramatic public way.

Was the bombing an act of terrorism, I asked him? Abouhalima thought for a moment, then explained that the whole concept was "messed up." The term seemed to be used only for incidents of violence that people didn't like or, rather, Abouhalima explained, for incidents that the media have labeled terrorist. "What about the United States government?," Abouhalima asked me. "How do they justify their acts of bombings, of killing innocent people, directly or indirectly, openly or secretly? They're killing people everywhere in the world: before, today, and tomorrow."

"How do you define that?," he asked. Then he described what he regarded as America's terrorist attitude toward the world. According to
Abouhalima, the United States tries to "terrorize nations," to "obliterate
their power," and to tell them that they "are nothing" and that they "have
to follow" America's lead. Abouhalima implied that any form of international political or economic control was a form of terrorism. With these
assertions Abouhalima indicated that he did not regard US power as legitimate. It is, in his mind, non-authoritative. He sought to challenge US
authority transnationally.

Abouhalima also gave specific examples of where he felt the United
States had used its power to kill people indiscriminately. "In Japan, for instance," Abouhalima said, referring to the atomic bomb blasts, "through
the bombs . . . that killed more than 200,000 people." Perhaps it was just
a coincidence, but the number that Abouhalima cited as having been
killed in Hiroshima and Nagasaki was exactly the number that is estimated would have been killed in the 2001 World Trade Center collapse if
both towers had toppled immediately and fallen into adjacent buildings
rather than imploded into themselves.

Was the Oklahoma City blast a terrorist response to the government's
terrorism? "That's what I'm saying," Abouhalima replied. "If they believe, if these guys, whoever they are, did whatever bombing they say they
did in Oklahoma City, if they believe that the government unjustifiably
killed the people in Waco, then they have their own way to respond."
"They absolutely have their own way to respond," Abouhalima added for
emphasis, indicating that the Oklahoma City bombing "response" was
morally justified. "Yet," I said, in an effort to put the event in context,
"it killed a lot of innocent people, and ultimately it did not seem to change
anything."

"But it's as I said," Abouhalima responded, "at least the government got
the message." Moreover, Abouhalima told me, the only thing that humans
can do in response to great injustice is to send a message. Stressing the
point that all human efforts are futile, and that those who bomb buildings
should not expect any immediate, tangible change in the government's
policies as a result, Abouhalima said that real change – effective change –
"is not in our hands," only "in God's hands."

This led to a general discussion about what he regarded as the natural connection between Islam and political order. Abouhalima said this
relationship had been weakened by modern leaders of Islamic countries,
such as those in his native Egypt, as a result of the influence of the West in
general and the United States in particular. The president of Egypt, for
example, was not really Muslim, Abouhalima implied, since he "watered
down" Islamic law. Leaders such as President Hosni Mubarak "said yes"

to Islamic law and principles, Abouhalima explained, but then turned around and "said yes" to secular ideas as well, especially regarding such matters as family law, education, and financial institutions (Muslim law prohibits usury).[3] He offered these examples of the deceitful character of many contemporary politicians: they pretended to be Muslim, but in practice followed secular – implicitly Western – codes of conduct.

Anti-America, anti-globalization

The enemy, in Abouhalima's view, was a kind of shadowy force of secularism out to destroy Islam. He and his colleagues, such as Osama bin Laden, thought that the United States was not only the prime example of anti-religion but also its chief supporter. Long before the bombing of the World Trade Center, Abouhalima's spiritual leader, Sheik Omar Abdul Rahman, expressed his disdain over America's role in propping up the Mubarak regime in Egypt. "America is behind all these un-Islamic governments," the sheik explained, arguing that the purpose of American political and economic support was "to keep them strong" and to try to "defeat the Islamic movements."[4] The Ayatollah Khomeini saw the shah and the American government linked together as evil twins: America was tarred by its association with the shah, and the shah, in turn, was corrupted by being a "companion" of "satanic forces" – i.e., America.[5] When Khomeini prayed to his "noble God for protection from the evil of every wicked traitor" and asked Him to "destroy the enemies," the primary traitor he had in mind was the shah, and the main enemy America.[6]

During a lengthy speech given in the courtroom at the end of the trial that convicted him of conspiracy in the 1993 bombing of the World Trade Center, Sheik Omar Abdul Rahman predicted that a "revengeful" God would "scratch" America from the face of the earth.[7] He was not alone, however, in his strident anti-Americanism. According to the RAND Chronicle of International Terrorism, each year since 1968 the United States has headed the list of countries whose citizens and property were most frequently attacked.[8] The US State Department's counterterrorism unit reported that, during the 1990s, 40 percent of all acts of terrorism worldwide were against American citizens and facilities.[9]

One of the world's best-known critics of America, Osama bin Laden, who was implicated not only in the 11 September 2001 attacks in New York City and Washington, D.C., but also in the attack on the USS *Cole* in Yemen in 1999, and in the bombing of American embassies in Kenya and Tanzania in 1998, explained in an interview in 1997 that America deserved to be targeted because it was "the biggest terrorist in the world."[10] It was an insult returned to bin Laden after the embassy bombings when

US National Security Advisor Samuel Berger labeled bin Laden "the most dangerous non-state terrorist in the world."[11] President George W. Bush, after the 11 September 2001 attacks, dubbed him "evil incarnate." The reason bin Laden gave for targeting America was its list of "crimes," which included "occupying the lands of Islam in the holiest of places, the Arabian Peninsula, plundering its riches, dictating to its rulers, humiliating its people, terrorizing its neighbors, and turning its bases in the peninsula into a spearhead through which to fight the neighboring Muslim peoples."[12] In response to what bin Laden regarded as a declaration of war on Muslims by America, he issued a *fatwa* calling on "every Muslim" as "an individual duty" to join him in what he felt was a righteous war "to kill the Americans and their allies." Their obligation was not only "to kill the Americans" but also to "plunder their money wherever and whenever they find it." He sealed his *fatwa* with the reassurance that "this is in accordance with the words of Almighty God," and that "every Muslim who believes in God and wishes to be rewarded" should "comply with God's order."[13] In these statements bin Laden was drawing upon what he regarded as the transcendent moral authority of Islam and his own convictions about God's will to justify his attack on the public authority of the most powerful Western secular state and its agents. In bin Laden's reasoning, a citizen of such a state is *de facto* an agent of this state.

It is not difficult to discern in these assertions an explicit appeal to the moral authority of the transcendent. Bin Laden claims, in essence, to know the mind of God, the ultimate moral authority, and to argue that this moral authority not only opposes America and its secular, Western popular and political culture, but commands Muslims to kill Americans and their allies, and plunder their property, wherever they are found. The authority of the secular state is not simply challenged by bin Laden's ideas and actions. It is so thoroughly obliterated by a transcendent moral authority that the agency on part of the secular Western state implied, somehow, by citizenship within it is judged by the moral authority of the transcendent to be punishable by death.

According to bin Laden's line of reasoning, even moderate Muslim leaders in Arab nations are manipulated by the United States in what amounts to a virtually global conspiracy to assert an American control – one that is perceived as having cultural and economic dimensions as well as military ones. The cultural argument is persuasive in a world where, increasingly, villagers in remote corners of the globe have access to MTV, Hollywood movies, and the internet. They are assaulted with images and values that are both secular and American. In Israel both conservative Jewish rabbis and Muslim mullahs have agreed that the United States was the "capital of the devil."[14] In a similar vein, Mahmud Abouhalima told me that he was bitter that Islam did not have influence over the global media the way that secular America did. America, he believed, was using its power of information to promote the immoral values of secular society.[15]

When Abouhalima linked America's control of the media with its economic power – thought to be in Jewish hands – he was echoing a sentiment earlier articulated by the Ayatollah Khomeini. When he identified the "satanic" forces that were out to destroy Islam, he included not only Israelis but also "more satanic" Westerners: corporate leaders with "no religious belief" who saw Islam as "the major obstacle in the path of their materialistic ambitions and the chief threat to their political power."[16] The ayatollah went on to claim that "all the problems of Iran" were due to the treachery of "foreign colonialists."[17] On another occasion, the ayatollah blended political, personal, and spiritual issues together in generalizing about the cosmic foe – Western colonialism – and about "the black and dreadful future" which "the agents of colonialism, may God Almighty abandon them all," have in mind for Islam and the Muslim people.[18]

What the ayatollah was thinking of when he prophesized a "black and dreadful future" for Islam was the global domination of American economy and culture. This fear of globalization is linked with the fear of America as a dominant military, economic, and cultural force. These apprehensions about globalization have been felt even within certain right-wing quarters of the United States where militias have been convinced that the "new world order" proclaimed by President George Bush was more than a mood of global cooperation: it was a conspiratorial plot to control the world. Accepting this paranoid vision of American leaders' global designs, the Aum Shinrikyo master, Shoko Asahara, linked the United States Army with the Japanese government, Freemasons, and Jews in the image of a global conspiratorial band.

Conspiracy theories aside, there is a certain amount of truth to the notion that globalization and American dominance are related. US culture and economy have influenced societies around the world in ways that have caused concern to protectors of local societies. The vast financial and media networks of American-backed corporations and information systems have affected the whole of the globe. There has indeed been a great conflict between secular and religious life throughout the world, and America does inevitably support the secular side of the fight. Financial aid provided to leaders such as Egypt's Hosni Mubarak has shored up the political power of politicians opposed to religious nationalism. Moreover, after the fall of the Soviet Union, the United States has been virtually the only coherent military power in the world. Hence it has been easy for it to be blamed when people have felt that their lives were going askew or were being controlled by forces that they could not easily see. The extreme form of this anti-Americanism is satanization: imagining America as a demonic entity. This gives its critics the license to strike American people and property as if they were cosmic foes.

New religious nationalism

By describing America as a great foe, religious activists like Osama bin Laden have implicitly placed themselves on an international playing field. Their scenario of cosmic war is designed not only to lower the United States, but also to elevate themselves to a level of national – or even transnational – importance. For this reason, some activist groups have gone to some effort to make themselves credible in the eyes of their opponents. Acts of violence, including the US Embassy bombings in Africa, have been perpetrated in part in order to fulfill threats made against their enemies. The Kashmiri rebels who killed their American and European hostages were said to have found themselves in a dilemma: not necessarily wanting to murder the young men, but feeling that they had an obligation to be true to their word when they threatened to kill them if their demands were not met.

Although it may appear as if these acts were meant as signs of respect to their opponents, they also showed something else: that the movements acted as if they were their opponent's equals. Kashmiri rebels thought themselves to be as important as the Indian government; Osama bin Laden's network imagined itself to be equal to the greatest superpower on earth. In a display of what René Girard has described as mimesis, they were not only imitating their rivals, but also showing their superiority in terms that they believed that their rivals would understand.[19] In doing so, they make an implicit claim to represent a form of authority that is morally superior to, and that competes with, the public authority of the secular Western state. Many activists used their courtroom trials as arenas to get across the notion that through their acts they were sparring with the government and taunting it by accusing it of abandoning the very values it professed. Timothy McVeigh, for example, cited Justice Brandeis in implying that the US government had set a bad example.[20] Defendants in the trials for the 1993 World Trade Center attack called the US Department of Justice the department of "injustice," and Paul Hill, during his trial in Miami for the murder of a provider of abortions on 4 October 1994 accused the US government that was convicting him of murder of being "unjust."[21]

In the same vein, the suicide bombings perpetrated by the Hamas movement in residential neighborhoods of Tel Aviv and Jerusalem were, as one Hamas leader described them, "letters to Israel." They were invasions of the most domestic of their rival's quarters, with messages intended to show that "Hamas cannot be ignored," and that "the security for Israel's people is zero."[22] In that sense the message was the medium in which it was sent: the bombing provided a moment of chaos, warfare, and victimage that the Hamas movement wanted Israeli society to experience. It made the point that war was at hand by providing a bloody scene of battle in Israel's own quiet neighborhoods.

What was buttressed in these acts of symbolic empowerment was not just the credibility of the leadership of the Hamas movement and their equality with government officials, but also the legitimacy of religious social order as an ideology of nationalism and as an alternative source of authority. Through the currency of violence they were drawing attention to what they thought was significant and true about the social arena around them. In the language of Bourdieu, they were creating a perverse "habitus," a dark world of social reality, and forcing everyone – Israelis and Palestinians alike – to take stock of their perception of the world.[23] Their acts of terror were aimed at displaying power that not only elevated them personally, but also forwarded the sociopolitical agenda of their groups. The very act of performing violence in public is a political act: it announces that the power of the group is equal or superior to that of the state. In most cases this is exactly the message that the group wants to convey. These are clearly authority claims, assertions regarding the legitimacy of a social order that is based upon a notion of moral truth that these actors hold.

Thus at the same time that acts of religious violence announce that their religious authority is in competition with that of the secular order, they also highlight chinks in the armor of the secular state. They explicitly attack the claim of the state to provide what John Herz has called a "hard shell of territoriality" to protect its citizens. To the extent that these actors demonstrate the inability of the secular state to provide this protection, they implicitly delegitimate the state and diminish its authority.

In Israel, for instance, the Jewish right has long accused the secular government of using its devotion to democracy as an excuse for not fully embracing the idea that Israel is a Jewish religious entity rather than a secular state. Years before his attack on innocent Muslims at the Shrine of the Patriarchs in Hebron, Dr. Baruch Goldstein, in a letter to the editor of the New York Times, wrote that "Israelis will soon have to choose between a Jewish state and a democratic one."[24] Goldstein's massacre, I was told by one of his followers, displayed how serious he was about that choice. The supporter went on to tell me that now "Jews will have to learn to worship in a national way."[25] One of Goldstein's colleagues, Yoel Lerner, agreed with this position, telling me that in his opinion Israel should not be a democracy but a "Tohracracy" – a society based on the principle of Jewish law.[26]

This idea of a nation based on religious law was on the minds of American religious activists as well. Several associated with the ideology of Christian Identity advocated the creation of a Christian Republic.[27] White supremacists from throughout the United States and Canada met in Idaho allegedly to plot the forcible overthrow of the federal government and to create a separate Aryan nation within the United States. A government indictment based on information gleaned from this meeting stated that they planned to "carry out assassinations of federal officials, politicians, and Jews, as well as bombings and polluting of municipal water supplies."[28]

The establishment of a rule based on religious law has been the primary aim of many Muslim groups. Members of Hamas regarded this as the main difference between their organization and the secular ideology of Fateh and other groups associated with Yasir Arafat's Palestinian Authority. A similar argument was made by activists associated with Egyptian groups. Mahmud Abouhalima told me that President Hosni Mubarak could not be a true Muslim because he did not make *shari'a* – Islamic law – the law of the land, and that their movement's goal was to purify Arab nations.[29] A cleric in Cairo's conservative Al-Azhar theological school told me he resented his government's preference for Western law. "Why should we obey Western laws when Muslim laws are better?," he asked me.[30] It was this position that was assumed by many Muslim activists: that Western political institutions and the ideology on which they were based should be banished from their territories. They wanted to rebuild their societies on Islamic foundations.

In some cases activist groups carried this critique to an extreme. They not only rejected secular political authority but also created alternatives to it. Aum Shinrikyo, for instance, designated the leaders in its organization with government administrative titles such as minister of defense, minister of intelligence, minister of internal affairs, and minister of science and technology. The idea was not only to show that their organization could do government's job, but also to prepare the movement for indeed doing that job after the arrival of the global catastrophe predicted by Shoko Asahara. When that dark day came, the government of Aum Shinrikyo would be the only entity remaining to administer civil order.

In India, during the height of the Sikh rebellion in the 1980s, militants were treated as if they possessed an authority rivaling that of police and other government officials. Villagers in terrorist zones around the Punjab cities of Batala and Tarn Taran were unwilling to report violent incidents to officials, and radical youth set up their own courts and governmental offices. "Politics can be beautiful," I was told by a former head priest of Sikhism's central shrine.[31] "But it must be the right kind of politics." By this he meant a politics fused with religion, where "religion dominated politics," rather than the other way around.[32] When the country of Khalistan was created and Sikh rule was established, one of the leaders of the movement told me, it would be a rule of law that would bring justice to all, not just Sikhs, in a regime that lauded the tenets of the Sikh scriptures, the Guru Granth Sahib, as supreme.[33] Exactly how this differed from the current form of political organization in India remained obscure. It was clear, however, that this new Sikh authority would be a form of public authority, albeit public authority with a "divine" source and sanction. Thus the claim, and goal, is an alternative conception of a moral public order.

One of the reasons why these activists wanted to create religious nations was to restore the ideological and organizational dominance of religion – a role that religion enjoyed before the Enlightenment concept of secular nationalism took hold around the world. By its nature, the secular state has been opposed to the idea that religion should have a role in public life. From the time that modern secular nationalism emerged in the eighteenth century as a product of the European Enlightenment's political values it did so with a distinctly anti-religious, or at least anti-clerical, posture. The ideas of John Locke about the origins of a civil community, and the social contract theories of Jean Jacques Rousseau required very little commitment to religious belief. Although they allowed for a divine order that made the rights of humans possible, their ideas had the effect of taking religion – at least institutional religion – out of public life.

At the time, religious "enemies of the Enlightenment" – as the historian, Darrin McMahon, described them – protested religion's public demise.[34] But their views were submerged in a wave of approval for a new view of social order in which secular nationalism was thought to be virtually a natural law, universally applicable and morally right. The result of religion's devaluation has been "a general crisis of religious belief," as Pierre Bourdieu has put it.[35] This causes a problem not just for believers but for society as a whole, for it has undercut the public's ability to rely on public symbols. Bourdieu describes this as "the collapse of a world of representations" and "the disintegration of an entire universe of social relations."[36]

In countering this disintegration, resurgent religious activists have proclaimed the death of secularism and reasserted the primacy of religious values in the public sphere. They have experienced what I once described as a "loss of faith" in secular politics.[37] They have dismissed the efforts of secular culture and its forms of nationalism to replace religion. They have challenged the notion that secular society and the modern nation-state are able to provide the moral fiber that unites national communities, or give it the ideological strength to sustain states buffeted by ethical, economic, and military failures. Their message has been easy to believe, and has been widely received because the failures of the secular state have been so real.

Acts of religious terrorism, therefore, have been more than hollow gestures. The very act of killing on behalf of a moral code is a political statement. Such acts break the state's monopoly on morally sanctioned killing. By taking the right to take life into their own hands, the perpetrators of religious violence make a daring claim of power on behalf of the powerless, a basis of legitimacy for public order other than that upon which the secular state relies. In doing so, they demonstrate to everyone how fragile public order actually is, and how fickle can be the populace's assent to the moral authority of the secular national public order.

Yet after over a decade of religious violence, the outlines of most attempts at asserting religious nationalism are still quite sketchy. Curiously, the goals are the most obscure among groups that are the most violent. In fact, no religious regime has ever been established through the means of terrorism: not in Afghanistan, Sudan, or Iran; not when Muslim activists were briefly in control in Turkey and Tajikistan; and not when they almost came to power in Algeria. These religious regimes rode into power on the vehicles of peaceful democratic elections or through well-organized military takeovers. It was not through the sporadic and extreme performances of power that characterize terrorist acts.

In fact, despite their bravado, groups associated with terrorism have largely shied from politics. They have eschewed elections. When given the opportunity to run for office they have rejected it, as Hamas did in Palestine in 1996 and radical Sikhs did in Punjab in 1992. Or if they did attempt to win at the polls, as Aum Shinrikyo did in 1990, they failed miserably. Nor have they attempted to develop effective fighting forces other than those needed for a hit-and-run style of terrorist bombing. The al Qaeda network of Osama bin Laden, for example, has no state, no political ideology, no army, and no military strategy.

While their claims that their goals are sanctioned by the moral authority of the transcendent have been quite clear, the images of political order that they yearned to create have been fuzzy – perhaps deliberately so. Sometimes they have been democratic, sometimes socialist, sometimes a sort of religious oligarchy. Although it was clear who the religious activists hated, nowhere in their program was a design for a political entity – Islamic or otherwise – that could actually administer the results of a victory over American and secular rule and the emergence of a religious revolution, should they have achieved it. My conclusion is that, despite their political potency, acts of religious terrorism are largely devices for symbolic empowerment in wars that cannot be won and for goals that cannot be achieved. For many, the notion of ideal political authority that fuels their imagination is not a national one, but one that is transnational and utopian: a righteous global political order, one slightly beyond the frame for mortal history.

Transnational networks

Islamic movements especially have held the illusion of waging a global struggle. The assemblage of al Qaeda activists coordinated by Osama bin Laden is profoundly multinational in membership: Egyptian, Palestinian, Jordanian, Saudi Arabian, Afghan, Algerian, Sudanese, Yemeni, and Pakistani. Their groups have been transnational in part because of the multicultural background of expatriate Muslims who have congregated in their movements. Similarly, the Hamas leader, Abdul Aziz Rantisi, told me that what distinguished his organization from Yasir Arafat's was that the Palestinian Authority was waging a "national struggle" whereas Hamas was "transnational."[38] It is supported by Muslims everywhere.

Compatriots from different parts of the world also make up the militant backing of movements such as Sinhalese and Tamil rebels in Sri Lanka and Sikh separatists in India. Although expatriate Tamils and Sikhs may find themselves on the periphery of society in Britain, Canada, the United States, and the many other parts of the world to which they migrated, militant movements provided them with the opportunity to display their commitment and prove their importance to the community in a powerful way. This phenomenon has been called "e-mail ethnicities": transnational networks of people tied together culturally despite the diversities of their places of residence and the limitations of national borders.[39] These ethnicities, united by web sites and the internet, have been not only extensions of traditional societies whose adherents and cultures are dispersed around the world, but harbingers of global cultures as well.[40] Among these expatriate groups have been some notoriously politically active ones.

Osama bin Laden and his lieutenants have trooped from Saudi Arabia to Sudan to Afghanistan. Sheik Omar Abdul Rahman, for instance, lived variously in Egypt, Sudan, and New Jersey, and other members of his network originated from diverse locations in the Muslim world. Among them was Mohammed Salameh, whose story was paradigmatic of the religious radical expatriate experience. Salameh lived virtually from hand to mouth, sharing addresses with several other people in Jersey City, in a busy working-class neighborhood that teemed with new immigrants from Haiti and the Middle East. The setting was in some ways not unlike the social situation and economic conditions in the crowded Palestinian refugee camps on the West Bank and in Jordan where Salameh was born and raised, and from which he departed in 1987 for America in order to improve his educational and financial situation. In the United States, where his limited English continued to be a social barrier, Salameh associated primarily with other Arabs. His life became focused around the local mosque, located above a Chinese restaurant, led by the charismatic Sheik Omar Abdul Rahman. The trajectory of his life led ultimately to his participation in the 1993 bombing of the World Trade Center, when the world came to know him as the terrorist who foolishly returned to the Ryder rental agency to retrieve his US$ 200 deposit for the van he had rented and had subsequently blown up, and was immediately caught by waiting agents of the FBI.[41]

The socially uprooted and dislocated Salameh found a new identity in a transnational community of radical Muslims. Appropriately, perhaps, they identified their miseries as global as well: the emerging transnational economy and the global culture seemingly promoted by the United States. It was a perception shared especially by those who were geographically dislocated, but their attitude of suspicion and cynicism was one that was widely experienced throughout the post-Cold War world. Even the United States saw a remarkable degree of disaffection with its political leaders and witnessed the rise of right-wing religious movements that fed on the public's perception of the inherent immorality of government. But the global shifts that have given rise to antimodernist movements have also affected less developed nations. Religious activists such as the Algerian leaders of the Islamic Salvation Front, the Ayatollah Khomeini in Iran, Sheik Ahmed Yassin in Palestine, Sayyid Qutb and his disciple, Sheik Omar Abdul Rahman in Egypt, L. K. Advani in India, and Sant Jarnail Singh Bhindranwale in India's Punjab have asserted the legitimacy of a postcolonial political identity based on traditional culture.[42]

In some cases these voices have been stridently nationalist; in others they hint at transnational political solutions. The al Qaeda network of Osama bin Laden sought no specific political goal but imagined itself embroiled in a global war. This uncertainty about what constitutes a valid basis for social order is on the one hand a kind of guerilla antiglobalism; on the other hand it is a political form of postmodernism.[43] In Iran it has resulted in the rejection of a modern Western political regime and the creation of a successful religious state. Yet, what lies beyond modernity is not necessarily a new form of political order, be it national or religious.

In regions formerly under Soviet control, for example, the specter of the future beyond the socialist form of modernity has been one of cultural anarchism. The fear that there will be a spiritual as well as a political collapse at modernity's center has, in many areas of the world, led to terror. Hence the rise of religious violence across geographic boundaries has been a sigh of distress. In the horrific destruction of the World Trade Center and other assaults on modern secular public life, it is a sign of vicious desperation. For at least some who perpetrate these actions, however, it has also been a tragic longing: a cry for social coherence and moral community in a time of global change.

NOTES

1 Mark Juergensmeyer, *Terror in the Mind of God: The Global Rise of Religious Violence*, (Berkeley: University of California Press, 2000). This essay includes revised excerpts from this book.
2 Interview with Mahmud Abouhalima, Federal Penitentiary, Lompoc, California, 30 September 1997.
3 Interview with Abouhalima, 19 August 1997. The topic of the relationship between Islam and public order was discussed in both interviews.
4 Sheik Omar Abdul Rahman, recorded on audiotape cassettes made in the United States and quoted in Kim Murphy, "Have the Islamic Militants Turned to a New Battlefront in the US?," *Los Angeles Times*, 3 March 1993, A20.
5 Imam [Ayatollah] Khomeini, *Collection of Speeches, Position Statements* (Arlington, Va.: Joint Publications Research Service, 1979), p. 24.
6 Ibid., p. 30.
7 John J. Goldman, "Defendants Given 25 Years to Life in New York Terror Plot," *Los Angeles Times*, 18 January 1996, A1.
8 RAND, "Chronicle of International Terrorism," reported in Bruce Hoffman, *Terrorism Targeting: Tactics, Trends, and Potentialities* (Santa Monica, Cal.: RAND Corporation Papers, 1992), p. 17.
9 State Department statistics cited by Robin Wright, "Prophetic 'Terror 2000' Mapped Evolving Threat," *Los Angeles Times*, 9 August 1998, A16.
10 Osama bin Laden, interviewed on an ABC News report, rebroadcast on 9 August 1998.
11 Samuel Berger, quoted in Osama bin Laden, *fatwa* issued February 1998, "Jihad Is an Individual Duty," *Los Angeles Times*, 13 August 1998, B9.
12 Excerpts from ibid.
13 Ibid.
14 Interview with Rabbi Manachem Fruman, Tuqua settlement, West Bank, Israel, 14 August 1995.
15 Interview with Abouhalima, 30 September 1997.
16 Khomeini, *Islam and Revolution: Writings and Declarations*, trans. and annotated by Hamid Algar (London: Routledge and Kegan Paul, 1985), pp. 27–28.
17 Khomeini, *Collection of Speeches, Position Statements*, p. 3.
18 Ibid., p. 25.

19 See René Girard, *Violence and the Sacred*, trans. by Patrick Gregory (Baltimore, Md.: Johns Hopkins University Press, 1977); and Girard, *The Scapegoat*, trans. by Yvonne Freccero (Baltimore, Md.: Johns Hopkins University Press, 1986); Walter Burkhert, René Girard, and Jonathan Z. Smith, *Violent Origins: Ritual Killing and Cultural Formation*, edited by Robert G. Hamerton-Kelly (Stanford: Stanford University Press, 1987).

20 Timothy McVeigh, quoted in Richard A. Serrano, "McVeigh Speaks Out, Receives Death Sentence," *Los Angeles Times*, 15 August 1997, A1.

21 Paul Hill, quoted in Mike Clary, "Suspect in Abortion Slayings Acts as Own Attorney at Trial," *Los Angeles Times*, 5 October 1994, A5.

22 Interview with Imad Faluji, journalist and member of the political wing of Hamas, in Gaza, 19 August 1995.

23 Pierre Bourdieu and Loic J. D. Wacquant, *An Invitation to Reflexive Sociology* (Chicago: University of Chicago Press, 1992), p. 131.

24 Dr. Baruch Goldstein, Letter to the Editor, *New York Times*, 30 June 1981.

25 Interview with Yochay Ron, Kiryat Arba, Israel, 18 August 1995.

26 Interview with Yoel Lerner, director of the Sannhedrin Institute, Jerusalem, 17 August 1995.

27 Leonard Zeskind, *The "Christian Identity" Movement: Analyzing Its Theological Rationalization for Racist and Anti-Semitic Violence* (New York: Division of Church and Society of the National Council of the Churches of Christ in the USA, 1986), pp. 35–42.

28 Reported in *Arkansas Gazette* (Little Rock, Ark.), 27 April 1987, quoted in Bruce Hoffman, *"Holy Terror": The Implications of Terrorism Motivated by a Religious Imperative* (Santa Monica, Cal.: RAND Corporation Papers, 1993), p. 8.

29 Interview with Abouhalima, 19 August 1997.

30 Interview with Dr. Muhammad Ibraheem el-Geyoushi, dean of the Faculty of Dawah, Al-Azhar University, Cairo, 30 May 1990.

31 Interview with Darshan Singh Ragi, former Jatedar, Akal Takhat, at Bhai Vir Singh Sadan, New Delhi, 13 January 1991.

32 Ibid.

33 Interview with Sohan Singh, leader of the Sohan Singh faction, Khalistan Liberation Force, Mohalli, Punjab, 3 August 1996.

34 Darrin McMahon, *Enemies of the Enlightenment: The French Counter-Enlightenment and the Making of Modernity* (New York: Oxford University Press, 2001).

35 Pierre Bourdieu, *Language and Symbolic Power* (Cambridge, Mass.: Harvard University Press, 1991), p. 116.

36 Ibid.

37 Mark Juergensmeyer, *The New Cold War? Religious Nationalism Confronts the Secular State* (Berkeley: University of California Press, 1993), p. 11.

38 Interview with Abdul Aziz Rantisi, cofounder and political leader of Hamas, in Khan Yunis, Gaza, 1 March 1998.

39 I do not know who coined the term "e-mail ethnicities." I first heard it used by the anthropologist Benedict Anderson, in comments made at a conference on nationalism held by the Center for German and European Studies, University of California, Berkeley, 15 March 1992.

40 I discuss further this notion of the global diaspora of religious cultures in my essay, "Thinking Globally About Religion," in Juergensmeyer (ed.), *Global Religion: A Handbook* (New York: Oxford University Press, forthcoming).

41 The story of Salameh's capture is told in Jim Dwyer, David Kocieniewski, Deidre Murphy, and Peg Tyre, *Two Seconds Under the Bomb. Terror Comes to America: The Conspiracy Behind the World Trade Center Bombing* (New York: Crown Publishers, 1994), pp. 89–101.

42 For a forceful statement of this thesis, see Partha Chatterjee, *The Nation and Its Fragments: Colonial and Postcolonial Histories* (Princeton, N.J.: Princeton University Press, 1993).

43 For the distinction between postmodernity as a social phenomenon and as a mode of analysis, see David Lyon, *Postmodernity* (Minneapolis: University of Minnesota Press, 1994).

Part IV

Illicit authority: mafias and mercenaries

8   Transnational organized crime and the state

Phil Williams

One of the most important characteristics of global politics at the beginning of the twenty-first century is the multiplicity of actors. An environment that, for a long time, was regarded as the domain of states is now seen by most commentators as much more complex: states share the stage with a wide variety of non-state or "sovereignty-free actors," ranging from transnational and multinational companies with global markets to non-governmental organizations concerned with good causes such as peace and disarmament, preventing further environmental degradation, famine and disaster relief, poverty alleviation, and the like.[1] There is also a new breed of criminal actor – transnational criminal organizations – that is interested not in the pursuit of good, but in the pursuit of wealth, and the use of criminal means to obtain it. Transnational criminal organizations are not new; they have been around as long as there has been a demand for the smuggling of goods across borders. The difference today, however, is that there are more of them, they are more varied, and they possess greater wealth and power than ever before. Furthermore, whereas most states in the past seemed to have the capacity to keep organized crime under control, this is no longer so obviously the case. Indeed, transnational organized crime has emerged as a major challenger to individual states – especially those in transition and those that are still developing economically – and to international governance. Against this background, this chapter seeks to do several things:

> to locate the relationship between organized crime and states in the broader context over the debate over the future of the state.
> to understand states from the perspective of transnational criminal organizations, which view states in terms of obstacles and impediments on the one hand and opportunities on the other. Transnational criminal organizations are concerned with both reducing or eliminating the obstacles and maximizing the opportunities. They do this in part through the use of corruption, which is the single most important instrument of organized

crime and one of the reasons organized crime during the 1990s aroused unprecedented concerns.

to highlight the vulnerabilities of weak states and states-in-transition to transnational organized crime, which finds such states congenial incubators and targets. The analysis develops the notion of capacity gaps and functional holes, and highlights ways in which criminal organizations exploit and fill these holes.

In the final section, the chapter speculates about the future of the relationship between states and transnational criminal organizations, suggesting that these organizations will continue to pose immense problems for many states and that one of the big divides in global politics will be between those states that tacitly or explicitly support or engage in organized crime and those that oppose and confront transnational criminal organizations.

The key issues and concepts

The meaning and future of the state

Some observers suggest that the period in which global politics has been dominated by the nation-state – a period ushered in by the Treaty of Westphalia in 1648 – has come to an end and that the Westphalian state is undergoing a long-term secular decline that will be impossible to reverse. Jessica Mathews, for example, has contended that the world is witnessing:

a novel redistribution of power among states, markets, and civil society. National governments are not merely losing autonomy in a globalizing economy, they are this time sharing powers, including political, social, and security roles that lie at the core of national sovereignty – with businesses, with international organizations, and with a multitude of . . . non-governmental organizations, or NGOs. The steady accumulation of power in the hands of states that began 350 years ago with the Peace of Westphalia is over, I believe, at least for a while. Increasingly, resources and threats that matter, whether they are money, information, pollution, popular culture, circulate and shape lives and economies with little regard for political boundaries.[2]

In a very similar vein, Susan Strange has talked about the retreat of the state.[3]

Many observers agree that globalization is challenging the dominance of states in international relations from above, while subnational forces are eroding it from below. In an important variant of the globalization argument, Saskia Sassen has contended that globalization threatens to undo the intersection of sovereignty and territory not least because electronic space, for the most part, is outside territorial jurisdiction.[4] For those who see the challenge as coming from above, there is a clear contraction in the domain of state authority. The state simply can no longer control many of the activities that, in the past, were within its mandate and power to control. There are also important challenges coming from below – from subnational groups that, for one reason or another, do not accept state authority and legitimacy. Indeed, some states, lacking legitimacy, simply dissolve into civil war, while those that lack basic elements of the capacity to govern become failed states, unable to fulfill the functions that are normally associated with states and characterized by chaos and disorder.

At the other extreme are those who argue that the state remains the dominant and defining entity in world politics. The state, in this assessment – which derives primarily, although not exclusively, from realist and neorealist assumptions – is essentially robust. Although there might be some contraction in the domain of state authority at the margin, the state, it is argued, is still the fundamental unit in international relations. Moreover, it is highly resilient in the face of globalization and various other challenges. From this perspective, civil wars and ethnic conflicts are usually about who controls the state, while transnational corporations and transnational social movements are often state-based and are an instrument of, rather than a challenge to, state power and authority.

One of the difficulties in the debate over the future of the state is that it is not always clear that observers are in full agreement on what constitutes a state. Indeed, it is possible to discern four major interpretations of the state:

> the state as a sovereign territorial entity controlling the area under its jurisdiction and who and what enters. This is also related to the notion of state as the major actor in global politics, which to some degree – and this is where opinions diverge sharply – is still territorially based.
>
> the state as a system of rules.[5] The state has both authority over its citizens and obligations toward them. The exercise of authority and the fulfillment of the obligations are embedded in a set of rules, norms, and laws that apply to all those within the territorial jurisdiction of the state.
>
> the state as a set of institutions and people who act on its behalf. Here the notion is that the state manifests itself through people and institutions who act as the representatives or guardians of the state and take decisions and implement policies in the name of the state.

the state as a set of functions that range from state as guarantor of order and security (through its monopoly of coercive power) to the state as manager of economic activity and provider of economic and social welfare.[6] These functions relate to the notion of state legitimacy, which is obtained and maintained in large part because the state meets certain basic needs of the citizenry.

The analysis here considers each of these notions of the state and shows how it relates to transnational organized crime. Before exploring the various relationships in more detail, however, it is necessary to elucidate more fully what is meant by transnational organized crime.

The nature of transnational organized crime

Within criminology, disputes over the nature and meaning of organized crime have spanned several decades. Out of this controversy, three approaches to the definition of organized crime have emerged: those which embody simple lists of characteristics; those with more sophisticated lists that identify some essential characteristics and some *à la carte* characteristics; and those that try to capture the essence of organized crime. The former can be found in almost any textbook on organized crime and usually includes such characteristics as enduring association for criminal purposes, a minimum number of people (often three), some kind of organizational structure and hierarchy, and the use of corruption and violence. The more sophisticated list approach distinguishes between primary characteristics, all of which have to be present, and secondary characteristics, only some of which will be present. The third kind of definition seeks to provide the essence of organized crime. An example of this is Interpol's definition, which sees organized crime in terms of "any group having a corporate structure whose primary objective is to obtain money through illegal activities, often surviving on fear and corruption."[7] An alternative and neo-Clausewitzian type of definition is to suggest that organized crime is simply the continuation of business by other means. Transnational organized crime is, then, criminal business that, in one way or another, crosses national borders. The border crossing can involve the perpetrators, their illicit products, people (either illegal migrants or women and children being trafficked illegally), their profits, or digital signals (a virtual border crossing).

Transnational organized crime and states

Organized crime both threatens states and exploits states. In terms of the threats to states, there are several aspects of transnational organized crime that need to be taken into account:

organized crime structures. These embody a concentration of illegal power in society that can significantly influence political, economic, and social life. In some countries organized crime is little more than a marginal problem, existing on the fringes of society and having little impact on the way that the society functions or is governed. In others, however, organized crime has succeeded in embedding itself not only in the social fabric and the economy but also in the political system. In some cases, organized crime and the state apparatus develop a deeply symbiotic and collusive relationship.

organized crime activities that provide the profits and that can range from drug trafficking and arms trafficking, to extortion and infiltration of licit business. These activities are generally against the law in most states. The irony, of course, is that prohibition or even regulation of some products that are in demand increases their price and encourages the development of criminal markets.

organized crime strategies and processes designed to manage the risks posed by governments and law enforcement agencies. Most transnational criminal organizations adopt some kind of risk management strategy that is designed to protect the organization and its activities. One of its most potent risk management tools is corruption, which is intended to neutralize the control powers of states but can also undermine their power and authority. Indeed, organized crime–corruption networks can be understood as the HIV virus of the modern state, circumventing and breaking down the natural defenses of the body politic.

It is clear from this that organized crime is a challenge to states, irrespective of whichever dimension or meaning is attributed to states. This is evident in table 4, which looks at how the three major aspects of organized crime impinge on the four dimensions of states elucidated above.

Transnational organized crime activities, for example, fundamentally challenge the territorial sovereignty of states and, in particular, any notion that states can determine who or what comes across their border, and what activities are permissible in the territory under their jurisdiction. Transnational criminal organizations typically circumvent border controls and, rather than negotiating with the government for access to legal markets (as transnational corporations do), operate clandestinely. Insofar as there is negotiation, it occurs with domestic organized crime groups that have readymade distribution networks for illegal goods and services. Indeed, alliances among criminal organizations are becoming increasingly important in allowing foreign groups to enter new domestic

Table 4: *Organized crime and the state*

Aspects of organized crime	Sovereign entity	System of rules	Institutions and people	Functions
Activities such as various forms of trafficking	Smuggling work with illegal power structure	Undermine and exploit prohibition of goods and services	Challenge and justification for resources for social control and criminal justice	Challenge to law and order
Power manifested in use of violence	Challenge state monopoly of coercive power and create no-go zones	Replace rule of law with rule of violence	Intimidate judiciary and law enforcement and ensure low penalties or acquittals for organized crime figures	Extortion threatens business and property supposedly protected by the state
Risk management strategies, especially corruption	Operational corruption to protect trafficking activities	Organized crime buys immunity from system of rules through corruption of law enforcement and judiciary	Corrosion of institutions such as police, judiciary, and the military as well as financial institutions	Corruption undermines good governance and democratic procedures

markets, compensating for their weaknesses and lack of local knowledge, and overcoming border restrictions. Ironically, although transnational criminal organizations violate national borders as a matter of routine, they also exploit these borders in several ways. In the first place, national borders often bring with them highly significant price differentials. A kilo of cocaine, for example, increases in value approximately sixfold once it has crossed the Mexican–United States border. Second, organized crime uses borders defensively. During one period when they were fighting extradition to the United States, for example, the leaders of the Medellin and Cali cartels became major champions of Colombian nationalism and sovereignty. Their arguments were resonant with the symbolism of sovereignty and reveal that, although drug trafficking groups and other transnational criminal organizations represent both private power and private authority, they are not averse to appealing to more traditional state authority when the need presents itself.

The hypocrisy of this, of course, is very striking given the routine way in which criminal organizations violate national borders and national laws. Indeed, in some cases, their challenge to state authority goes even further and the state has to accept that there are "no-go zones" in which it has no authority and little, if any, presence. Criminal activities also challenge the system of rules that states attempt to impose. There is another deep irony here: criminal organizations operate in criminal markets that are particularly lucrative because they are a direct product of state policies of prohibition and regulation of certain goods and services. The challenge to state institutions and functions from criminal activities is more tangential but still significant – to the extent that law enforcement institutions fail to stem these activities and provide order and safety for citizens, then questions about the efficacy of the state apparatus come to the fore. At the same time, criminal activities provide a rationale for strengthening state institutions and devoting more resources to the functions of social control and border control.

The power of criminal organizations is a threat to the state as sovereign entity in that the state claims a monopoly of coercive power; criminal organizations also exercise such power and use violence to remove competitors and obstacles to their businesses. In a few cases, criminal organizations have launched major assaults on the state, using terror tactics in an effort to intimidate the authorities. Criminal violence is a frontal attack on the notion of the state as a system of rules and its concomitant, the rule of law. This violence is sometimes directed at particular state institutions such as the judiciary or law enforcement agencies. In effect, criminal organizations seek to use what Thomas Schelling once called "the power to hurt" to neutralize social control and criminal justice institutions that threaten them.[8] Violence and the threat of violence by criminal organizations are also often directed against large and small businesses as part of extortion. To the extent that this succeeds, the state has failed in one of its major functions, securing the safety and prosperity of its citizens.

If violence is the most dramatic manifestation of the power of organized crime, the wealth that criminal organizations often have available is another form of power – and is used as the basis for risk management strategies by criminal organizations. The wealth of criminal organizations is used for corruption, in ways that undermine the very foundations of good governance. Although corruption is often treated as a condition, in this context it has to be seen as a very powerful instrument used by criminal organizations to ensure that the risks to them and to their activities are minimized. Corruption is used to undermine border control efforts, to ensure that organized crime, in effect, can operate outside the system of rules that apply to other citizens, to neutralize state institutions and people combating organized crime, and to inhibit the proper functioning of the criminal justice system. The targets and objectives of corruption are examined more fully below.

If transnational criminal organizations, in some respects, pose major challenges to the functioning of states, in other ways their activities and behavior acknowledge the continued importance of the state. Indeed, transnational criminal organizations in effect accept and use states in several ways. In the first place a state – particularly one that has been neutralized by the power of organized crime – can provide a safe haven, i.e., protection from other states and a base from which the criminal organizations can operate with impunity. The capacity to provide safe havens or sanctuaries actually makes states very important to criminal organizations. Another attraction is that states have access to all sorts of resources that criminal organizations might want to obtain or export. In such cases, criminal organizations will seek access to institutions and people who formally control these resources. Indeed, from the perspective of criminal organizations, states can be understood in terms of four categories: home, host, transshipment, and service. Home states are in some respects the most important – they provide the location from which criminal organizations operate their transnational businesses. Consequently, a congenial, low-risk environment is critical.

This is less true of host or market states which are the destination for many of the illegal products of criminal organizations that are shipped across borders. Host or market states generally have lucrative markets or other targets for their criminal activity – with the result that criminal organizations are sometimes willing to incur a significant level of risk in order to operate within them. Moreover, there are some things that give transnational criminal organizations an advantage in host states, compensating for the difficulties of establishing corruption networks of the kind that are so potent in the home state. Among these are the capacity to operate within ethnic enclaves, which provide cover and recruitment and which are difficult for law enforcement to penetrate because of language and cultural barriers. States that act as hosts or markets for organized crime rarely face fundamental challenges in the way that home states do – partly because ethnic-based criminal organizations are not rooted in local or national power structures.

Before illegal products reach their final destination in the market states, they generally have to pass through one or more transshipment states. These states are located on major transit routes for certain kinds of illicit commodities such as drugs, arms, or illegal aliens, and become the transshipment states because of their access to the target (i.e., the market or final destination for the illicit products) and the ease of transit, which is largely a function of state capacity for interdiction.[9] Such states suffer from the violation of their sovereignty and are particularly vulnerable to operational corruption (i.e., corruption designed to facilitate the movements of illicit goods through the state).

The other kind of state, from the perspective of criminal organizations, is what might be termed a service state. Service states generally have particular sectors of activity – usually the financial sector – that can be exploited by criminal organizations to move, hide, and protect the proceeds of their illegal activities. Those states which make up the offshore banking world – a world that incorporates many Caribbean states and European states such as Luxembourg, Austria, Monaco, Switzerland, and Cyprus, and that extends to minuscule South Pacific jurisdictions such as Vanuatu, Niue, and Nauru – offer bank secrecy and pose few problems for criminal organizations seeking to hide and protect their money. The biggest challenge to the small service states is corruption, which is used to resist any efforts to clean up their activities and develop banking safeguards such as know-your-customer rules. The irony here – as with the notion of home states as sanctuaries – is that transnational criminal organizations are fully exploiting the sovereignty of some states for defensive purposes even as their trafficking activities are grossly violating the sovereignty of others.

Any analysis of the relationship between transnational criminal organizations and states is complicated by the fact that some states fulfill several roles simultaneously. Russia, for example, is a home state for as many as 10,000 indigenous criminal organizations, yet is also a host state for Nigerian criminal groups involved in drug trafficking and fraud, as well as a transshipment state for drug trafficking groups from Central Asia and a service state for Italian criminal organizations looking for safe ways to launder the proceeds of crime. South Africa is in a similar position. In addition to acting as home state for indigenous criminal organizations, it also acts as host to Nigerian groups involved in drug trafficking, fraud, and control of prostitution, Italians involved in money laundering, Chinese networks trafficking in abalone and endangered species, and Ukrainian and Russian groups involved in arms trafficking and the illegal diamond trade. The critical point about both these states, however, is that they are states-in-transition, and, as such, share certain characteristics that make them particularly vulnerable to organized crime.

Transnational organized crime and weak states

It became increasingly clear throughout the 1980s and the 1990s that the rise of transnational organized crime was inextricably connected with the weakness of many states in the international system. Yet state weakness is not a new phenomenon. Nor is the link between weak states and organized crime particularly novel. The weakness of the Italian state in the nineteenth century facilitated the rise of the mafia in Sicily: with the state incapable of providing protection and arbitration for business, the mafia developed to fill the vacuum.[10] Similarly, but of more recent vintage, during the 1970s and 1980s, the weakness of the Colombian state and its lack of control over territory nominally under its jurisdiction was a major factor in explaining the rise of Colombia as the corporate headquarters of the South American cocaine industry. State weakness gave Colombian drug trafficking organizations a comparative advantage over their counterparts in Peru and Bolivia.[11]

Perhaps the most dramatic examples of state weakness providing ideal conditions for the rise of criminal organizations, however, are to be found in the states of the former Soviet Union. The collapse of the Soviet state resulted in a major upsurge of organized crime in Russia and other former republics, providing both unprecedented opportunities for criminal organizations and incentives and pressures for citizens to engage in criminal activities. Similarly, the political transition in South Africa has been accompanied by the growth of indigenous criminal organizations and the influx of groups from outside the country. Part of the reason is that transitions are characterized by the collapse and reestablishment of state structures; major shifts in the principles underlying economic management; a redefinition of the principles and values on which society operates (e.g., who is eligible for participation in political affairs); and a reorientation of relationships with the outside world, usually involving an opening of the economy and the society. As a result, states-in-transition have certain weaknesses and vulnerabilities that are readily exploited by transnational organized crime.

As well as being the result of a sudden collapse of an old regime, state weakness can also reflect a more long-term failure to develop viable, legitimate, and effective state institutions. Whatever the short- or long-term causes of weakness, however, weak states tend to share certain characteristics: there is a low level of state legitimacy; border controls are weak; rules are ineffective; the institutions and people who represent the state put other goals above the public interest; there is little economic or social provision for the citizenry; business is not legally regulated or protected; social control through a fair and efficient criminal justice system is lacking; and other typical state functions are not carried out with either efficiency or effectiveness. Not surprisingly, these weaknesses provide a greenhouse effect for organized crime. This section seeks to elucidate this effect. It contends, in essence, that weak states suffer from capacity gaps, and that

Table 5: *Capacity gaps, functional holes, and transnational organized crime*

Capacity gaps	Functional holes	Implications for organized crime
Social control	Ineffective criminal justice system	Organized crime operates with impunity
Social welfare	Lack of provision for citizens	– Migration to illegal economy – Organized crime recruitment – Paternalism substitute for state
Business regulation	Lack of regulatory framework	– Organized crime as arbitrator, protector, and debt collector
Oversight and accountability	Lack of control and transparency	– Opportunity for extensive use of corruption – Hijacking of privatization processes
Border control	Weak interdiction capability	– Use state for transshipment of various illegal products
Legitimacy	Lack of authority and affiliation	– Build on patron–client links and other relationships that are more important than loyalty to the state
Electoral norms and patterns	Campaign financing	– Opportunity to influence election outcomes and cut deals with politicians

capacity gaps lead to functional holes (i.e., a failure of the state to fulfill certain basic functions that are normally associated with states and that are expected by the citizenry). Capacity gaps and functional holes are exploited by criminal organizations in one of two ways – either by filling them and, in effect, substituting or compensating for the state, or by exploiting the room for maneuver that they provide. In effect, functional holes provide space that can either be filled by organized crime or in which organized crime can operate virtually unhindered. The ways in which capacity gaps and the resulting functional holes are exploited by criminal organizations is summarized in table 5.

Organized crime tends to develop in response to a particular combination of opportunities on the one side and pressures and incentives on the other. Capacity gaps and functional holes feed all aspects of this equation, offering multiple opportunities for – and few constraints on – organized criminal activity.

One aspect of state weakness with particular relevance to the development of organized crime has been the inadequate development of effective criminal justice systems that are efficient, effective, fair, and equitable and that incorporate measures specifically designed to prevent and control various forms of racketeering and money laundering. This capacity gap has been evident in a number of states-in-transition including Russia and

South Africa. This is hardly surprising. As Durkheim argued, most societies have regulatory mechanisms to restrain criminal behavior through both formal sanctions and social norms, "but when society is disturbed by some painful crisis or by beneficent but abrupt transitions" it becomes incapable of enforcing restraint – at least temporarily.[12] The problem is sometimes one of laws – and in particular the absence of legislation specifically directed against organized crime – and sometimes one of resources. Most states-in-transition, for example, "are faced with a plethora of economic and political problems that they must address" and "severe resource constraints that limit the training and equipping of effective law enforcement organizations."[13] The resulting functional holes mean that organized crime can operate with a high level of impunity or, at the very least, a minimum of risk. The prospects that major organized crime figures will be caught and incarcerated are minimal. Although rank-and-file members of criminal enterprises might be arrested, the organizers and leaders are often able to operate with remarkable freedom. And even when they are arrested, they are often able to buy acquittals or remarkably light sentences.

The legal capacity gaps are not confined to criminal law. The failure of some states to provide adequate and appropriate regulatory frameworks for business can have profound implications for organized crime, offering opportunities either to fill or to exploit the resulting functional hole. In Russia, for example, the lack of an appropriate regulatory framework for business providing recourse for debt collection and effective and peaceful arbitration of disputes has been a huge problem during the move toward a free market economy. In the absence of such a framework, there is neither protection nor contract enforcement, a condition that allows organized crime to become a surrogate for government.[14] The change in the principles on which the economy is based preceded the development of appropriate regulatory and legal provisions and led some businessmen to turn to criminal organizations to collect outstanding debts or to settle disputes. Recourse to these unorthodox methods had two consequences: it gave criminal organizations an *entrée* into the business world, thereby creating a seamless web between the licit and the illicit, and it encouraged legitimate businesses to resort to increasingly ruthless methods against their competitors. Indeed, one result of the capacity gaps and functional holes in Russia has been the emergence of an "iron triangle" in which politicians and government officials, businessmen, and criminals are bound together in complex relationships that are enormously difficult to disentangle, but clearly highly damaging to the transition and to Russia's reputation in the world. Collusion and even integration of the three groups both results from and accentuates a blurring of the public and private, of legitimate and criminal enterprises, and of money laundering and capital flight.

A variant on this theme of regulatory gaps can be found in several African states where the lack of regulations in key economic sectors, including those involved in the extraction of minerals and other natural resources, fuels criminal activity by leaders, by domestic and transnational criminal organizations, and by rebel armies and warlords. While a well-defined regulatory framework might not be a sufficient condition for stopping criminal looting of state resources, it is almost certainly a necessary one. Moreover, the absence of such a framework gives the problem a self-perpetuating quality: political or territorial control of certain regions not only yields rich rewards to criminals (or rebel groups) but also deprives governments of resources that could help to fuel economic growth, infrastructure improvements, and the like. The result is a lack of resources to reduce the capacity gap and fill the functional hole and which in turn contributes to its continued exploitation.

Another capacity gap that is often overlooked concerns economic management and social welfare. The resulting functional hole is a lack of provision for the welfare of the citizens. While other dimensions of weakness offer opportunities for criminal behavior, this type of weakness creates pressures and incentives for citizens to engage in criminal activities – a notion that is consistent with what Joel Migdal termed "survival strategies."[15] Amidst conditions of economic hardship caused by unemployment and hyperinflation, there is a tendency to turn to extra-legal means of obtaining basic needs. Illicit means of advancement offer opportunities that are simply not available in the licit economy. During the 1990s this took a unique form in Russia as a result of the decline in status of some of the central institutions of the state, such as the military and the intelligence agencies. Not surprisingly, therefore, corruption in the Russian military has become pervasive, with all ranks engaging in their own entrepreneurial activities and selling both light and heavy weapons to anyone with the money to pay.[16] Equally if not more striking was the migration into organized crime of specialists in violence – former special forces and KGB operatives – who were trained and then discarded by the state. Many contract killings in Russia have the hallmark of former KGB agents and, for important victims at least, reap relatively high rewards.

Another variant on the social welfare hole is that some criminal organizations and criminal leaders engage in a form of paternalism that earns them considerable gratitude and at least tacit support from members of the populace. In Colombia during the 1980s, for example, Pablo Escobar initiated a program called Medellin Without Slums that provided new houses for poor people. Very visible, and sometimes even ostentatious, support for charities is another aspect of the same tendency. In effect, organized crime becomes a surrogate for the state. Although the functional hole is filled to only a very modest extent by organized crime, the benefits from this are considerable – and the contrast between criminal provision and the apparent ineptitude or indifference of the state could hardly be more marked.

Another capacity gap in weak states is the inability to control borders. In states-in-transition this is often a major shift from the state of affairs in the old regime when the state was isolated from the world. Not only do such states generally display a greater degree of openness to the outside world, but they also encourage external trade and investment. The difficulty is that, when borders are opened, controlling who and what enters and distinguishing between licit and illegitimate business activity become much more difficult. Criminal organizations take advantage of this and states that have holes in their border control are prime candidates for transshipment of illegal goods.

There are, of course, other capacity gaps and functional holes providing opportunities that are readily exploited by transnational criminal organizations. The discussion here offers a sampling of the problem rather than a comprehensive analysis. One of the critical points, however, is that such conditions are attractive to criminal organizations. Consequently, these organizations will do everything they can to perpetuate a situation in which the risks they face are low and controllable, and the opportunities are very considerable. As one close observer and former practitioner has shrewdly noted, "organized crime may begin to grow in a country due to gaps in laws or enforcement. But over time these gaps have to be forced open into ever larger holes in governance to make room for the criminals' greed."[17] Perhaps even more important than greed in this enlargement process, however, is the desire of the criminals to retain a low-risk environment in which they are safe from arrest and from which they can engage in a variety of transnational criminal enterprises. It is in this connection that corruption becomes particularly important.

Transnational organized crime and corruption

One of the problems with many discussions of corruption is that it is treated simply as a condition or pathology that needs to be corrected. In the present context, it makes much more sense to treat corruption as an instrument. The key then becomes a matter of determining who is corrupting whom for what purposes and using what means. Although much corruption stems from officials intent on using public office for private gain, organized crime groups use corruption as a major instrument

Table 6: *Targets and objectives of corruption*

Target of corruption	Objective of corruption
Executive branch	– Create a safe haven – Obtain protection and support – Obtain information
Legislature	– Obtain favorable legislation – Block unfavorable initiatives – Obtain informal support group
Political parties	– Ensure tacit support through funding – Receive favors in return for votes – Create obligations for new government members
Judiciary	– Obtain dismissal of cases – Obtain light sentences – Overturn guilty verdicts
Police	– Obtain information and advance warning – Obtain time for countermeasures – Create capacity for sabotage – Persuade police to act against rivals
Customs	– Neutralize inspections – Protect shipments of drugs – Obtain information on standard search procedures
Banks	– Obtain approval for money laundering – Meet "know-your-customer" requirements – Avoid filing of suspicious activity reports
Businesses	– Obtain opportunities for money laundering through legitimate companies – Develop opportunities for false invoicing – Develop legitimate cover for trafficking
Civil society	– Develop reputation for paternalism – Obtain legitimacy – Obtain public support – Acquire information
Media outlets	– Influence public debate – Develop lobbying capacity – Enhance legitimacy

to ensure both a congenial environment and the success of their activities. As suggested above, corruption is one of the most important instruments used by criminal organizations as part of their risk management strategies. Not surprisingly, they have some very specific targets for corruption. Some of these are identified in table 6, which provides a generic overview of potential targets of corruption along with the benefits that can be obtained by criminal groups.

Among the specific objectives of criminal organizations in using corruption is the neutralization of border control authorities in the home state, in transshipment states, and in destination or market states. This involves what might be termed operational corruption and is designed to ensure that the trafficking process itself is subjected to as little interference, interdiction, and damage as possible. More serious is the use of "systemic" corruption to neutralize the punitive powers of the state. Criminal organizations essentially want a congenial low-risk environment from which they can operate with impunity. Consequently, they have many targets for corruption, including the police and the military, the judiciary (to ensure favorable verdicts or, at the very least, lenient penalties), the legislature (to inhibit the passage of effective and stringent laws), and the executive branch (to obtain protection and support). The best of all positions for criminal organizations is to have political protection at very high levels. This, in effect, offers not simply a risk management approach but risk prevention. To the extent that this approach succeeds, there is less need for the criminals to initiate countermeasures to offset law enforcement and the like. It is also particularly corrosive of the state.

Corruption, of course, is not confined to state structures. It can also extend to the private sector where criminal organizations seek to infiltrate, corrupt, and control companies that can provide an apparently legitimate cover for their activities. In addition, criminal organizations often seek to corrupt and coopt financial institutions to ensure that they can be used to move and hide the proceeds of drug trafficking and other criminal activities. In effect, corrupting bank officials is a means of circumventing the impact of regulations relating to suspicious transactions and due diligence. The Russian banking system, for example, has been heavily infiltrated by organized crime, which has used a mixture of violence and corruption to obtain control of a significant number of banks – some of which have developed correspondent banking relationships with many Western banks.

Whatever the target, however, corruption invariably involves exchange relationships and mechanisms.[18] In some cases this will simply be money for favors – payoffs that allow the recipients a lifestyle that is far more lavish than their income can support. For those being corrupted, the obligation is to provide tacit support for criminal organizations, to provide these organizations with critical information, and to ensure that there is little interference with their activities. For the criminal organizations, although this might require a substantial portion of the proceeds of their crimes, the investment can be understood simply as one of the necessary costs of illegal enterprise. As suggested above, in some cases politicians will sell their covert protection and support in return for mobilization of voters in elections or financial support for electoral campaigns. In this connection, it is worth emphasizing that some of the trends of the 1990s, particularly those toward democratization and decentralization, provided new opportunities for corruption. In many countries where democratization is moving ahead, for example, politicians need campaign finance and a capacity to mobilize voters. This offers organized crime a major opportunity to play a major role in the political system.

In some cases, the use of corruption goes beyond neutralization and, in effect, enables organized crime to capture the state through the development of what Roy Godson has termed a "political–criminal nexus."[19] In captured states there is a symbiosis between politicians and criminals: the criminals provide money and help to mobilize political support for the politicians; the politicians provide protection, information, and support for the criminals. In some cases, the state apparatus is gradually enmeshed in a fully symbiotic relationship with criminal organizations, becoming a real partner in these activities rather than merely a relatively passive beneficiary. In a collusive relationship of this kind, high-level representatives of the state go beyond protecting the organization to working closely with it in the furtherance of its criminal enterprise. There are some collusive relationships, however, in which the collusion is relatively low-key and covert and others in which it is more overt. Japan during the Cold War provided an example of low-key collusion between state authorities and home state criminal organizations. Italy under successive Christian Democrat governments from the 1950s through to the 1980s offered a classic example of a protection-for-votes deal, although one that fell apart in the 1980s. Another classic example of high-level political support for criminal organizations occurred in Mexico where Raul Salinas, brother of President Salinas, became the protector of drug trafficking organizations, and in return was able to deposit well over US$100 million in Swiss bank accounts.

If Mexico can be considered a captured state, so too can Russia, where the "iron triangle" of politicians, businessmen, and criminals has become one of the dominating features of the postcommunist system. The criminals provide "muscle," support, protection, and plausible deniability for both businessmen and members of the political and administrative elites; the businessmen provide resources and access to the legal economy for the criminals; and the political and administrative figures offer the legitimacy and cloak of the state.[20] Crime and politics are also connected at very high levels in Turkey. In 1996 the Susurluk incident – a car accident in which a major criminal and a political figure were in the same car, along with documents and weapons that were traced back to a minister – exposed connections between organized crime and the political elite, connections that were subsequently underlined by allegations that a former prime minister and her husband were heavily involved in various criminal activities.

One of the key issues in these collusive or highly symbiotic relationships that is insufficiently understood – and rarely even discussed – concerns the distribution of power. Since it is the weaknesses of the state, however, that lead to the dynamic growth of organized crime, it would not be surprising if the criminals – with their capacity for violence – were not, in some respects at least, the dominant element in the relationship. In effect this reverses the relationship in strong states such as the USSR, where organized crime operated, but within parameters determined by the state and its officials.

The model of vulnerable states under siege or captured by organized crime is not the only possible representation of the relationship between organized crime and the state. Another variant that also needs to be considered, if only briefly, concerns what might be called the criminal state. This involves the state itself not just benefiting from or actively participating in organized criminal activities but actually directing and controlling such activities. Prime examples of the state itself engaging in criminal enterprises are Nigeria and North Korea. In the case of Nigeria, the military government, especially during the Abacha era, ran criminal enterprises under the guise of the state apparatus. Recent revelations that the Swiss Federal Police have discovered US$ 654 million in various Swiss banks accounts belonging to former president Abacha and his family suggest that both defrauding the state and using the state as a cover for crime were very lucrative, to say the least. North Korea has been less successful, but provides another example not of organized crime taking over the state, but of the state taking over organized crime – and using opium cultivation and heroin trafficking, various forms of smuggling, and counterfeiting as revenue sources. In both cases state officials have initiated and managed a variety of organized criminal activities for personal enrichment.

Conclusions

Charles Tilly in an oft-quoted comment once noted that the state was simply the most efficient and effective form of organized crime.[21] In effect, the state legitimized organized crime by transforming extortion into taxation, brute force into authority, and rule by fear into rule by consent of the governed. The implication of the preceding analysis, however, is that in the last decade or so there have been signs that organized crime has been fighting back and that the state is not as successful as it was in the period of state-building so trenchantly dissected by Tilly. The issue remains, however, as to whether transnational organized crime is appropriately understood as an example of private authority or is simply a case of private power that seeks to masquerade as public authority.

The answer to this question has to go beyond a simple dichotomy, to recognize that organized crime combines elements of power and authority in ways that are very distinctive. On the one side, it is clear that organized crime relies heavily on power and has actually turned the capacity for coercion into a highly lucrative art form through its strategies for extorting business. Moreover, organized crime very clearly challenges the government monopoly of violence. In the two cases where this has been particularly overt and brutal – Italy and Colombia – organized crime lost much of its popular support and the state was ultimately able to mobilize even greater power and beat back the challenge. It is also clear that organized crime, whether operating domestically or transnationally, has distinctive features that set it apart from other private actors. It lacks accountability, and for the most part operates covertly. Moreover, unlike other private authorities, it seeks to undermine or circumvent international norms, rules, and regulations. Furthermore, the clandestine activities that are an essential part of organized crime, by their very nature, do nothing to build authority or legitimacy.

Yet there are dimensions of organized crime that suggest authority rather than power. The wealth that organized crime accrues through its operations in some cases is used to create a base from which it is sometimes possible to develop a degree of legitimacy that can be parlayed into authority structures. Similarly, the exploitation of functional holes in ways that substitute for the state, for example, gives organized crime some degree of legitimacy and, at the domestic level at least, provides a crude form of governance in certain areas where it would otherwise be absent. Similarly, the occasional use of paternalism to build domestic support can be understood as an attempt to transform power based on fear into more legitimate notions of authority and approval, if not actually consent. It is also clear that organized crime flourishes in societies where family, kinship, clan relations, and patron–client relationships are the primary points of reference and loyalty. In this sense, organized crime can be understood as an alternative forum to the state for allegiance and affiliation. This is also true in diaspora communities. Ethnic migrants are often marginalized in their new home, and as a result develop little loyalty for the political authorities and little trust in law enforcement. Instead, they develop coping mechanisms that include organized crime, black market activities, and, in the Chinese case, their own underground banking system sometimes referred to as "flying money." The underground banking system is particularly interesting in that it is based on trust and ostracism for those who betray it. Moreover, in some immigrant communities, organized crime figures are likely to have considerable authority and influence at least within the confines of the community. Insofar as authority involves allegiance that is given voluntarily rather than coerced, then it is clear that, in some communities, organized crime can be understood in terms of private authority. In other words, when public authority is weak, and state legitimacy is low, other less formal, often illicit forms of authority will thrive. Organized crime can be understood as one of these. In sum, there are some grounds for treating organized crime as private illicit authority.

In some ways, however, the most intriguing aspect of transnational organized crime is the tendency of at least some criminal organizations to cloak their power in the mantle of state authority. This is not to suggest that the criminal symbiosis will determine all aspects of state behavior. In instances in which the state is captured by organized crime, the state will still carry out many of its traditional functions in international relations in the normal way. At the same time, the state authorities will take measures to ensure that organized crime functions unhindered and uninhibited in its pursuit of wealth. In domestic terms this will mean doing little to close the capacity gaps or fill the functional holes; organized crime must be allowed to continue to function unhindered and in a low-risk environment. The implication is that there will continue to be states that provide sanctuaries or safe havens for criminal organizations. Indeed, their number could well increase as transnational criminal organizations continue to entrench themselves in weak states in the former Soviet Union, Africa, Latin America, and parts of Asia.

Because of differing degrees of vulnerability, however, some states are not only strong enough to resist transnational organized crime but also willing to confront criminal organizations, seeking to reduce their power, to stem their activities, and to dismantle their organizational structures. Not surprisingly, those states that adopt a confrontational strategy toward transnational criminal organizations are usually both strong and legitimate. In effect, this suggests a differentiated state approach that acknowledges that some states are in retreat but that others are not. This is consistent with the analysis of Linda Weiss that focuses on different domains of activity but highlights the adaptation rather than the retreat of the state.[22] If some states are fighting back against transnational organized crime, the task will not be easy – not least because weak and captured states will seriously hinder multilateral efforts to combat transnational organized crime. Efforts to provide global regimes or multilateral attacks on organized crime will suffer from the problem of defecting states. The defections themselves will take various forms. In the case of weak states there will be tacit defections, as nominal adherence to global regimes and multilateral efforts is not accompanied by substantive actions. There will also be overt defections by captured and criminal states. Such defections will have serious consequences, ensuring that regimes aimed at combating transnational organized crime will be seriously incomplete, and that criminal organizations will continue to enjoy geographic and jurisdictional loopholes. The result will be not the containment of criminal activity but its displacement – geographical and methodological. In short, multilateral efforts by states to combat transnational organized crime will continue to exhibit serious deficiencies. Sanctuary or safe-haven states will continue to put transnational criminal organizations out of the reach of those states whose laws they have violated and whose populations provide customers for their illicit products and services.

There is another possible consequence that is even more disturbing: it is not inconceivable that the major global divide will be caused not by competing ideologies, the struggle for power, or Huntington's "clash of civilizations," but by clashes between states that uphold law and order and those that are dominated by criminal interests and criminal authorities.

NOTES

1 James Rosenau, *Turbulence in World Politics* (Princeton, N.J.: Princeton University Press, 1990).
2 See "The Changing Role of the State," transcript from the 75th Anniversary Symposium of a keynote address given by Jessica Mathews at the Harvard School of Public Health. The transcript is available at *www.hsph.harvard.edu/digest/mathews.html.*
3 Susan Strange, *The Retreat of the State: The Diffusion of Power in the World Economy* (Cambridge: Cambridge University Press, 1996).
4 See Saskia Sassen, *Losing Control?: Sovereignty in an Age of Globalization,* 1995 Columbia University Leonard Hastings Schoff Memorial Lectures (New York: Columbia University Press, 1996).
5 This is one of the notions touched on ibid.
6 Sassen has an excellent discussion of this in terms of the notion of citizenship. See ibid.
7 Fenton Bressler, *Interpol* (London: Mandarin, 1993),.
8 The "power to hurt" is one of the main themes explored in Thomas C. Schelling, *Arms and Influence* (New Haven and London: Yale University Press, 1967).
9 Richard Friman, "Just Passing Through: Transit States and the Dynamics of Illicit Transshipment," *Transnational Organized Crime,* 1 (1) (Spring 1995), 65–83.
10 Diego Gambetta, *The Sicilian Mafia: The Business of Private Protection* (Cambridge, Mass.: Harvard University Press, 1993).
11 Francisco E. Thoumi, *Political Economy and Illegal Drugs in Colombia* (Boulder, Colo.: Lynne Rienner, 1995), pp. 172–73.
12 Quoted in Richard Lotspeich, "Crime in the Transition Economies," *Europe–Asia Studies,* 47 (4) (June 1995), 569.

13 See Graham H. Turbiville, *Mafia in Uniform: The Criminalization of the Russian Armed Forces* (Fort Leavenworth, Kansas, 1996).

14 This is a theme in the work of Diego Gambetta and has been applied to Russia by Federico Varese, *The Russian Mafia* (Oxford: Oxford University Press, 2001).

15 See Joel S. Migdal, *Strong Societies and Weak States* (Princeton, N.J.: Princeton University Press, 1988), for the development of this notion.

16 Graham H. Turbiville, "Organized Crime and the Russian Armed Forces," *Transnational Organized Crime*, 1 (4) (Winter 1995), 57–104.

17 Jonathan Winer, "International Crime in the New Geopolitics: A Core Threat to Democracy," in W. F. McDonald (ed.), *Crime and Law Enforcement in the Global Village* (Cincinnati, Ohio: Anderson, 1997), p. 46.

18 This notion is developed in Donatella della Porta and Alberto Vannucci, *Corrupt Exchanges* (New York: Aldine De Gruyter, 1999).

19 Roy Godson, "Political–Criminal Nexus: Overview," *Trends in Organized Crime*, 3 (1) (Fall 1997), 4–7.

20 The author would like to express his appreciation to William Cook and Gregory O'Hayon for these observations.

21 Charles Tilly, "War Making and State Making as Organized Crime," in Peter B. Evans, Dietrich Rueschemeyer, and Theda Skocpol (eds.), *Bringing the State Back In* (Cambridge: Cambridge University Press, 1985), pp. 169–91.

22 Linda Weiss, *The Myth of the Powerless State* (Ithaca, N.Y.: Cornell University Press, 1998).

The return of the dogs of war?
The privatization of security in Africa

Bernedette Muthien and Ian Taylor

In the current era, neoliberalism has emerged as the defining economic program by which state administrations are held accountable. This has gone hand in hand with the globalization process, building a "market civilization" whereby states are more and more subject to the apparent arbitrary whim of "the market."[1] At the same time, technological advances have facilitated a compression of time and space within the global political economy.[2] The autonomy of the state has, in a varied but dialectical action, been reduced and the ability of administrations in the South to resist prescriptions emanating from the developed world (but increasingly transnational in character) has been diminished. "Faced with the power of globalized production and international finance, including debt structures, leaders are constrained to concentrate on enhancing national conditions for competing forms of capitalism," the dominant being neoliberalism.[3] This process is partial and incomplete, but is particularly strong and most energetic in the periphery of the global economy, where the hegemonic agenda has strenuously pushed for states to abandon any (remaining) *dirigiste* pretensions they may possess and instead "open up" their economies to international capital flows. At the same time, the national budget has been framed by advocates of the neoliberal solution as a source of many of the state's woes, and tight fiscal constraints are placed on its activities, with obvious social implications. This has been particularly so in Africa, where international lending agencies have placed strict conditionalities on state administrations seeking funds to (try to) help them out of the economic malaise they currently suffer.[4]

Such constraints on the national budget have increasingly served to stimulate a turn toward the privatization of everyday life, while at the same time emasculating the state's authority to regulate the social sphere. Though uneven in its effect on spatial territories, state administrations have increasingly had to contend with public and private forms of transnational governance.[5] National, and *nationalist*, developmental projects in the South have, since the demise of the NIEO (New International Economic Order) movement, increasingly been abandoned. This process has sometimes been voluntary, but mostly it has been under disciplinary pressure from international financial institutions and other donor sources, and administrations in the South have had to adopt a variety of strategies to survive.[6] As this has occurred, space has opened up for a more individualist, indeed private, model of accumulation for elites in the developing world.

This has had important implications for the stability of a number of weak states on the African continent, in some case stimulating a downward spiral into anarchy and civil war. Causality can be traced if one argues that neoliberal programs have eroded the neopatrimonial state that came into being in the postcolonial period, and have subsequently invited the elites largely to abandon formal state-derived authority and prestige: to "privatize" their activities, as it were. This has arisen in a situation in which a rent-seeking state is no longer capable of being used in the usual neopatrimonial fashion of "buying off" opponents. The extent to which this has occurred is, of course, specific to each state. Certainly, the larger the state, the greater the amount of space is created for elites to secure power and privilege via the diversion of funds, awarding of sinecures, and the creation of client–patron relationships, etc.

Yet in the era of globalization, the neoliberal project assails the very base upon which a neopatrimonial state is predicated and, by rolling back the state, dissolves the elaborate patron–client relationships built up within the framework of an expanded state. As Hoogvelt points out, neoliberal programs and the "manner of reining in the rent-seeking state and its officials [dissolve] the patrimonial glue that holds the society together. It brings about fragmentation as erstwhile clients are now forced to seek their own benefits independent from the central authority."[7] As the impulses generating such moves intensify, the state's position within society is peeled back, and personal – and private – networks of accumulation and power develop in the absence of any strong legitimating authority. What is left is a rump state, with the symbols and trappings of authority remaining to be captured, but very little else.

This of course is not to say that the state "withers away" totally: authority does not become altogether privatized, although formal structures may be highly circumscribed in their effectiveness. What usually features is an uneasy "shadowing" of the formal, with patrons of private sites of authority often crossing from one to the other, profoundly blurring the distinction between state and non-state activity. Chabal and Daloz remark that "patrons [become] 'licensees' of violence in that they possess that attribute – the exercise of coercion – which in more politically institutionalized societies is the strict preserve of the state. Control of and protection from violence, or coercion, are thus unofficially devolved.

Patrons can access or restrain official force, most notably in military regimes, while at the same time maintaining their own corps of armed men to protect clients and counter the violence of competitive networks."[8] This scenario describes situations that have recently occurred in the Democratic Republic of the Congo and Sierra Leone, to name but two.

In states that have endured particularly intrusive disciplinary neoliberal programs, or where the state was weak in the first place, even the monopoly on violence dissolves, and security – and the ability to use force as a means of accumulation – becomes the realm of those who can afford it. This cannot but be negative. As Clapham asserts:

The use of power over other people for purposes essentially of private gain is corrupt, not merely because it fails to correspond to formal rules of essentially Western origin, or to meet the demands of "good governance" laid down by external aid donors, but because of its impact on the lives of the people most harshly affected by it. This impact is in turn all too clear from an examination of those parts of Africa [such as] Liberia, Nigeria, Sierra Leone, Zaire ... where it has been most evident.[9]

The theme we have sketched above obviously has important ramifications for security in a number of African countries that have been particularly affected by the onrush of globalization. The situation in many senses reflects the intensification (to an extreme, to be sure) of the privatization of authority that is increasingly marking notions of governance throughout the world, as globalization reconfigures the global political economy and as "the market" stimulates the retreat of the state.[10] The (re-turn to the) private as a source of security, in an era in which the state has been "rolled back" from much of its traditional involvement in society and in which the authority of the state has been substantially eroded, is the subject of this chapter.

The return of private armies: privatizing security

With the end of the Cold War, a disturbing increase in the reemergence of private armies in Africa has been witnessed. Much of these seemingly spring from the refuse thrown out as apartheid died, with a plethora of former South African "troopies" now seeking an outlet for their redundant security skills in places as far apart as Angola and Sierra Leone. This phenomenon needs to be placed within the wider global context of the privatization of authority. In doing so, the notorious firm Executive Outcomes and its role in conflicts in Angola and Sierra Leone is particularly highlighted as a case in point. Before doing so, however, we first define the concepts "security" and the "privatization of security."

"Security" is a generic term, suggesting notions of "protection from harm," while emphasizing the liberal concerns related to the protection of citizens and their private property. This responsibility has historically been the domain of the state – the state has traditionally been entrusted with providing security for individuals. However, due to the intensification of factors such as the global decline of state power and authority (particularly in the developing world), the concept of security has shifted more recently from the state providing security for individuals (state security) to individuals providing their own security. In territories where the state is seemingly now incapable of guaranteeing the security of its citizens, non-state initiatives are rapidly filling the vacuum. Indeed, "the erosion of a government's administrative capacity brings in its train the delegitimization of public authority, a precursor to its confiscation by private actors."[11] This is reflected in a whole gamut of private activities, ranging from neighborhood patrols and vigilantism, to the employment of technologically advanced security equipment, private security personnel, and gated communities. In such a scenario, security has been transformed from being a service provided by the state for all citizens, to being a market good for those who can afford it: a reflection of the privatization of everyday life, with all the profound implications this has for those who cannot afford the luxury of private security arrangements.

At this point, it is important to note a conceptual distinction. The privatization of security, while generic, refers in the context of this chapter to those private security concerns involved in effective civilian policing. This includes operations such as the guarding of corporate installations, embassies, and, in South Africa at least, the ubiquitous 24-hour rapid response units who patrol the mostly white suburbs of South Africa's towns and cities. In contrast to these commercial concerns, we are more concerned with the privatization of war – the private military firms that offer their services to perform military functions hitherto reserved as the prerogative of the state, including armed combat, the training of ostensibly state military units, the gathering of intelligence, and the effective replacement of state authority "on the ground" in large geographical areas. As we will show, the private armies now reemerging in Africa play a crucial role in a number of territories on the continent. As national economies become more and more outwardly linked to the global market, and as the dominant ideology of neoliberalism demands the rolling back of the state, the neopatrimonial framework which has held certain fragile states within Africa together has begun to unravel. As this has occurred, such territories have become increasingly open and subject to exploitation by undemocratic but powerful individuals, as well as by unscrupulous irregulars. At the same time, transnational corporations have frequently stepped in to take advantage of this situation, often working in tandem with the emerging sites of private authority. In many cases, the usage of services offered by private armies has gone hand in hand with such developments, with private security companies being engaged to guard mining installations a prime example.

Criticism of such developments has invariably focused on the mercenary nature of their activities. The word "mercenary," with very negative connotations in Africa, includes memories of "Mad Mike" Hoare in the Congo, Colonel Callan in Angola, or Bob Denard in the Comores. These stir up images of white "dogs of war" embarking on killing sprees, toppling governments, and generally undermining the sovereignty and indeed credibility of post-independent African states.[12] It is important therefore to ask critically whether private armies such as Executive Outcomes are mercenaries. Nathan distinguishes mercenaries as soldiers hired by a foreign government or rebel movement to contribute to the prosecution of armed conflict – whether directly by engaging in hostilities, or indirectly through training, logistics, intelligence, or advisory services – and who do so outside the authority of the government and defense force of their own country.[13] Article 47 of the 1997 Additional Protocol I of the Geneva Convention considers someone who is specifically recruited locally or abroad in order to fight in an armed conflict as a mercenary. The protocol adds that a mercenary is someone who takes direct part in the hostilities essentially by the desire for private gain, and who, in fact, is promised remuneration above that paid to soldiers of similar ranks and functions in the contracting armed forces, and who is neither a national of a party to the conflict nor a resident of a territory controlled by a party to the conflict. Subparagraph (c) of Article 47 clearly excludes what some analysts have called "ideological mercenaries," citing Che Guevara and the International Brigades of the Spanish Civil War during the 1930s.

Clearly then, members of standing armies engaged by countries that are not their own – the French and Spanish Foreign Legions and the Gurkhas of the British Army – are excluded from this working definition of what constitutes a mercenary. However, many of those who are thought of as mercenaries invariably deny their involvement in active combat, instead claiming to be employed in training, logistics, or advisory capacities. This being so, Nathan's definition is more inclusive (and incidentally is closer to South Africa's Regulation of Foreign Military Assistance Act of 1998). This act defined foreign military assistance as advice or training; personnel, financial, logistical, intelligence, or operational support; personnel recruitment; medical or paramedical services; or procurement of equipment. This broad definition continues in paragraph (iv) to define "mercenary activity" as "direct participation as a combatant in armed conflict for private gain," in line with Article 47 above. Such a broad definition of who and what is a mercenary was specifically enacted to stop private armies becoming embroiled in regional conflicts. This was sparked by a desire to put a stop to various South Africans' continued support for UNITA in Angola by supplying arms and pharmaceuticals during the postapartheid period, as explored below.

Be that as it may, it is clear that companies such as Executive Outcomes *are* mercenaries, for their market, as it were, is dependent upon the breakdown of state capacity, invariably triggered by war or violent conflict. Indeed, the private security companies discussed in this paper operating in Africa, whether for the purposes of guarding installations, supplying, and servicing military equipment or actual combat, are intricately connected, by nature of their shared employee pool, and the men, predominantly former combatants, who run them and profit from the conflicts in their areas of operation. As Francis puts it, "[t]hese companies thrive on conflict, and it is these conflicts that provide market opportunities for them, without which they are failed business ventures."[14]

Obviously, protestations of innocence wrapped around the cloak of legality have been standard fare of firms involved in the business of war. According to one account, Italian mercenaries in the Middle Ages "often organized themselves like other commercial guilds at the time ... As men of business, they studied their trade, the available markets and their competitors."[15] In short, whether the "Free Companies" of medieval Europe or Executive Outcomes of contemporary Africa, such firms are effective private armies. Pech refers to them as "corporate armies" and argues that they are:

A privately owned military group whose finances, personnel, offensive operations, air wing division and logistics are all handled within a single group or through interlinked companies and enterprises. In its most basic form, it would be managed by a common pool of directors and have a small permanent corps of staff, serving its own commercial interests and those of affiliated entities. Such a group of companies would typically be owned, organised, paid and deployed by the controlling shareholders of one or more private companies, which, in turn, may be transnational conglomerates. As such, the traditionally state-owned powers and instruments for effecting political and social change through the use of force are transferred through privatisation to a corporate entity or group. These powerful entities function at both a corporate, suprastate and the transnational level thus transferring the powers of a global city-state to a corporate group that is essentially accountable only to laws of profit and those of supply and demand.[16]

Such corporate or private armies may now establish mining and drilling companies with international ties, registered offshore with occasional listings on international stock exchanges. They have diversified widely to include in their repertoire not only the provision of security and military training, but construction and civil engineering as well. Numerous companies are formed in joint venture partnerships with government leaders and the families of these leaders, creating monopolies in the economies of the regions in which they are involved. Indeed, in many territories the private army "constitute[s] an advance guard for the construction of new corporate empires."[17]

Certainly, private armies like South Africa's Executive Outcomes are effective corporate networks, and have become transnational by definition, from their diverse areas of operation, to their multiple stock exchange listings, offices, and representatives internationally. It is not too much to suggest that they could be classed as transnational corporations. Like conventional transnational corporations, they also employ each other's services, as Sandline and Branch Energy have employed Executive Outcomes and its subsidiary companies. Whether government- or privately employed, private armies ultimately aim to secure a geographic area in order to facilitate resource extraction. What unites private armies and transnational corporations in the exploration business is their profit motive. This process is exacerbated by globalization and the dominance of neoliberalism. Indeed, the decline of state capacity and the push for a continual retreat of the state from economic management facilitates the rise of private security concerns, particularly in territories where state authority was never particularly strong in the first place. Interestingly, in many ways, this can be seen as a return to a scenario that marked Africa before the development of the formal colonial state in Africa, a theme to which we shall now turn.

Private armies in Africa's past

During the colonial period, private companies such as the Dutch East India Company, the British East Africa Company, or Cecil John Rhodes's British South Africa Company made use of privately recruited men to protect and guard territories under the various companies' surveillance. These effective private armies patrolled the territories that at first were purely commercial concerns but that rapidly became subsumed within the wider – and more official – state-led imperial project. The history of Zimbabwe, for example, is dominated by the activities of the British South Africa Company (BSAC) and its attendant administrators and soldiers.

During mid-1890, 196 men of the "Pioneer Column" of the British South Africa Company crossed from South Africa into what was later to become Southern Rhodesia. Lured by tales of gold and other mineral wealth, the Pioneer Column was funded by Rhodes on the pretext that colonial intervention was required in Mashonaland to protect the indigenous Shona people against the Ndebele, a branch of the Zulus who had crossed into the region several decades earlier. Rhodes had earlier (in 1889) negotiated with the British government for a royal charter for the British South Africa Company. This charter gave him the right to occupy and exploit the land and mineral resources, including the gold deposits reputed to be in abundance throughout the area. With the promise of mining concessions and guarantees of land, the 196 volunteers he recruited into a *de facto* private army penetrated to the heart of Mashonaland, and on 12 September 1890 raised the British flag at what was to be called Fort Salisbury, named after the prime minister of the time.[18]

Guarded by these private men-at-arms, Southern Rhodesia was rapidly invaded by a flood of prospectors, settlers, and adventurers from further south. Within a few years, the BSAC had constituted itself into an effective government and established an administrative and legal infrastructure to run the country, with much of the financing being raised by the imposition of taxes on local people. Refusal to pay resulted in confiscation of their land, enforced by the private BSAC police. The confiscated land was then turned over to white settlers. Another important aim of the taxation system was to produce a supply of black workers for the mines and white farms. Indeed, black peasants were effectively forced to look for wage labor in order to pay the various taxes demanded by the private authorities administering Southern Rhodesia. The same story was repeated in Northern Rhodesia (now Zambia) where the BSAC also effectively ran a private reserve. It was only in 1923 and 1924 that the Southern and Northern Rhodesias officially became British colonies respectively.

What this demonstrates is that private armies and the large-scale privatization of authority in Africa has a long history, particularly as part of the settler involvement in the southern African region. This tradition of relying on private men-at-arms was resuscitated during the Second Chimurenga (Zimbabwean war of independence) when Rhodesia's standing army engaged the services of a number of mercenaries, especially in its elite Special Air Services. Most of these soldiers later joined the apartheid-era South African Defence Force after their country became Zimbabwe. In another continuation, the ideology of white supremacy and other leftovers from the colonial period was particularly evident in the exodus of white Rhodesians to South Africa, who saw black rule as equaling disaster and incompetence. The apartheid regime was obviously well-placed to tap into these sentiments, and eagerly recruited ex-Rhodesians as *de facto* mercenaries into its armed forces. Some of these rose to notoriety as they became involved in the struggle against black liberation forces. For instance, British mercenary Tyrone Chadwick was later imprisoned in South Africa after admitting to a London reporter his and other mercenaries' roles in several murders while serving on an apartheid hit squad farm.[19] A former Executive Outcomes officer, now a restaurateur in Cape Town, was stationed at the most extreme apartheid-era killing farm, Vlakplaas, subject of intense investigation by South Africa's Truth and Reconciliation Commission. Pech notes that EO's founder, Eben Barlow, while a senior officer with the Civil Co-operation Bureau (CCB), a unit known for assassinations of anti-apartheid activists, "was also engaged in sanctions-busting efforts in Europe which brokered the procurement of military equipment on behalf of the SADF [South African Defence Force]."[20] Further, Barlow recruited his lieutenant at EO, Lafras Luitingh, "while he evaded South African authorities who wanted him for questioning in connection with the murder of anthropologist and ANC [African National Congress] activist, David Webster in Johannesburg in 1989."[21]

Along with self-confessed mercenary Donald Acheson, Johan Niemoller, ex-CCB, has been implicated in the murder of Namibian anti-apartheid activist Anton Lubowski. An established businessman and supplier of equipment to the apartheid-era Defence Force, Niemoller planned to "kick the white communists out of Africa and put the white man back in power."[22] During 1997 Niemoller was responsible for the spate of arms thefts on the new National Defence Force's armories. This was an attempt to channel arms to UNITA as part of a decades-old pattern of apartheid and right-wing support for UNITA in Angola. In addition, Niemoller continued to supply medicines and other equipment as well as former Defence Force mercenaries to UNITA, and received remuneration in uncut diamonds. South African arms were also sold and transported widely to the rest of the continent, including the Democratic Republic of Congo, with involvement by Niemoller, and several other ex-CCB operatives, in particular ex-EO employee and now Stabilco Security boss, Mauritz le Roux. Since at least 1995 Ibis, the air wing of Executive Outcomes and Sandline International, has been operating from the Johannesburg Airport quarters of Simera, the aviation division of Denel, South Africa's largest recently privatized arms corporation.[23] What unites these mercenaries, secret agents, arms dealers, and mining corporations is their quest for personal profit and power, and their concomitant disdain for black rule. This has continued to this very day as the privatization of authority runs its course.

Contemporary private armies in Africa

Although the end of the Cold War and the demise of apartheid saw an overall process of demilitarization in the region, South Africa's recent and massive arms purchases have reinvigorated the regional arms race (albeit at a lower level than during apartheid). At the same time, conflict over control of mining and drilling interests throughout Africa has led to a remilitarization of the region in a very short space of time.[24] This is especially true in the case of central Africa, Sierra Leone, and Angola. Accompanying this phenomenon has been the rise of private armies, which have increasingly begun to operate throughout the continent. In southern Africa these mercenaries are predominantly demobilized former apartheid soldiers, many of whom consider themselves marginalized by the new democratic regime in South Africa.

The existence of such people fits with a scenario in which policing by the state has become more and more constrained by budgetary and other limitations. In such a milieu, private domestic security companies are being used increasingly by governments, corporations, and private individuals to protect their assets. Indeed, the privatization of domestic security parallels the external privatization of war in the form of mercenaries. As wealthier states move increasingly toward demilitarization, and cash-strapped countries cannot afford adequate domestic security, a trend is developing by which private security firms like Executive Outcomes increasingly meet the clamoring need among especially African states for assistance against insurgents.

Interestingly, private interventions by firms such as Executive Outcomes are generally viewed as being negative and to be avoided, even if such intrusions bring a modicum of peace to an area (a point to which we shall return later). In contrast, public, i.e. state-led, peacekeeping initiatives are generally applauded. The division between public and private peacekeeping ventures (and the greater efficiency of the latter) is a moot point, however, and perhaps points more to the jealousy by which state elites guard their monopoly on violence rather than any disinterested evaluation of the effectiveness in helping the victims of civil wars and the collapse of formal administrations.

Returning to the rise of private sites of authority, even developed Western states have been faced with having to decrease state spending, and the traditional concept of social security has been under sustained attack, sparking a proliferation of private security companies and professional security associations. This has become a multibillion dollar industry, with Shearer reporting that "US citizens spent $90 billion on private security in 1995, against the $40 billion of public funds allocated to national police forces," and that Russia during 1997 had 4,500 companies employing 155,000 to 1,000,000 personnel.[25] Developing countries are under even greater pressure to roll back state involvement, bolstering the argument that in the contemporary era security is no longer a service by the state for all its citizens, but has become a market good. Graphically, by

1996 private security guards in South Africa outnumbered the full-time military by more than two to one,[26] while Angola has seen an increase in private security companies from 2 in 1992 to over 100 in 1998, with contracts to protect assets, installations, embassies, diamond mines, and international organizations working there.[27]

This encroachment of the private into areas formerly reserved for the state has been facilitated by Africa's traditionally porous borders, and made worse by regional state fragility. In often chaotic situations, the traffic of mercenaries, illegal arms, uncut diamonds, drugs, and other contraband has gone unmolested. Such extreme social problems and large-scale civil unrest have certainly been exacerbated (and in many case stimulated) by structural adjustment programs of the International Monetary Fund (IMF) and the World Bank.[28] Sadly, too, the fragility of states in Africa has been certainly worsened by poor management, nepotism, and corruption. Yet outside involvement has often served to encourage the further privatization of security. For instance, the IMF *approved* Sierra Leone's payments to Executive Outcomes as part of its complete funding package to the cash-strapped country.[29] At best the IMF sought stability in Sierra Leone, as well as to ensure state revenue from the recaptured diamond mines. At worst, they exacerbated the dire situation within the country and contributed to the further erosion of state authority.

Following this line, a shift in inquiry from the state to the international system underscores the significance of global financial markets as the locus of power, a system wherein international financiers have displaced states in the core–periphery continuum of political and economic decision-making. In this view, some states are more equal than others and those states at the bottom of the hierarchy are particularly vulnerable to outside interference and – as the IMF involvement in Sierra Leone demonstrates – effective undermining. Certainly, within the global hierarchy, state structures operate as the means for particular groups to influence the functioning of global markets. A state's "strength" or capacity in this respect is attributable to its economic strength, as well as military capacity and bureaucratic efficiency, and this is largely reflected in its position in the global hierarchy.[30]

In this context, fragile and weak African states are blessed with vast natural resources while cursed with bankruptcy, corruption, and strife. These are ideal conditions for unscrupulous entrepreneurs to achieve maximum profits, as the regulatory framework that surrounds sound state administrations is largely absent, or can easily be circumnavigated. However, the profitability and success of such ventures are hampered by insurgent movements and the lack of state capacity to provide security. Hence they source their own private armies, not unlike Rhodes with his

British South Africa Company, to maximize profit extraction and ensure the safety of their (usually transient) investments.

It is true to say that, in numerous parts of Africa at present, private companies are using their own resources to protect installations, enforce regulations, and discipline staff on compounds little touched by local laws. Authority has become truly privatized in the most benighted parts of the continent. Perhaps the most detrimental effect of these corporate mercenaries is to be found in their monopolization of the economies of the countries in which they are active, from security, to mining and drilling, to construction, engineering, and telecommunications. This usage of private security, however, can be seen by foreign-based shareholders as highly attractive. As Pech writes, "it is problems with geology that drives down the cost of shares, not association with mercenaries. In fact when Diamond Works' connection to mercenaries was made public in Canada, the share prices went up immediately. The risks may be high, but so are the potential profits."[31] Even international humanitarian organizations have started taking an interest in employing private armies in situations in which the state security apparatus cannot be trusted or has collapsed. During 1999 CARE Canada released a policy discussion document which recommended that international "NGOs should consider the privatisation of security for humanitarian purposes."[32]

Ultimately, the question of whether private armies serve a constructive role is central to any serious assessment of their activities. They *do* secure areas temporarily, which can at times facilitate peace-brokering between conflicting parties, such as in Angola and Sierra Leone. They can also allow international non-governmental organizations and other humanitarian agencies to enter areas of conflict, even rescuing child soldiers in Sierra Leone and delivering them to a rehabilitation centre. Harding mentions that in Sierra Leone Executive Outcomes prepared logistics for "an international aid agency to manage the return of roughly 8,000 displaced civilians" and provided the aid agency's field workers with air transport: "wherever they went, civilians stopped dying."[33] Nevertheless, Harding also points out that "the trouble [with Executive Outcomes] was that they only went where the payoff was high. The children they had brought to Nahims [rehabilitation] centre came from Kono. If you did not live in one of Sierra Leone's mineral-rich enclaves, and yet you were beset by rebels and soldiers, EO was not disposed to help you."[34] Echoing the views of international humanitarian agencies, Rubin asks, "is it wrong to let the Sierra Leonians keep their limbs by keeping their mercenaries?"[35] This is a thorny question for critics of private authority, when authority in any guise has evaporated and people's lives are at stake. Having said that, it is surely wrong that a person's life is dependent upon profits and their good fortune of living in an area rich in minerals, while those who do not cannot count on protection. As one commentator has remarked on Executive Outcomes' record in Sierra Leone:

EO's humanitarianism in Sierra Leone stopped abruptly at the fringe of the mineral areas. Even as the diamond mines churned out stones in Kono, the rebels were continuing to terrorise villages twenty miles away. "It was a pact with the devil," an anthropologist in Freetown explained . . . "Everyone prospered bar the ordinary Sierra Leoneans."[36]

Conclusion

The privatization of security in Africa is perhaps the most extreme manifestation of a global trend turning toward sources of private authority. This has had unfortunate consequences for many African states, as in the case of Sierra Leone where corrupt, unpopular, and/or unrepresentative governments, instead of embarking on significant transformation, hired private armies to enrich themselves through commissions from the allocation of mineral and oil concessions. Furthermore, employing mercenaries perpetuates the myth that force is an acceptable and even desirable solution to problems – something which has bedeviled postcolonial Africa and which the continent can most certainly do without. The involvement of private armies is invariably a stopgap measure which can do little to address structural crises within the territories concerned. It is said that Executive Outcomes' operations in Angola precipitated the Peace Accords, and that UNITA reneged on the peace agreements only after the private army was expelled from the country. This temporary peace is symptomatic of mercenary engagement specifically, and the use of force generally: unless the root causes of conflict are addressed, a lasting peace is not possible. As Cleary puts it:

There is no doubt that EO's engagement by the [Angolan army] in 1993 contributed to the prolongation of the war – greatly worsening the suffering by Angola's civilian population. It diverted attention from the need to address the root causes of the conflict and helped to create an Angolan military capability that has not been wisely used in regional affairs since then . . . Worse yet, peace is still not at hand in Angola, or its surrounding region, in part because the Angolan government, just as the old South African government, appeared to believe that it could resolve its domestic challenges by internal suppression and military pressure on its neighbours . . . Persons associated with EO, in whatever corporate guise thereafter, were still engaged in the Angolan government's efforts to resolve the conflict by military means in 1998.[37]

The privatization of authority, then, has profound implications for a number of states within Africa. This is intensified if and when security becomes privatized and private armies are engaged. Unlike state military units, private military firms are not subject to governmental control or scrutiny, partly because they are not beholden to any government. The military's standard policy of confidentiality also precludes transparency. Thus private armies are being hired in circumstances in which surveillance of their operations is weak or even non-existent. This has profound implications for the power of the formal state and may contribute to the further erosion of authority invested in its traditional location: government. In countries where the state has been despotic, the erosion of its ability may not be overly mourned.

However, this is a short-term viewpoint for, once it has broken down, it is very difficult for the state to rebuild itself – as the difficulties faced by Sierra Leone and Somalia attest. In such a vacuum the emergence of privatized sites of authority may bring stability in the short term, as we have outlined, but it is evident that peace secured through the use of mercenaries is temporary and totally devoid of legitimacy – the prolonged affair in Comores being a case in point.[38] Furthermore, mercenary involvement may temporarily mask the underlying causes of conflict and prolong an unstable if not capricious regime – as one commentator remarked on the situation in Sierra Leone, "even if EO's role in Sierra Leone proves to be beneficial, it may lead to a situation where any [despotic] government in a difficult position can hire mercenaries to stay in power."[39] Yet the temporary pause in fighting is bound to reignite when the private armies depart, if the question of why private security was needed in the first place is not addressed. Ultimately sustainable peace is possible only if the root causes of conflict are addressed and peace-building is a significant part of the process of social reconstruction.

If one believes in the democratic ideals of accountability, as well as in transparency for public and governmental scrutiny, one should also hope that these private security corporations and their employers, both states and transnational corporations, should be held answerable for their actions, and accountable to international and domestic legislation. This is deeply problematic vis-à-vis private armies. As Nathan asserts:

[Private armies' claims of accountability] inspire no confidence whatsoever... They amount to this: trust me, I'm a mercenary... Who determines whether Executive Outcomes personnel have committed a crime? Who investigates allegations of criminal conduct?... The answers to these questions are no one [and] no one.[40]

Having said that, even if this is so, private armies are a poor long-term substitute for the state in the provision of security for individuals and, taken to their logical conclusion, threaten the very foundations of the

Westphalian state system – a project that is already under severe attack by the forces of globalization. Furthermore, unaccountable as they are to wider society, private armies are able, in the most extreme cases, to asset-strip a country with virtual impunity, leading to irreversible ecological degradation, the illicit export of resource commodities, and the general encouragement of a culture of criminality within the host country that further diminishes the legitimacy of the state.

The turn to private security arrangements is, however – and this needs to be reiterated – reflective of the impulses of globalization and neoliberalism. In an era in which the state is rolled back, the emergence of private sites of authority is inevitable, particularly in territories where the state was weak in the first place but where attractive profits may be made by entrepreneurs willing to pay for private security – which characterizes much of Africa. At the same time, in an era where the dominant global powers have effectively disengaged themselves from an activist role on the continent, the recourse to private security arrangements can be seen as reflecting frustration with a world that now seems no longer to care what happens in Africa. In this sense, the return of private armies to Africa is a symptom rather than a cause of the continent's milieu and it is the wider environment – both at the domestic and international/structural level – that needs to be addressed before mercenaries and private armies can finally be eliminated from the list of Africa's woes.

NOTES

1 Stephen Gill, "Globalization, Market Civilization, and Disciplinary Neo-Liberalism," *Millennium: Journal of International Studies*, 24 (1995), 399–423.
2 David A. Held, Anthony G. McGrew, D. Goldblatt, and J. Perraton, *Global Transformations* (Cambridge: Polity Press, 1999).
3 James Mittelman, "The Dynamics of Globalization," in Mittelman (ed.), *Globalization: Critical Reflections. International Political Economy Yearbook*, vol. 9 (Boulder, Colo.: Lynne Rienner, 1996), p. 7.
4 K. Mengisteab and B. Logan, *Beyond Economic Liberalization in Africa: Structural Adjustment and the Alternatives* (London: Zed Books, 1995).
5 Richard Stubbs and Geoffrey Underhill (eds.), *Political Economy and the Changing World Order*, 2nd edn. (Oxford and New York: Oxford University Press, 2000).
6 F. Adams, S. Gupta, and K. Mengisteab (eds.), *Globalization and the Dilemmas of the State in the South* (London: Macmillan, 1999).
7 A. Hoogvelt, *Globalization and the Postcolonial World: The New Political Economy of Development* (Baltimore, Md.: Johns Hopkins University Press, 1997), pp. 175–76.
8 P. Chabal and J.-P. Daloz, *Africa Works: Disorder as Political Instrument* (Oxford: James Currey, 1999), p. 80.

9 C. Clapham, *Africa and the International System: The Politics of State Survival* (Cambridge: Cambridge University Press, 1996), pp. 251–52.

10 Susan Strange, *The Retreat of the State: The Diffusion of Power in the World Economy* (Cambridge: Cambridge University Press, 1996).

11 J.-F. Bayart, S. Ellis, and B. Hibou, *The Criminalization of the State in Africa* (Oxford: James Currey, 1999), p. 96.

12 The fear of such activities by state elites in Africa should not be underestimated. Indeed, Africa is the only continent to enact a specific law to outlaw mercenaries on a pan-continental basis – the Convention on the Elimination of Mercenarism in Africa, adopted in Libreville in 1977 and entered into force in 1985.

13 L. Nathan, "Lethal Weapons: Why Africa Needs Alternatives to Hired Guns," *Track Two*, 6 (2) (August 1997), 10.

14 D. Francis, "Mercenary Intervention in Sierra Leone: Providing National Security or International Exploitation?," *Third World Quarterly*, 20 (2) (April 1999), 327.

15 C. Botha, "Soldiers of Fortune or Whores of War? The Legal Position of Mercenaries with Specific Reference to South Africa," *Strategic Review for Southern Africa*, 15 (2) (1993), 77.

16 K. Pech, "Executive Outcomes: A Corporate Quest," in J. Cilliers and P. Mason (eds.), *Peace, Profit or Plunder? The Privatisation of Security in War-Torn African Societies* (Halfway House, South Africa: Institute for Security Studies, 1999), p. 83.

17 Ibid., p. 82.

18 D. Martin and P. Johnson, *The Struggle for Zimbabwe* (Harare: Zimbabwe Publishing House, 1981).

19 The apartheid government maintained several farms for its security establishment where detained anti-apartheid activists and captured liberation movement combatants were held and "turned into" apartheid spies and operatives. Many detained and/or captured anti-apartheid activists and/or insurgents were tortured and/or killed, and their remains discovered and deaths investigated by the post-apartheid Truth and Reconciliation Commission. The farms were also used as bases from which to launch internal and external attacks on sites of resistance against apartheid, as well as to host recreational activities for various apartheid security forces: e.g., some apartheid operatives were known to dispose of detainees' corpses on huge bonfires, while simultaneously holding a barbecue with much alcohol consumption and revelry.

20 Pech, "Executive Outcomes," p. 84.

21 Ibid., p. 85.

22 K. Pech, W. Boot, and A. Eveleth, "South African Dogs of War in Congo," *Mail & Guardian* (Johannesburg), 28 August 1998, 7.

23 K. Pech and D. Beresford, "Africa's New-Look Dogs of War," *Mail & Guardian* (Johannesburg), 24 January 1997.

24 I. Taylor and P. Williams, "South African Foreign Policy and the Great Lakes Crisis: African Renaissance Meets Vagabondage Politique?," *African Affairs*, 100 (399) (April 2001), 265–86.

25 D. Shearer, *Private Armies and Military Intervention*, Adelphi Paper No. 316 (New York: Oxford University Press, 1998), pp. 24–26.

26 M. Malan, "Security Firms or Private Armies?," *The Star* (Johannesburg), 30 August 1996.

27 M. Malan, "Can Private Peacekeeping Deliver 'Executive Out-comes'?," *Indicator SA*, 1 (2) (1997), 12–15; K. Pech, "Bill to Crack Down on SA Mercenaries," *The Star* (Johannesburg), 19 September 1997; Shearer, *Private Armies*.

28 Taylor and Williams, "South African Foreign Policy."

29 Shearer, *Private Armies*, p. 68.

30 Immanuel Wallerstein, *After Liberalism* (New York: New Press, 1995).

31 Pech, "Executive Outcomes," p. 92.

32 M. Bryans, B. Jones, and J. Gross Stein, "Mean Times: Humanitarian Action in Complex Political Emergencies: Stark Choices, Cruel Dilemmas," *Coming to Terms*, 1 (3) (1999), *www.care.ca*.

33 J. Harding, "The Mercenary Business: 'Executive Outcomes,'" *Review of African Political Economy*, 24 (71) (1997), 96.

34 Ibid., 93.

35 E. Rubin, "Saving Sierra Leone, at a Price," *New York Times*, 4 February 1999.

36 A. Russel, *Big Men, Little People: Encounters in Africa* (Basingstoke: Macmillan, 1999), p. 186.

37 S. Cleary, "Angola: A Case Study of Private Military Involvement," in Cilliers and Mason, *Peace, Profit or Plunder?*, p. 166.

38 S. Weinberg, *Last of the Pirates: The Search for Bob Denard* (London: Jonathan Cape, 1994).

39 M. Ashworth, "Africa's New Enforcers," *Independent* (London), 16 September 1996.

40 Nathan, "Lethal Weapons," 11.

Part V

Conclusions and directions

10   Private authority as global governance

Thomas J. Biersteker and Rodney Bruce Hall

Private locations of authority have begun to influence a growing number of issues in our contemporary world. Authoritative private actors are not only important players in the international political economy; they are increasingly beginning to play a critical role in the governance of other important spheres of social and political life. They are engaged in the establishment of standards, the provision of social welfare, the enforcement of contracts, and the maintenance of security. The essays in this volume illustrate well the extent of the phenomenon, its complex character, the controversies surrounding its definition, and some of its implications. While the very meanings of the "private," of "authority," and of "private authority" themselves remain controversial, we think we have made some important progress in our understanding of these phenomena.

Rather than define the realm of the private in an abstract, theoretical sense, most of the contributors to this volume define the private sector in terms of what it is not. For Claire Cutler, private actors are increasingly engaged in authoritative decision-making that was previously the prerogative of sovereign states, while for Saskia Sassen the domain of the private is taking over functions once enclosed in national legal frameworks. Ronnie Lipschutz and Cathleen Fogel differentiate the private sector from the public, while Mark Juergensmeyer locates it in opposition to the government. Thus, whether it is differentiated from the sovereign state, the government, the national legal framework, or the public sector, the private sector is typically defined in terms of some residual of the national state.

Illustrations of private actors abound throughout the essays included in this volume. For those with a primary interest in private market authority, firms, private international regimes, networks, or transnational private arenas (composed of regulatory agencies and/or networks) are primary examples of private, market-associated authority. For contributors with a primary interest in what we term moral authority, non-governmental organizations, transnational regimes, or religious transnationalists are examples of private actors that have assumed authoritative functions. In the realm of security, organized crime syndicates, private armies, and private security agencies are different illustrations of private locations of authority.

In what sense, however, do any of these private actors possess authority? In chapter 1 of this volume, we differentiated authority from power, arguing that, to have authority, actors must be perceived as legitimate. In order to claim any rights of legitimacy, actors in authority must obtain some form of obligation from those subject to their authority. As Claire Cutler argues in her contribution to this volume, there must be an obligatory acceptance of the legitimacy of as well as respect for an authority "as a specialist, a scholar, or an expert" (p. 28 above). Authority thus requires both the recognition by, and the consent of, those governed by that authority. Drawing further on the work of Cutler and others, we also described the importance of the public social recognition of claims of authority. Authority, however, need not be accorded exclusively to public actors. As long as there is consent and social recognition, an actor – even a private actor – can be accorded the rights, the legitimacy, and the responsibilities of an authority.

While Louis Pauly forcefully challenges the very idea of private authority, and Phil Williams remains doubtful about whether transnational organized crime possesses authority, rather than simple, brute power, most of the contributors to this volume discuss what they term the growing authority of private actors. For Stephen Kobrin (and to some extent, for Saskia Sassen), the market itself is becoming increasingly authoritative. Sassen describes "accommodations on the part of the national state" to the requirements of the global capital market (p. 105 above). She argues further that the state has participated in the creation of private authority through its withdrawal, not, as Pauly maintains, only through its delegation of authority. Sassen also discusses some of the new normative roles assumed by the growing authority of non-state actors (p. 106 above).

Ronnie Lipschutz and Cathleen Fogel also describe the normative (as well as functional) roles filled by private actors. They consider explicit and implicit delegations of social authority to private actors who operate with "less formalized systems of norms, rules, and procedures that pattern behavior without the presence of written constitutions or material power" (p. 123 above). For Lipschutz and Fogel, private actors whose expertise is acquired through global networks of knowledge and practice are taking over responsibilities no other actor wants, resulting in a "very diffuse" system of globalizing governance (ranging from entirely private to mixed public and private ventures). Mark Juergensmeyer similarly describes how religious transnationalists challenge the state's monopoly on morally sanctioned violence and construct for themselves "a basis of legitimacy for public order other than that upon which the secular state relies" (p. 152 above). During the height of the Sikh rebellion of the 1980s, Juergensmeyer argues that the "militants were treated as if they possessed an authority rivaling that of police and other government officials" (p. 150 above).

Though he is wary about characterizing organized crime as possessing authority, rather than power, Phil Williams similarly describes how capacity gaps and functional holes are filled by criminal organizations that, in effect, substitute or compensate for the state. In transitional states like contemporary Russia, the lack of an appropriate regulatory framework means that there is "neither protection nor contract enforcement, a condition that allows organized crime to become a surrogate for government" (p. 172 above). With reference to Colombia, Williams goes even further to describe how the paternalism of the Medellin cartel earns the gratitude of the people "and at least tacit support from members of the populace" (p. 173 above). Thus, they are accorded certain rights of legitimate authority through the social recognition and public consent of the governed, granting them a form of private authority, as defined above.

Bernedette Muthien and Ian Taylor describe a market-driven return to the precolonial era within some states of contemporary Africa, to a period when large trading companies constituted themselves "into an effective government and established an administrative and legal infrastructure to run" countries (p. 190 above). In some parts of Africa today, "private companies are using their own resources to protect installations, enforce regulations, and discipline staff on compounds little touched by local laws." As they conclude, "[a]uthority has become truly privatized" (p. 194 above).

Although private authority is not always equivalent to and/or does not always exceed the authority of the national state, the contributors to this volume present a persuasive argument about the extent, the significance, and the complexity of the emergence of private authority in the international system. Markets, market actors, transnational movements, mafias, and mercenaries are each recognized socially as possessing authority within certain issue domains. Their authority is legitimate to the extent that they obtain the consent of the governed and exercise certain rights within those domains.

How did private authority emerge? Was it delegated by the state, negotiated with the state, enabled by the state, allowed by the state, or seized from the state? The contributors to this volume are generally divided between those who contend that authority was yielded, implying that the state had little or no choice (Kobrin, Lipschutz and Fogel, and Muthien and Taylor) and those who argue that authority was seized deliberately by private actors (Juergensmeyer and Williams). Saskia Sassen stakes a middle position on the issue, arguing that private authority has been enabled by states. Only Louis Pauly maintains that authority is delegated deliberately by the state (and only in good times), rendering it a momentary, temporary, or fleeting phenomenon.

These different assessments of how private authority emerged do not correspond directly to the three principal forms of private authority (market, moral, or illicit authority) considered in this volume. Among those interested primarily in private market authority, there is an implicit debate between the views of Stephen Kobrin, who describes the retreat of the state, and the skeptical views of Louis Pauly, who describes the state's strategic delegation of authority. Within the domain of moral authority, Mark Juergensmeyer's description of the seizure of authority by private transnational religious movements differs from Ronnie Lipschutz and Cathleen Fogel's characterization of the ways in which the state has yielded its regulatory authority. In the area of illicit authority, Phil Williams's assessment of the explicit challenges posed by mafias contrasts with Bernedette Muthien and Ian Taylor's assessment of the ways in which private armies have moved into the vacuum left by the state. Despite their different assessments of how it came about, however, nearly all of the contributors included in this volume agree that private locations of authority have emerged in the international system.

Implications of the emergence of private authority for global governance

What are some of the implications of the emergence of private authority in the international system? What are its implications for the changing role of the state, for the institution of state sovereignty, and for the prospects of accountability and global governance? There are a number of important insights contained within the work of the contributors to this volume that begin to answer some of these important questions about the emergence, the nature, and the functioning of private authority in the international system. These insights often extend across the threefold typology of market, moral, and illicit forms of private authority that serves as the organizing principle of the volume.

Private authority and the role of the state

Louis Pauly and Saskia Sassen agree that the state remains the ultimate guarantor of property rights (though they do not consider in detail the situation in transitional states, as described by Phil Williams). Sassen develops this argument when she examines the role of the state in the neoliberal globalization process. She asks whether the state is simply reducing its authority to market-based forms of decision-making, or whether it has a crucial role to play in the production of a new international legal-institutional framework that is conducive to the emerging international capital mobility regime. She argues strongly for the latter case, essentially agreeing with Pauly that the technical, administrative capacity of the state is irreplaceable in the context of guaranteeing property rights. However, she provides an important caveat to this argument by suggesting that the act of guaranteeing is itself becoming privatized to an important extent. She draws our attention to the impressive growth of international commercial arbitration as an example. Her observation suggests the potential for market authority to challenge sovereign authority as the sole guarantor of the "adequately firm political foundations" that Pauly (and others) argue that markets require (p. 83 above). Similarly, Claire Cutler, who emphasizes the broad and far-reaching effects of private market authority, notes that in many cases private actors turn to the state for assistance in enforcing regime norms.

In a similar vein, Ronnie Lipschutz and Cathleen Fogel argue that firms take advantage of different (and, typically, less restrictive) regulatory regimes across states. However, this imposes transaction costs for them, and hence they prefer a single global set of regulatory standards to mitigate these transaction costs. Drawing upon the work of Karl Polanyi, in a fashion that similarly resonates strongly with Louis Pauly's analysis, Lipschutz and Fogel argue that markets require rules for orderly functioning. Thus they argue that, while market actors may desire *domestic* deregulation, they do not desire the elimination of all rules at the *international* level because this would subvert the orderly functioning of global markets, and drive up cost of transactions within these markets. Transnational market actors resist transnational social regulation on this basis as well. Thus market authority appears to have a strong influence in determining how some forms of transnational rules are formulated, while other forms are dismantled. Claire Cutler, similarly, emphasizes the self-regulatory nature of private authority, suggesting that market authority is acquiring the capacity to structure a transnational regulatory environment that is conducive to its operations.

Ronnie Lipschutz and Cathleen Fogel also agree with Louis Pauly when it comes to their assessment of some of the consequences of the emergence of private authority for the domestic political practices of the state. Lipschutz and Fogel discuss the social purpose of transnational regulatory harmonization provided by international regimes, and argue that the resulting regulatory harmonization is intended to "eliminate politics" by removing from the domestic realm to the international realm. Similarly, Pauly contends that references to market "authority" are intended to allocate politics to the market. One of the questions posed in the introductory essay of this volume was that of whether and why the state is complicit in the devolution of its authority to private actors. Pauly, in particular, provides us with an answer. State managers may wish to avoid responsibility and domestic accountability for painful domestic adjustments generated by their liberalization policies. The invocation of the authority of the market permits them to deflect responsibility to the abstract entity of the global markets, which are not obviously accountable to a national citizenry, a point to which we will return in a later section.

Private authority and the transformation of state sovereignty

There is strong agreement among most of the contributors to this volume that the emergence of private authority has affected the operational meaning of state sovereignty. In the realm of market authority, Stephen Kobrin and Saskia Sassen emphasize different practices in their respective contributions, but both argue that, in Sassen's lexicon, globalization generates an emerging "set of practices that destabilize another set of practices, i.e., some of the practices that... constitute national sovereignty" (p. 104 above). Kobrin sees this as a transition from a modern to a post-modern mode of organization. With the "end of geography" accompanying global financial integration, he argues that "the meaning of sovereignty will evolve"; he invokes the medieval period as analogous, where "[b]orders are diffuse and permeable," "[r]elationships are increasingly networked," and "[m]ultiple and competing loyalties result" (p. 65 above). This is a far cry from the Westphalian ideal of state sovereignty. Sassen argues that global financial integration is a process involving "multiple policy, analytic, and narrative negotiations" that have been "coded as 'deregulation'" (p. 104 above). Both Kobrin and Sassen agree that there is a new grid of economic transactions that has been superimposed over traditional, geographic-economic patterns of organization. But Sassen is more circumspect than Kobrin (though less so than Louis Pauly) regarding the long-term consequences of this development for international organization and global governance.

Stephen Kobrin argues that transnational networks of private capital actors are replacing hierarchies and national markets as the basic form of organization, and he emphasizes the migration of markets into cyberspace. His analysis implies that not only is market authority supplanting sovereign authority, but also that "the real question is whether the spatial concepts of borders, territory, and jurisdiction apply to electronically organized global networks" (p. 61 above). Saskia Sassen argues that because the global economy has to be produced, reproduced, serviced, and financed somewhere, its structure is not purely a function of the power of transnational firms or of markets. She emphasizes the extent to which the global economy materializes in national territories, in "global cities," where financial networks and their support infrastructures provide the command and control functions of the global economy. This requires that the globalization process be negotiated with the state.

Saskia Sassen argues that these negotiations leave territorial boundaries intact, "but do transform the institutional encasements of that geographic fact" (p. 103 above). Thus in its manifestation as market authority, private authority transforms both the state and state sovereignty. However, the state participates in this transformation. We agree and would argue that market (private) authority does not simply supplant sovereign (public) authority, but that sovereign authority accommodates the burgeoning demands for market authority by participating in its own transformation. Louis Pauly argues that the globalization process enhances some state capacities, while Stephen Kobrin and Saskia Sassen contend that it diminishes others. Ronnie Lipschutz and Cathleen Fogel maintain that the state will remain an important actor for some time to come, but this does not mean that the state will remain the same institution that it has been in the past. They suggest that states are yielding "substantial" amounts of regulatory authority to transnational regulatory regimes. Thus, our contributors provide a preliminary response to the question about the future of state sovereignty posed in the introductory chapter of this volume. Most argue that we are witnessing a transformation, rather than the replacement, of state sovereignty.

In the form of private authority that we have termed moral authority, Ronnie Lipschutz and Cathleen Fogel discuss the emergence of overlapping sets of authorities arising to challenge the regulatory monopoly of the state that characterized much of the twentieth century. Like Stephen Kobrin, they see an emerging "globalizing 'heteronomy' " (p. 124 above), in which regulatory authority is distributed across actors, but is focused on specific issues and problems. This form of private authority is developing because specific private actors, particularly NGOs, are shouldering responsibilities that other actors, including state actors, no longer wish to take on. Authority is accruing to NGOs on the basis of their technical expertise, or what Kratochwil has termed "consensual knowledge."[1] In this instance, NGOs perform an "epistemic function" by providing the consensual knowledge necessary for the formation and maintenance of transnational regulatory regimes. State managers share regulatory authority with NGOs, whose moral authority is translated into regulatory authority, as well as with transnational market actors, whose market authority is translated into regulatory authority.

In our other illustration of moral authority, Mark Juergensmeyer points out that transnational religious movements employ strategic violence to attack state authority directly, in an effort to demonstrate that the state no longer possesses a monopoly over the legitimate means of violence. To the extent that these groups, movements, and ideologies succeed in demonizing the secular, Western (Westphalian) state, and particularly the transnationally culturally influential United States, they undermine Weberian empirical statehood. The secular, Western state is, in their eyes, illegitimate. Since they regard their own actions as not merely legitimate, but divinely sanctioned, their actions may be seen as a dramatic and destructive way to establish that the entire model of the Westphalian state sovereignty is illegitimate. Juergensmeyer argues powerfully that the act of killing on behalf of a moral code is overtly political, because it attacks the state's monopoly of legitimate violence. Each of the groups Juergensmeyer examined in his contribution to this volume advances claims of transnational moral authority immanent within their doctrines that they believe are morally superior to the bases of the secular, Western state, and that provide the basis for viable alternatives to the Westphalian conception of sovereignty.

Within the realm of illicit (private) authority, the contributors to this volume demonstrate how actors such as mafias and mercenaries capitalize on the failures of sovereign (public) authority to fulfill certain basic functions or to provide fundamentally vital public goods for the citizenry. Phil Williams identifies common characteristics of weak states, which facilitate their penetration by transnational criminal organizations. He argues that they tend to possess low levels of state legitimacy, porous borders, ineffective legal structures and criminal justice systems, and corrupt civil administrations. All of these features presage low levels of Weberian empirical statehood and sovereign legitimacy. Thus he suggests these "capacity gaps" of weak states generate certain "functional holes" that appear to undermine the legitimacy of public authority. Illicit (private) authority in the form of transnational organized crime rushes into the vacuum created by these gaps. He notes that some criminal organizations and leaders "engage in a form of paternalism that earns them considerable gratitude and . . . support from members of the populace" and that their sometimes "[v]ery visible, and sometimes even ostentatious, support for charities is another aspect of the same tendency." The consequence for state sovereignty here is that illicit (private) authority becomes "a surrogate" for state (public) authority (pp. 170–174 above).

Bernedette Muthien and Ian Taylor argue similarly that in many of the weak states of mineral rich sub-Saharan Africa, "security is no longer a service [provided] by the state for all its citizens, but has become a market good" (p. 186 above). Their discussion of characteristics of weak African states, and how their weaknesses facilitate their penetration by private armies and mercenary forces, resonates strongly with Williams's descriptions of the public authority failures that enable penetration by mafias. However, Muthien and Taylor note that, in some instances, the private provision of security services to embattled states has been legitimated by transnational international agencies such as the International Monetary Fund. While highly critical of most illicit mercenary arrangements, Muthien and Taylor consider whether they might serve a positive role in some instances (as the IMF seems to believe), ostensibly in the defense of an endangered public authority. Like the expansion of transnational criminal organizations, the introduction of mercenary forces also undermines the authority of the sovereign state and raises profound questions about the operational meaning of state sovereignty.

Private authority and democratic accountability

Many of the contributors to this volume raise explicit concerns about the limited degree (or virtual absence) of accountability of private authority. Claire Cutler contends that, as firms begin to function like governments, this raises major issues for democratic and representative theories of governance. She maintains that private entities are not normatively entitled to act authoritatively for the public, because they are not subject to mechanisms of political accountability, but rather are only subject to the accountability of their private members. Ronnie Lipschutz and Cathleen Fogel similarly raise questions about the privatization of global regulatory authority and conclude that the trend in the future "is likely to be toward greater privatization of regulation and less democracy and accountability around the world" (p. 121 above). Bernedette Muthien and Ian Taylor voice the same concern and warn that, because they are unaccountable to wider society, "private armies are able, in the most extreme cases, to asset-strip a country with virtual impunity, leading to irreversible ecological degradation, the illicit export of resource commodities, and the general encouragement of a culture of criminality" (p. 197 above).

In the domain of market authority Stephen Kobrin argues that, with globalization, emergent forms of private authority such as networked oligopolies are able to extract unprecedented regulatory concessions from host governments, to which multinational corporations had previously been relatively responsive. Louis Pauly notes the "discipline" imposed on autonomous state action by market authority in the form of floating exchange rates and international capital mobility. He also suggests that this has implied cutting back on the welfare state, in spite of the fact that its services remain in high demand and enjoy high levels of popular support in most advanced, industrialized states. However, Pauly challenges the assertion that no one could be held accountable for a financial catastrophe resulting from truly integrated global financial markets. He argues that the authority to manage global finance either has been dispersed to supranational institutions or has been privatized. However, in the event of a major financial crisis, agencies like the IMF take on the role of scapegoat to buffer the political crises attending financial crisis to prevent a legitimation crisis of the global, socioeconomic order. The vituperative criticism attending the IMF's handling of the Asian financial crisis of 1997, from economists and commentators of all stripes, appears to bear Pauly out in this context.[2] In the final analysis, however, Pauly contends that justice and legitimacy are inextricably linked, and that governments will not be able to shift ultimate political authority to what we are calling market authority. He remains skeptical of the long-term causal significance of market authority and argues that markets are a tool of policy (of sovereign authority) rather than a substitute for it.

Saskia Sassen addresses the relationship between democratic accountability and the growth of private authority in the brief description of her new research oriented toward tracing the microhistory of US legal accommodations to the globalization process. The increased coordination of regulatory standards is being conducted in a manner that is largely hidden from the global public, and Sassen argues that there is a need for the state to do much more than it is doing to increase the level of accountability built into the global economy. Sassen issues a call for a "new politics of accountability" (p. 107 above). Perhaps the strong levels of protest seen at the meetings of the World Trade Organization in Seattle, and the IMF and World Bank in Washington in 2000, could be described as a popular echo of Sassen's call.

In the realm of moral authority, Ronnie Lipschutz and Cathleen Fogel provide a somewhat hopeful assessment of the prospects for greater accountability when they note the "growth in neofunctional authority" resulting from the proliferation of non-corporate NGOs with emancipatory goals and some influence in the global regulatory process. These organizations are accorded a certain degree of moral authority because of their non-state nature, their substantive expertise, and their positive normative commitments. However, Lipschutz and Fogel are concerned that those forms of global regulation that serve the narrow self-interests of specific actors may be legitimated via transnational processes that pass for global governance. Like Saskia Sassen, they call for a countervailing movement to bring public scrutiny and participation to bear on these global regulatory processes. The application of more moral authority is seen as a democratic prescription for the undemocratic application of market authority.

Mark Juergensmeyer's study of the moral authority of transnational religious movements suggests that adherents of these movements wish precisely to attack the legitimacy of secular, democratically accountable public authority. The private application of religious violence ultimately aims to reconstruct both transnational and domestic public authority on transcendental bases. It does this with a combination of a dramatic demonstration of the weakness of public secular authority, coupled with an appeal to the moral authority of a transnational, transcendental creed to which "democracy" is either anathema, or is conceived in a radically different fashion than in the secular West. While they may promise a form of accountability (before God), transnational religious movements are not accountable in this world.

In the realm of illicit authority matters are somewhat simpler. Democracy has already been subverted by the partial or complete collapse of the public authority of weak sovereign entities. Illicit (private) authority steps in to provide public goods and to meet needs and responsibilities that the sovereign (public) authority has neglected or eschewed. To the extent that mafias and mercenaries are visible and successful in providing these public goods, they may enjoy the partial, popular legitimation of their exercise of private authority. However, it is difficult to see how these outcomes may be described as democratic or accountable (beyond the basic provision of public goods). The intervention by private military forces in Sierra Leone had some positive outcomes, but, as Bernedette Muthien and Ian Taylor suggest, "they only went where the payoff was high" (p. 194 above). The people who lived in the mineral-rich areas benefited from the protection provided by the mercenary force, but those who did not had to fend for themselves. Private entities in strong possession of the means of violence, whether these means are either locally or transnationally perceived as legitimate or as illegitimate, are ultimately accountable to no one.

The reversibility of private authority

Can the emergence of private authority be reversed? Louis Pauly argues forcefully that, since markets ultimately rely on stable political foundations, public authority may seize back its perquisites at any moment, and is likely to do so in the advent of bad times. He argues that the responsibilities of a public authority to attend to the welfare of its citizenry may be displaced for a time, but it can never be completely avoided. Pauly concludes that "it is always easy to say 'Let the market work.' But it is politically unthinkable actually to do it" (p. 87 above). Having elaborated on the definition, the forms, and the implications of the emergence of private authority in the international system, we now need to examine the conditions under which the emergence of private authority might be reversed. In order to understand the potential for the reversal of different forms of private authority, we also need to understand the different bases (and types) of each of the three forms of private authority considered in this volume.

The potential reversal of private market authority

There are two principal types of private market authority considered in this volume: institutional and normative. Institutional market authority refers to the capacity of private actors to set standards that are recognized and adhered to by others. Normative market authority refers to the general acceptance of the more abstract idea that markets should determine decision-making over important issues.

Claire Cutler concentrates on institutional market authority in her contribution to this volume. She argues that institutional market authority ranges in degree of institutionalization from informal industry norms and practices on the low end of the continuum to highly institutionalized private international regimes on the other. The authority of private institutional actors is based on their capacity to establish technological, manufacturing, and regulatory standards that become recognized and adhered to by other actors. The proliferation of ISO standards generated by transnational market actors and the commercial regulatory authority adhering to burgeoning agency of corporate NGOs are both examples of institutional private market authority.

Normative market authority is based on the acceptance of essentially market-based modes of decision-making among important political actors. While social recognition is necessary to constitute authority, this form of private authority rests upon the power inherent in the private control of mobile, productive, and portfolio capital, along with the capacity to generate new productive technologies. The oligopolistic networks of transnational corporations that are featured in Stephen Kobrin's analysis are exemplars of this type of private market authority, managed from the command and control centers of Saskia Sassen's "global cities." Louis Pauly refers to them as the international capital mobility regime.

How might the emergence of these different types of private market authority be reversed? Private market authority would most likely revert to public authority in the event of a major normative delegitimation of the market mechanism. A global financial crisis affecting the major financial centers or a broader crisis of global market capitalism could create the conditions under which, as Pauly suggests, the state might take unilateral action to seize back that which it has ceded (or delegated) to private, market-oriented actors. Public authorities would presumably revise their statements about the power and inevitability of global market forces in an effort to reassure the citizenry to whom Pauly suggests they remain accountable. However, the probability of this scenario is likely to be sharply contested by market optimists and observers who maintain that globalization is driven by irreversible technological developments. Institutional types of private market authority would be easier to reverse, particularly if their capacity to set and enforce standards were diminished by new players. However, the effects of this reversal would be less extensive and would most likely be contained within individual economic sectors.

The potential reversal of private moral authority

As with private market authority, there are different types of private moral authority, reflecting the different claims on which it is based: expertise, neutrality, or normative superiority. Some private actors possess moral authority because of their capacity to provide expertise on an important issue. Others claim moral authority because of a combination of their possession of expertise and the plausibility of their claims of neutrality on a controversial issue. Still other private actors claim moral authority because of more general normative claims that they are socially recognized to represent progressive or, in some instances, morally superior, transcendent social and political positions. The emerging regulatory authority of non-corporate NGOs featured in the work of Ronnie Lipschutz and Cathleen Fogel combines elements of all three (expertise, neutrality, and moral transcendence), while the claims of adherents of the transnational religious movements discussed by Mark Juergensmeyer are based primarily on claims of moral transcendence.

As in the case of the potential reversibility of different types of private market authority, the reversal of different examples of private moral authority is closely linked to the bases of their claims of moral authority. One circumstance under which the exercise of the moral authority of private actors might revert to a public authority would involve a normative delegitimation of the private actor through its own actions or through the strategic discursive efforts of other actors. For example, an action taken by a non-governmental organization, or a socially recognized, discursive claim by its adversaries that it had abandoned its neutrality or become unable to generate expertise, could result in a crippling withdrawal of the social recognition of the moral authority of the NGO. Similarly, action by or socially recognized discursive claims against activist adherents to transnational religious movements could have similar effects. The exclusion of NGOs from input into transnational regulatory processes might temporarily enhance their moral authority in the view of their supporters, but would at the same time negate their regulatory authority. In as much as authority remains the legitimate use of power, the negation of the power to act necessarily negates the authority to act. However, the negation of legitimacy in action can be more crippling to the capacity to act authoritatively, because prohibitions that remove the capacity to act may ultimately enhance the legitimacy of the excluded actor.

The excluded actors' loss of capacity to act can itself be reversed by external pressure from outraged third parties who continue to grant social recognition to the legitimacy of the excluded actor. For example, the imprisonment of Nelson Mandela by the apartheid regime of South Africa negated his capacity or power to act against the regime directly by virtue of the fact of his incarceration and isolation. This actually enhanced his normative legitimacy and moral authority among reformist elements of the South African polity. His ultimate release from prison reversed his incapacity to act, and he emerged as an even stronger political actor in view of the moral authority that adhered to him for having suffered under the apartheid regime. He was consequently accorded the pinnacle of political (public) authority upon the delegitimation and collapse of the previous South African public authority.

The potential reversal of private illicit authority

The claim to authority of private illicit actors in the international system rests upon their capacity to provide public goods and their private control of the means of violence that competes with, or supercedes, the capacity of public authority. The social recognition of illicit authority is also essential to its emergence as private authority, not simply its possession of power. Accordingly, there are two principal ways in which private illicit authority might be reversed: either a normative delegitimation or a nullification of the capacity or power to act.

Failure to provide the public goods underprovided by public authority, either through conscious decision or through incapacity, might result in the normative delegitimation and local withdrawal of social recognition of illicit authority. For example, the mafias and mercenaries that fail to provide public goods such as the enforcement of contracts and the provision of security tend to be viewed, even by prospective recipients of these public goods, as mere predators and parasites. Mafias and mercenaries most successfully penetrate weak states; hence, the emergence of private illicit authority might also be reversed by the success of state-building or institution-building efforts oriented toward strengthening state capacities to provide public goods to the citizenry. Unfortunately, state-building is a long-term project and is not terribly easy to accomplish. Finally, external intervention and/or policing by transnational public authorities could produce the same outcome as successful state- and institution-building. By generating a competing normative legitimacy for public authority, enabling state capacity to replace private violence capacity, and undermining the fiscal basis of illicit authority, external intervention could also reverse the emergence of private illicit authority, at least in the short term.

In table 7 we present a summary of the preceding discussion of the bases of each major subtype of private authority considered in this volume. We also suggest some major examples of each type of private authority. In the final column we derive, from the logic of the arguments about the bases of these different subtypes of private authority, some of the conditions under which the different types of private authority might be reversed.

Ideas for future research on private authority and the international system

The preceding discussion of the conditions under which private authority might be reversed suggests a rich agenda for future research. Many of the logical assertions summarized in table 7 could be converted into testable hypotheses about the nature and future direction of authority in the international system. At the same time, the research included in this volume has illuminated many questions that were obscured when we began. We believe we have made a useful beginning in exploring the phenomenon of private authority and its importance for the contemporary international system. We can now see more clearly some of the exploratory paths down which we could tread, paths that were obscured before we had conducted some reconnaissance of the general intellectual terrain.

There is clearly more conceptual work to be done. In this volume, we have provided a provisional typology of three forms of private authority that are being exercised in the contemporary international system: market, moral, and illicit authority. We have considered their bases, identified subtypes within each category, listed examples, and suggested some of the conditions under which we might anticipate a potential reversal of each form of private authority. However, our review of the chapters

Table 7. *Typology of private authority*

Type of private authority	Bases of private authority	Examples of private authority	Sources of potential reversal of private authority
Market authority	Capacity to set standards recognized and adhered to by others (*institutional market authority*) Acceptance of market-based decision-making (*normative market authority*)	ISO standards Corporate NGO regulatory authority Networks of transnational corporations International capital mobility regime	Normative delegitimation: – global financial crisis – crisis of global capitalism Breakdown of networks Unilateral action by public authority
Moral authority	Capacity to provide expertise (*authorship*) Status of non-state, non-self interested actor or neutral (*referee*) Claim to represent socially progressive or morally transcendent position (*normative*)	Non-corporate NGO regulatory authority Transnational religious movements	Normative delegitimation of non-state NGO action capacity Exclusion of non-state NGOs by market and public authority Normative delegitimation of transnational religious movements in view of adherents
Illicit authority	Capacity to provide *public goods* underprovided by public authority Control of private *means of violence*	Penetration of weak public authorities by transnational criminal organizations and private armed forces	Normative delegitimation via failure to provide public goods Successful state-/ institution-building to strengthen public authority Successful intervention/ policing by transnational public authority

included in this volume suggests to us that each form of private authority in our typology might be conceptually disaggregated and further theorized in ways that could provide us some directions for future theoretical and empirical research.

In the realm of market authority, the distinctions raised in the introductory essay and in Claire Cutler's summation of her collaborative work on private regimes are highly suggestive of one way in which the concept of market authority might be further explored. As discussed above, two major subtypes of market authority present themselves. Cutler, Haufler, Porter, and their collaborators have recently studied one subtype: the authoritative consequences of constructing institutions of and by market actors, especially private transnational regimes and the norms, rules, principles, decision-making procedures, and institutions which comprise them. Their work is the definitive study to date of what we call *institutional market authority*. We regard their suggestions for future research into these institutions as excellent and refer the reader to their proposed research program designed to garner further insights into this subtype of market authority.

However, a second subtype of market authority, perhaps even more pervasive, is suggested by the normative acceptance of market-based modes of decision-making in general. This entails research into the following questions. By what processes have transnational market actors and, in many cases, public authorities normatively legitimated the neoliberal vision of a globalized economy? What discursive battles have been waged to effect this normative legitimation? Should we (or how shall we) theorize economics as ideology rather than as "science"? As the economist Robert Heilbroner has argued, the notion of economics "as ideology forces us to confront directly . . . the constitutive basis of what we call the economy and the pronouncements about it that comprise economics."[3] How does the language of economics, employed in these discursive battles, help to "construct" the neoliberal globalized economy? As the economic historian, Deirdre McCloskey, has observed so adeptly, the rhetorical style in which economics is written relies upon a highly intersubjective set of social meanings. The reader (or listener) is intended to avail herself of these meanings as she draws "truth value" from the rhetorical style.[4] In short, by what means does "market authority" acquire, for many actors, through discursive and operational construction, its own "moral authority" as a normatively legitimate means of allocating, for example, the painful economic adjustments that attend the neoliberal globalization process? We have labeled this subtype of market authority *normative market authority*. Note that we are not claiming our own adherence to the normative legitimacy of these market-based processes and outcomes. We are suggesting that the observed levels of market authority exercised in the international system are inconsistent with purely coercive processes of allocating market-based adjustment costs. In other words, if these market-based processes and outcomes did not enjoy significant levels of normative legitimacy, this form of market authority could not be exercised.

Even more clearly than market authority, the form of private authority that we have designated as moral authority needs conceptual unbundling. As suggested in the introductory chapter, the concept of "moral authority" has been applied, in the context of the study by Ronnie Lipschutz and Cathleen Fogel, as well as that of Mark Juergensmeyer, in at least four specific contexts. First it has been applied to the authority that adheres to those who possess useful expertise. We call this the *authority of authorship.* Second, it has been applied to the authority that adheres to those who can claim the moral high ground, or status, of neutrality as an actor in a highly contested or conflictual social environment. It may also entail a claim of altruism, or at least an absence of personal or institutional, pecuniary or political self-interest.

Both the claim to expert status (specifically when it is accompanied by a discursive claim to the "scientific," thus "neutral," status of the expertise provided) may entail an implicit or explicit claim to hold the moral high ground in a contested social interaction. Thus we are comfortable in designating both as "moral" claims. Further, both of these claims must enjoy social recognition to function socially as claims to "authority" as opposed to simple "capacity" or "power." We are therefore happy that both are forms of "authority." Yet the variation in the source of these claims to moral authority is sufficiently significant that we deem it useful to delineate between them. We designate the second form of moral authority claim, which adheres to those claiming neutral status in a contested social dynamic, as the *authority of the referee.*

Two further distinctions arise in the work of our contributors that we believe suggests a further subtypology of moral authority. Let us first suggest that there is a generic form of the subtype. It entails a moral claim to a normatively legitimate social purpose in the course of social action. We shall, then, simply designate the third subtype of moral authority as *normative moral authority.* Among our contributors to this section we have two distinctive examples of the subtype. The first is the illustration by Ronnie Lipschutz and Cathleen Fogel of the moral claim on behalf of non-corporate NGOs to the secularly normatively legitimate claim to regulate and certify ecologically responsible manufactures. We could, then, designate this claim as *"secular" normative moral authority,* though we could just as easily further specify the context and designate it as "ecologically" normative moral authority. The illustration of normative moral authority provided by Mark Juergensmeyer's study of the proclaimed social purposes of transnational religious movements can similarly be designated as a claim to *"transcendent" normative moral authority*.

In spite of the claims advanced by any social actor to possessing moral authority, or any form of private authority for that matter, the social recognition of these claims must be demonstrated to justify their claim to the actual exercise of private authority. The claims that non-corporate NGOs exercise private authority may not be recognized by corporate NGOs, or even by many public authorities. Yet they are valid to the extent that social recognition of the claims by other actors or publics lend the NGO agency that makes it effective in participating in the construction of regulatory frameworks for ecologically responsible manufactures, and in certifying these frameworks. The claim of these NGOs to the authority of authorship appears to enjoy somewhat unproblematic social recognition. The claims of NGOs to the authority of the referee, or to the possession of normative moral authority, are more likely to be contested by important actors, even if they enjoy social recognition from some of them. Social recognition of all relevant actors is not necessary to sustain a claim to legitimate and effective private authority. Whose recognition is required to sustain the claim is contingent upon the structure of each, unique, social interaction environment.

The forms of illicit private authority explored by Phil Williams and by Bernedette Muthien and Ian Taylor find their basis in the capacity of private actors to provide public goods that are underprovided by weak or inadequately institutionalized public authorities. The other major source of their authority is a high capacity for delivering the means of violence. Capabilities are a source of power, and they may be a source of authority when, as is the case of the Weberian empirical state, the entity in possession enjoys a socially recognized monopoly over the means of their employment. In the cases of mafias and mercenaries, any monopoly enjoyed through the means of private violence tends to be temporary, and social recognition of the monopoly of its use is likely to be spare among the citizenry, and grudging where it is accorded. Nevertheless, it is possible to disaggregate illicit private authority in accordance with the types of public goods, or social services, provided by that form of private authority.

There is clearly more theoretical and empirical work to be done. Our intention with the publication of this volume is to advance the debate and understanding of the emergence of private authority. In the final analysis, authority (private or public) is a social construct. The terms of its construction are always contingent upon the self-understandings of actors, in addition to their social understandings of one another. Like state sovereignty, both public and private authority are social conventions.

Social conventions may be strongly institutionalized or they may be weakly institutionalized. State sovereignty is highly institutionalized in most states, but it is so weakly institutionalized in others that private actors can exploit that weakness, and may enjoy a measure of private authority for delivering public goods that the state fails to provide. Similarly, private authority is weakly institutionalized in many of its manifestations. However, private authority may be so highly institutionalized in some of its manifestations, such as private regimes, that public authority may be forced to transform its institutional and regulatory environment in order to enjoy the "public goods" provided by the operations of transnational networks.

NOTES

1 Friedrich Kratochwil, "Regimes, Interpretation, and the 'Science' of Politics: A Reappraisal," *Millennium: Journal of International Relations*, 17 (2) (1988), 263–84, and Kratochwil, *Rules, Norms, and Decisions: On the Conditions of Practical and Legal Reasoning in International Relations and Domestic Affairs* (Cambridge: Cambridge University Press, 1989), pp. 60–61.
2 Martin Feldstein, "Refocusing the IMF," *Foreign Affairs*, 77 (2) (March/ April 1998), 20–32; Paul Krugman, *The Return of Depression Economics* (New York: Norton, 1999); Joseph Stiglitz, "Must Financial Crises Be This Frequent and This Painful?," McKay Lecture, University of Pittsburgh, Pittsburgh, Penn., 23 September 1998, *www.worldbank.org/html/extdr/extme/js-092398/*; Stiglitz, "Back to Basics: Policies and Strategies for Enhanced Growth and Equity in Post-Crisis East Asia," delivered 19 July 1999, Shangri-la Hotel, Bangkok, Thailand; Stiglitz, "Whither Reform? Ten Years of the Transition," keynote address for the World Bank Annual Bank Conference on Development Economics, Washington, D.C., 28–30 April 1999; Stiglitz, "The Insider: What I Learned at the World Economic Crisis," *New Republic*, 17 & 24 April 2000, 56–60; Robert Wade and Frank Veneroso, "The Asian Crisis: The High Debt Model Versus the Wall Street–Treasury–IMF Complex," *New Left Review*, 228 (March/April 1998), 3–24.
3 Robert Heilbroner, "Economics as Ideology," in Warren J. Samuels (ed.), *Economics as Discourse: An Analysis of the Language of Economists* (Boston: Kluwer, 1990), p. 106.
4 Deirdre N. McCloskey, *The Rhetoric of Economics* (Madison: University of Wisconsin Press, 1998), p. 6.

Bibliography

Adams, F., S. Gupta, and K. Mengisteab (eds.), *Globalization and the Dilemmas of the State in the South*, London: Macmillan, 1999.

Albrow, Martin, *The Global Age: State and Society Beyond Modernity*, Stanford: Stanford University Press, 1997.

Aman, Alfred C. Jr., "The Globalizing State: A Future-Oriented Perspective on the Public/Private Distinction, Federalism, and Democracy," *Vanderbilt Journal of Transnational Law*, 31 (4) (1998), 769–870.

Anderson, James, "Nationalism and Geography," in Anderson (ed.), *The Rise of the Modern State*, Brighton, UK: Harvester Press, 1986, pp. 115–42.

Appadurai, Arjun, *Modernity at Large: Cultural Dimensions of Globalization*, Minneapolis and London: University of Minnesota Press, 1996.

Arrighi, Giovanni, *The Long Twentieth Century: Money, Power, and the Origins of Our Times*, London: Verso, 1994.

Ashworth, M., "Africa's New Enforcers," *Independent* (London), 16 September 1996.

Attali, J., "The Crash of Western Civilization: The Limits of Market and Democracy," *Foreign Policy*, 107 (Summer 1997), 54–63.

Baker, Wayne E., "Market Networks and Corporate Behavior," *American Journal of Sociology*, 96 (3) (1990), 589–625.

Baldwin, Richard E., and Phillipe Martin, "Two Waves of Globalization: Superficial Similarities, Fundamental Differences," Working Paper 6904, National Bureau of Economic Research, 1999.

Barber, Benjamin, *Jihad vs. McWorld: How Globalism and Tribalism Are Reshaping the World*, New York: Ballantine Books, 1995.

Barkin, J. Samuel, and Bruce Cronin, "The State and the Nation: Changing Norms and the Rules of Sovereignty in International Relations," *International Organization*, 48 (1) (1994), 107–30.

Bartleson, Jens, *A Genealogy of Sovereignty*, Cambridge: Cambridge University Press, 1995.

Bartlett, Robert, *The Making of Europe*, Princeton: Princeton University Press, 1993.

Bass, S., and M. Simula, "Independent Certification/Verification of Forest Management," background paper for the World Bank/WWF Alliance Workshop, Washington, D.C., 9–10 November 1999, *www-esd.worldbank. org/wwf/sim-bass.doc* (5/11/00).

Bayart, J.-F., S. Ellis, and B. Hibou, *The Criminalization of the State in Africa*, Oxford: James Currey, 1999.

Beck, Robert J., Anthony C. Arend, and Robert D. Vander Lugt, *International Rules: Approaches from International Law and International Relations*, New York and Oxford: Oxford University Press, 1996.

Bhagwati, Jagdish, "Trade and the Environment: The False Conflict?," in D. Zaelke, P. Orbuch, and R. F. Houseman (eds.), *Trade and the Environment: Law, Economics, and Policy*, Washington, D.C.: Island Press, 1993, pp. 159–90.

Biersteker, Thomas J., and Cynthia Weber (eds.), *State Sovereignty as a Social Construct*, Cambridge: Cambridge University Press, 1996.

Bin Laden, Osama, *fatwa* issued February 1998, "Jihad Is an Individual Duty," *Los Angeles Times*, 13 August 1998, B9.

  interview, *ABC News* report rebroadcast, 9 August 1998.

Blumental, W. Michael, "The World Economy and Technological Change," *Foreign Affairs*, 66 (1988), 529–50.

Bonacich, E., and R. Appelbaum, *Behind the Label: Inequality in the Los Angeles Apparel Industry*, Berkeley: University of California Press, 2000.

Botha, C., "Soldiers of Fortune or Whores of War? The Legal Position of Mercenaries with Specific Reference to South Africa," *Strategic Review for Southern Africa*, 15 (2) (1993), 75–91.

Boughton, James, *Silent Revolution: The International Monetary Fund, 1979–1989*, Washington, D.C.: International Monetary Fund, 2001.

Bourdieu, Pierre, *Language and Symbolic Power*, Cambridge, Mass.: Harvard University Press, 1991.

Bourdieu, Pierre, and Loic J. D. Wacquant, *An Invitation to Reflexive Sociology*, Chicago: University of Chicago Press, 1992.

Braithwaite, J., and P. Drahos, *Global Business Regulation*, Cambridge: Cambridge University Press, 2000.

Bratton, William, Joseph McCahery, Sol Picciotto, and Colin Scott (eds.), *International Regulatory Competition and Coordination: Perspectives on Economic Regulation in Europe and in the United States*, Oxford: Clarendon Press, 1996.

Braudel, Fernand, *Afterthoughts on Material Civilization and Capitalism*, Baltimore, Md.: Johns Hopkins University Press, 1977.

  The Perspective of the World Civilization and Capitalism: 15th–18th Century, vol. III, New York: Perennial Library, Harper and Row, 1986.

Bressand, Albert, Catherine Distler, and Kalypso Nicolaidis, "Networks at the Heart of the Service Economy," in Bressand and Nicolaidis (eds.), *Strategic Trends in Services*, New York: Ballinger, 1989, pp. 17–33.

Bressler, Fenton, *Interpol*, London: Mandarin, 1993.

Bromley, D. W. (ed.), *Making the Commons Work*, San Francisco: ICS Press, 1992.

Brown, Clarence J., "New Concepts for a Changing International Economy," *Washington Quarterly*, 11 (1) (1988).

Brown, Michael E., Sean Lynn-Jones, and Steven E. Miller, *The Perils of Anarchy: Contemporary Realism and International Security*, Cambridge, Mass.: MIT Press, 1995.

Bryans, M., B. Jones, and J. Gross Stein, "Mean Times. Humanitarian Action in Complex Political Emergencies: Stark Choices, Cruel Dilemmas," *Coming to Terms*, 1 (3) (January 1999), *www.care.ca*.

Bryant, Ralph, *Turbulent Waters: Cross-Border Finance and International Governance*, Washington, D.C.: Brookings Institution, forthcoming.

Bull, Hedley, *The Anarchical Society: A Study of Order in World Politics*, New York: Columbia University Press, 1977.

Burkhert, Walter, René Girard, and Jonathan Z. Smith, *Violent Origins: Ritual Killing and Cultural Formation*, edited by Robert G. Hamerton-Kelly, Stanford: Stanford University Press, 1987.

Burley, Anne-Marie, "Regulating the World: Multilateralism, International Law, and the Projection of the New Deal Regulatory State," in John G. Ruggie (ed.), *Multilateralism Matters*, New York: Columbia University Press, 1993, pp. 125–56.

Caldwell, D. J., "Ecolabeling and the Regulatory Framework: A Survey of Domestic and International Fora," prepared for the Consumer's Choice Council, Washington, D.C. (discussion draft), 30 October 1998, at *www.consumerscouncil.org/ccc/*.

Callaghy, Thomas M., "Globalization and Marginalization: Debt and the International Underclass," *Current History*, 26 (613) (November 1997), 392–96.

Camilleri, Joseph, and Jim Falk, *The End of Sovereignty?*, Cheltenham, UK: Edward Elgar, 1992.

Carr, E. H., *The Twenty Years' Crisis, 1919–1939*, New York: Harper and Row Publishers, 1964 [1946].

Cascio, J., G. Woodside, and P. Mitchell, *ISO 14000 Guide: The New International Environmental Management Standards*, New York: McGraw-Hill, 1996.

Castells, Manuel, "The Informational Economy and the New International Division of Labor," in Martin Carnoy, Manuel Castells, Stephen S. Cohen, and Fernando Henrique Cardoso (eds.), *The New Global Economy in the Information Age*, University Park, Penn.: Penn State University Press, 1993, pp. 15–43.

The Rise of the Network Society, Malden, Mass.: Blackwell, 1996.

Castells, Manuel, and Jeffrey Henderson, "Techno-economic Restructuring, Socio-political Processes and Spatial Transformation: A Global Perspective," in Henderson and Castells (eds.), *Global Restructuring and Territorial Development*, London: Sage, 1987, pp. 1–117.

Cerny, P. G., *The Changing Architecture of Politics*, London: Sage, 1990.

Chabal, P., and J.-P. Daloz, *Africa Works: Disorder as Political Instrument*, Oxford: James Currey, 1999.

Chatterjee, Partha, *The Nation and Its Fragments: Colonial and Postcolonial Histories*, Princeton, N.J.: Princeton University Press, 1993.

Cilliers, J., and P. Mason (eds.), *Peace, Profit or Plunder? The Privatisation of Security in War-Torn African Societies*, Halfway House, South Africa: Institute for Security Studies, 1999.

Clapham, C., *Africa and the International System: The Politics of State Survival*, Cambridge: Cambridge University Press, 1996.

Clapp, Jennifer, *Toxic Exports: The Transfer of Hazardous Wastes and Technologies from Rich to Poor Countries*, Ithaca, N.Y.: Cornell University Press, 2001.

Clary, Mike, "Suspect in Abortion Slayings Acts as Own Attorney at Trial," *Los Angeles Times*, 5 October 1994, A5.

Cleary, S., "Angola: A Case Study of Private Military Involvement," in Cilliers and Mason, *Peace, Profit or Plunder?*, pp. 141–74.

Clegg, Stewart R., *Modern Organizations*, London: Sage, 1990.

Cohen, Benjamin J., *The Geography of Money*, Ithaca, N.Y.: Cornell University Press, 1998.

Cooper, Richard N., *Economic Policy in an Interdependent World*, Cambridge, Mass.: MIT Press, 1986.

Council on Foreign Relations Independent Task Force, *Safeguarding Prosperity in a Global Financial System*, Washington, D.C.: Institute for International Economics, 1999.

Cox, Robert W., "Social Forces, States, and World Orders: Beyond International Relations Theory," in Cox with Timothy Sinclair, *Approaches to World Order*, Cambridge: Cambridge University Press, 1996, pp. 85–123.

Coy, Peter, Neil Gross, Silvia Sansoni, and Kevin Tilley, "R&D Scoreboard," *Business Week*, 3378 (27 June 1994), 78–103.

Cutler, A. Claire, "Artifice, Ideology, and Paradox: The Public/Private Distinction in International Law," *Review of International Political Economy*, 4 (2) (1997), 261–85.

"Critical Reflections on Westphalian Assumptions of International Law and Organization: A Crisis of Legitimacy," *Review of International Studies*, 27 (2) (2000), 133–50.

"Global Capitalism and Liberal Myths: Dispute Settlement in Private International Trade Relations," *Millennium: Journal of International Studies*, 24 (3) (Winter 1995), 377–97.

"Globalization, Law, and Transnational Corporations: A Deepening of Market Discipline," in Theodore Cohn, Stephen McBride, and David Wiseman (eds.), *Power in the Global Era: Grounding Globalization*, Basingstoke: Macmillan, 2000, pp. 53–66.

"The 'Grotian Tradition' in International Relations," *Review of International Studies*, 17 (1991), 41–65.

"Locating 'Authority' in the Global Political Economy," *International Studies Quarterly*, 43 (1) (March 1999), 59–81.

"Private Authority in International Trade Relations: The Case of Maritime Transport," in Cutler, Haufler, and Porter, *Private Authority and International Affairs*, pp. 283–329.

Private Power and Global Authority: Transnational Merchant Law and the Global Political Economy, Cambridge: Cambridge University Press, forthcoming.

"The Privatization of Global Governance and the New Law Merchant," in Héritier, *Common Goods*.

"Public Meets Private: The International Unification and Harmonization of Private International Trade Law," *Global Society*, 13 (1) (1999), 25–48.

Cutler, A. Claire, Virginia Haufler, and Tony Porter, "The Contours and Significance of Private Authority in International Affairs," in Cutler, Haufler, and Porter, *Private Authority and International Affairs*, pp. 333–76.

"Private Authority and International Affairs," in Cutler, Haufler, and Porter, *Private Authority and International Affairs*, pp. 3–28.

(eds.), *Private Authority and International Affairs*, Albany, N.Y.: SUNY Press, 1999.

Davis, Diana E. (ed.), "Chaos and Governance," *Political Power and Social Theory*, 13, Part IV: Scholarly Controversy, Stamford, Conn.: JAI Press, 1999.

Deibert, Ronald J., "Harold Innis and the Empire of Speed," *Review of International Studies*, 25 (1999), 273–89.

Dezalay, Yves, and Bryant Garth, *Dealing in Virtue: International Commercial Arbitration and the Construction of a Transnational Legal Order*, Chicago and London: University of Chicago Press, 1996.

Dicken, Peter, "The Roepke Lecture in Economic Geography. Global–Local Tensions: Firms and States in the Global Space-Economy," *Economic Geography*, 70 (2) (1994), 101–28.

Dombrowski, Peter, and Richard Mansbach, "From Sovereign States to Sovereign Markets?," working paper, Department of Political Science, Iowa State University, 1998.

Doremus, Paul N., William W. Keller, Louis W. Pauly, and Simon Reich, *The Myth of the Global Corporation*, Princeton, N.J.: Princeton University Press, 1998.

Dunning, John, *Globalization, Economic Restructuring and Development: The Sixth Raul Prebish Lecture*, Geneva: UNCTAD, 1994.

Multinational Enterprises and the Global Economy, Reading, Mass.: Addison-Wesley, 1993.

Dwyer, Jim, David Kocieniewski, Deidre Murphy, and Peg Tyre, *Two Seconds Under the Bomb. Terror Comes to America: The Conspiracy Behind the World Trade Center Bombing*, New York: Crown Publishers, 1994.

Economist, "The Global Firm: RIP," 6 February 1993, 69.

Eichengreen, Barry, *Toward a New International Financial Architecture*, Washington, D.C.: Institute for International Economics, 1999.

Evans, Bryan, "Technical and Scientific Elements of Forest Management Certification Programs," paper prepared for the conference on Economic, Social and Political Issues in Certification of Forest Management, University of Pertanian, Malaysia, 12–16 May 1996, at *www.forestry.ubc.ca/concert/evans.html*.

Evans, Peter, "The Eclipse of the State? Reflections on Stateness in an Era of Globalization," *World Politics*, 50 (1) (1997), 62–87.

Evans, P. B., H. Jacobson, and R. Putnam (eds.), *Double-Edged Diplomacy: International Bargaining and Domestic Politics*, Berkeley: University of California Press, 1993.

Evans, Peter B., Dietrich Rueschemeyer, and Theda Skocpol (eds.), *Bringing the State Back In*, Cambridge: Cambridge University Press, 1985.

Falk, Richard, *On Humane Governance*, University Park, Penn.: Penn State University Press, 1995.

Predatory Globalization: A Critique, Cambridge: Polity Press, 1999.

Feldstein, Martin, "Refocusing the IMF," *Foreign Affairs*, 77 (2) (March/April 1998), 20–32.

Fischer, Stanley, "On the Need for an International Lender of Last Resort," *Essays in International Economics*, No. 220, International Economics Section, Department of Economics, Princeton University, Princeton, N.J., November 2000.

Francis, D., "Mercenary Intervention in Sierra Leone: Providing National Security or International Exploitation?," *Third World Quarterly*, 20 (2) (April 1999), 319–38.

Friedman, R. B., "On the Concept of Authority in Political Philosophy," in Raz, *Authority*, pp. 56–91.

Friman, Richard, "Just Passing Through: Transit States and the Dynamics of Illicit Transshipment," *Transnational Organized Crime*, 1 (1) (Spring 1995), 65–83.

Gambetta, Diego, *The Sicilian Mafia: The Business of Private Protection*, Cambridge, Mass.: Harvard University Press, 1993.

Garai, Gabor, "Leveraging the Rewards of Strategic Alliances," *Journal of Business Strategy*, 20 (2) (1999), 40–43.

Garrett, Geoffrey, "Global Markets and National Politics: Collision Course or Virtuous Circle?," *International Organization*, 52 (4) (Autumn 1998), 787–824.

Gereffi, Gary, "Global Production Systems and Third World Development," in Barbara Stallings (ed.), *Global Change, Regional Response: The New International Context of Development*, New York: Cambridge University Press, 1995, pp. 100–42.

Giddens, Anthony, *The Consequences of Modernity*, Cambridge: Polity Press, 1990.

Gill, Stephen, "Globalization, Democratization, and the Politics of Indifference," in Mittelman, *Globalization*, pp. 205–28.

"Globalization, Market Civilization, and Disciplinary Neo-Liberalism," *Millennium: Journal of International Studies*, 24 (1995), 399–423.

"Structural Change and the Global Political Economy: Globalizing Elites and the Emerging World Order," in Yoshikazu Sakamoto (ed.), *Global Transformation: Challenges to the State System*, Tokyo: United Nations University Press, 1994, pp. 169–99.

Gilpin, Robert, *Global Political Economy*, Princeton, N.J.: Princeton University Press, 2001.

Girard, René, *The Scapegoat*, trans. by Yvonne Freccero, Baltimore, Md.: Johns Hopkins University Press, 1986.

Violence and the Sacred, trans. by Patrick Gregory, Baltimore, Md.: Johns Hopkins University Press, 1977.

Godson, Roy, "Political–Criminal Nexus: Overview," *Trends in Organized Crime*, 3 (1) (Fall 1997), 4–7.

Goldman, John J., "Defendants Given 25 Years to Life in New York Terror Plot," *Los Angeles Times*, 18 January 1996, A1.

Goldstein, Dr. Baruch, Letter to the Editor, *New York Times*, 30 June 1981.

Goldstein, Morris, "Strengthening the International Financial Architecture: Where Do We Stand?," Working Paper 00-8, Washington, D.C.: Institute for International Economics, 2000.

Gomes-Casseres, Benjamin, "Computers: Alliances and Industry Evolution," in David B. Yoffee (ed.), *Beyond Free Trade: Firms, Governments and Global Competition*, Boston: Harvard Business School Press, 1993, pp. 79–128.

Goodwin, Geoffrey L., "The Erosion of External Sovereignty?," in Ghita Ionescu (ed.), *Between Sovereignty and Integration*, New York: John Wiley and Sons, 1974, pp. 100–17.

Gordon, David M., "The Global Economy: New Edifice or Crumbling Foundations?," *New Left Review*, March–April 1988, 24–65.

Goshal, Sumantra, and Christopher A. Bartlett, "The Multinational Corporation as a Strategic Network," *Academy of Management Review*, 15 (1990), 603–25.

Graham, E. M., *Global Corporations and National Governments*, Washington, D.C.: Institute for International Economics, 1996.

Greven, Michael Th., and Louis W. Pauly (eds.), *Democracy Beyond the State? The European Dilemma and the Emerging Global Order*, Lanham, Md., and Toronto, Ont.: Rowman & Littlefield Publishers and University of Toronto Press, 2000.

Guehenno, Jean-Marie, "Asia May Offer a New Model of Politics," *International Herald Tribune*, 16 May 1994.

Haas, Ernst, *Beyond the Nation-State*, Stanford: Stanford University Press, 1964.

Hagedoorn, John, "Understanding the Role of Strategic Technology Partnering: Interorganizational Modes of Cooperation and Sectoral Differences," *Strategic Management Journal*, 14 (5) (1993), 371–85.

Haggard, Stephan, and Sylvia Maxfield, "The Political Economy of Financial Internationalization in the Developing World," *International Organization*, 50 (1) (1996), 35–68.

Hall, Rodney Bruce, "Moral Authority as a Power Resource," *International Organization*, 51 (4) (Autumn 1997), 591–622.

National Collective Identity: Social Constructs and International Systems, New York: Columbia University Press, 1999.

Harding, J., "The Mercenary Business: 'Executive Outcomes,'" *Review of African Political Economy*, 24 (71) (1997), 87–97.

Harvey, David, *The Condition of Postmodernity: An Enquiry into the Origins of Cultural Change*, Cambridge, Mass., and Oxford: Blackwell Publishers, 1990.

Hasenclever, Andreas, Peter Mayer, and Volker Rittberger, *Theories of International Regimes*, Cambridge: Cambridge University Press, 1997.

Haufler, Virginia, "Crossing the Boundary Between Public and Private: International Regimes and Non-State Actors," in Rittberger with Mayer, *Regime Theory and International Relations*, pp. 94–111.

Public Role for the Private Sector: Industry Self-Regulation in a Global Economy, Washington, D.C.: Carnegie Endowment for International Peace, 2001.

Heilbroner, Robert, "Economics as Ideology," in Warren J. Samuels (ed.), *Economics as Discourse: An Analysis of the Language of Economists*, Boston: Kluwer, 1990, pp. 101–16.

Held, David, and Anthony McGrew, "Globalization and the Liberal Democratic State," *Government and Opposition*, 28 (2) (1993), 261–88.

Held, David, Anthony McGrew, D. Goldblatt, and J. Perraton, *Global Transformations*, Cambridge: Polity Press, 1999.

Helleiner, Eric, *States and the Reemergence of Global Finance*, Ithaca, N.Y.: Cornell University Press, 1994.

Héritier, Adrienne (ed.), *Common Goods: Reinventing European and International Governance*, Boulder, Colo.: Rowman & Littlefield, 2002.

Hirst, Paul, and Graham E. Thompson, "The Problem of Globalization: International Economic Relations, National Economic Management and the Formation of Trading Blocs," *Economy and Society*, 21 (4) (1992), 357–96.

Hobsbawm, Eric J., *The Age of Extremes: A History of the World, 1914–1991*, New York: Pantheon Books, 1994.

Hoffman, Bruce, *"Holy Terror": The Implications of Terrorism Motivated by a Religious Imperative*, Santa Monica, Cal.: RAND Corporation Papers, 1993.

Terrorism Targeting: Tactics, Trends, and Potentialities, Santa Monica, Cal.: RAND Corporation Papers, 1992.

Hoffman, Mark, "Critical Theory and the Inter-Paradigm Debate," *Millennium: Journal of International Studies*, 16 (2) (1987), 231–49.

Holland, Kelley, and Paula Dwyer, "Technobanking Takes Off," *Business Week*, 3399 (18 November 1994), 52–53.

Hoogvelt, A., *Globalization and the Postcolonial World: The New Political Economy of Development*, Baltimore, Md.: Johns Hopkins University Press, 1997.

Horn, Norbert, and Clive Schmitthoff (eds.), *The Transnational Law of International Commercial Transactions*, Deventer, Netherlands: Kluwer, 1982.

Horsman, Mathew, and Andrew Marshall, *After the Nation-State: Citizens, Tribalism and the New World Disorder*, London: Harper-Collins, 1994.

Hurd, Ian, "Legitimacy and Authority in International Politics," *International Organization*, 53 (2) (Spring 1999), 379–408.

Hurrell, Andrew, "International Society and the Study of Regimes: A Reflective Approach," in Rittberger with Mayer, *Regime Theory and International Relations*, pp. 49–72.

Ikenberry, G. John, *After Victory*, Princeton, N.J.: Princeton University Press, 2000.

"Rethinking the Origins of American Hegemony," *Political Science Quarterly*, 104 (3) (1989), 375–400.

International Organization, P. Haas (ed.), Special Issue: Knowledge, Power, and International Policy Coordination, 46 (1) (1992).

Special Issue: Legalization of World Politics, 54 (3) (Summer 2000).

Jameson, Frederic, *Postmodernism or the Cultural Logic of Late Capitalism*, Durham: Duke University Press, 1991.

Jankowski, J. E. Jr., *National Patterns of R&D Resources*, NSF 92-330, Washington, D.C.: National Science Foundation, 1992.

Jarillo, J. Carlos, "On Strategic Networks," *Strategic Management Journal*, 9 (1988), 31–41.

Johns, Fleur, "The Invisibility of the Transnational Corporation: An Analysis of International Law and Legal Theory," *Melbourne University Law Review*, 19 (1994), 893–921.

Jones, Candace, and William S. Hesterly, "A Network Organization: Alternative Governance Form or a Glorified Market?," presented at the Academy of Management meeting, Atlanta, Ga., August 1993.

Juergensmeyer, Mark, *The New Cold War? Religious Nationalism Confronts the Secular State*, Berkeley: University of California Press, 1993.

Terror in the mind of God: The Global Rise of Religious Violence, Berkeley: University of California Press, 2000.

"Thinking Globally About Religion," in Juergensmeyer (ed.), *Global Religion: A handbook*, New York: Oxford University Press, forthcoming.

"The Worldwide Rise of Religious Nationalism," *Journal of International Affairs*, 50 (1) (Summer 1996), 1–20.

Kahler, Miles, *International Institutions and the Political-Economy of Integration*, Washington, D.C.: Brookings Institution, 1995.

"Inventing International Relations: International Relations Theory After 1945," in Michael W. Doyle and G. John Ikenberry (eds.), *New Thinking in International Relations Theory*, Boulder, Colo.: Westview Press, 1997, pp. 20–53.

Kapstein, Ethan B., "Workers and the World Economy," *Foreign Affairs*, 75 (3) (May/June 1996), 16–37.

Keck, Mary, and Kathryn Sikkink, *Activists Across Borders: Advocacy Networks in International Politics*, Ithaca, N.Y.: Cornell University Press, 1998.

Kennedy, Paul, *Preparing for the Twenty-First Century*, New York: Random House, 1993.

Keohane, Robert O., *After Hegemony: Cooperation and Discord in the World Political Economy*, Princeton, N.J.: Princeton University Press, 1984.

"International Institutions: Two Approaches," in Keohane, *International Institutions and State Power*, pp. 158–79.

(ed.), *International Institutions and State Power: Essays in International Relations Theory*, Boulder, Colo.: Westview Press, 1989.

"Neoliberal Institutionalism: A Perspective on World Politics," in Keohane, *International Institutions and State Power*, pp. 1–20.

"Sovereignty, Interdependence, and International Institutions," in Linda B. Miller and Michael Joseph Smith (eds.), *Ideas and Ideals: Essays on Politics in Honor of Stanley Hoffman*, Boulder, Colo.: Westview Press, 1993, pp. 91–107.

Keohane, Robert O., and Joseph S. Nye, *Power and Interdependence*, Boston: Little Brown, 1977, Glenview, Ill.: Scott Foresman and Company, 2nd edn., 1989.

Khomeini, Imam [Ayatollah], *Collection of Speeches, Position Statements*, Arlington, Va.: Joint Publications Research Service, 1979.

Islam and Revolution: Writings and Declarations, trans. and annotated by Hamid Algar, London: Routledge and Kegan Paul, 1985.

Kindleberger, Charles, *The World in Depression, 1929–1939*, Berkeley: University of California Press, 1986.

Kobrin, Stephen J., "The Architecture of Globalization: State Sovereignty in a Networked Global Economy," in John Dunning (ed.), *Governments, Globalization and International Business*, Oxford and New York: Oxford University Press, 1997, pp. 146–71.

"Electronic Cash and the End of National Markets," *Foreign Policy*, 107 (Summer 1977), 65–77.

"An Empirical Analysis of the Determinants of Global Integration," *Strategic Management Journal*, 12 (1991), 17–31.

"Neo-Medievalism and the Post-Modern World Economy," *Journal of International Affairs*, 51 (2) (Spring 1998), 361–87.

"You Can't Declare Cyberspace National Territory: Economic Policy Making in the Digital Age," in Don Tapscott, Alex Lowy, and David Ticoll (eds.), *Blueprint to the Digital Economy*, New York: McGraw-Hill, 1998, pp. 355–70.

Konici, Steve, "Covisint Books Impressive Procurement Volume," Information-week.com, 18 July 2001 (*www.informationweek.com*).

Korten, D., *Globalizing Civil Society: Reclaiming Our Right to Power*, New York: Seven Stories Press, 1998.

Krasner, Stephen D. (ed.), *International Regimes*, Ithaca, N.Y.: Cornell University Press, 1983.

"Power Politics, Institutions, and Transnational Relations," in Risse-Kappen, *Bringing Transnational Relations Back In*, pp. 257–79.

Sovereignty: Organized Hypocrisy, Princeton, N.J.: Princeton University Press, 1999.

"Structural Causes and Regime Consequences: Regimes as Intervening Variables," in Krasner, *International Regimes*, pp. 1–22.

"Westphalia and All That," in Judith Goldstein and Robert O. Keohane, *Ideas and Foreign Policy: Beliefs, Institutions, and Political Change*, Ithaca, N.Y., and London: Cornell University Press, 1993, pp. 235–64.

Kratochwil, Friedrich, "Regimes, Interpretation, and the 'Science' of Politics: A Reappraisal," *Millennium: Journal of International Relations*, 17 (2) (1988), 263–84.

Rules, Norms, and Decisions: On the Conditions of Practical and Legal Reasoning in International Relations and Domestic Affairs, Cambridge: Cambridge University Press, 1989.

"Of Systems, Boundaries, and Territoriality: An Inquiry into the Formation of the State System," *World Politics*, 39 (1) (1986), 27–52.

Kratochwil, Friedrich, and John G. Ruggie, "International Organization: A State of the Art on the Art of the State," *International Organization*, 40 (1986), 753–75.

Krieger, Leonard, "The Idea of Authority in the West," *American Historical Review*, 82 (2) (April 1977), 249–70.

Krugman, Paul R., "A Global Economy Is Not the Wave of the Future," *Financial Executive*, March–April 1992, 10–13.

The Return of Depression Economics, New York: Norton, 1999.

Laurence, Henry, *Money Rules: The New Politics of Finance in Britain and Japan*, Ithaca, N.Y.: Cornell University Press, 2001.

Leatherman, J., R. Pagnucco, and J. Smith, "International Institutions and Transnational Social Movement Organizations: Transforming Sovereignty, Anarchy, and Global Governance," Working Paper 5:WP3, Kroc Institute for International Peace Studies, University of Notre Dame, August 1994.

Lee, Thomas H., and Proctor P. Reed (eds.), *National Interests in an Age of Global Technology*, Washington, D.C.: National Academy Press, 1991.

Levy, M. A., O. R. Young, and M. Zürn, "The Study of International Regimes," *European Journal of International Relations*, 3 (1) (1995), 267–330.

Linklater, Andrew, "The Question of the Next Stage in International Relations Theory: A Critical-Theoretical Point of View," *Millennium: Journal of International Studies*, 21 (1) (1992), 77–98.

Lipschutz, Ronnie D., *After Authority: War, Peace and Global Politics in the 21st Century*, Albany, N.Y.: SUNY Press, 2000.

"Doing Well by Doing Good? Transnational Regulatory Campaigns, Social Activism, and Impacts on State Sovereignty," in John Montgomery and Nathan Glazer (eds.), *Challenges to Sovereignty: How Governments Respond*, New Brunswick, N.J.: Transaction, 2002, pp. 291–320.

"From Local Knowledge and Practice to Global Governance," in M. Hewson and T. J. Sinclair (eds.), *Approaches to Global Governance Theory*, Albany, N.Y.: SUNY Press, 1999, pp. 259–83.

"Reconstructing World Politics: The Emergence of Global Civil Society," *Millennium: Journal of International Studies*, 21 (3) (Winter 1992), 389–420.

"Reconstructing World Politics: The Emergence of Global Civil Society," in Jeremy Larkins and Rick Fawn (eds.), *International Society After the Cold War*, London: Macmillan, 1996, pp. 101–31.

"Why Is There No International Forestry Law? An Examination of International Forestry Regulation, Both Public and Private," *UCLA Journal of Environmental Law and Policy*, 19 (1) (2000/01), 155–82.

Lipschutz, Ronnie D., with Judith Mayer, *Global Civil Society and Global Environmental Governance*, Albany, N.Y.: SUNY Press, 1996.

Lipsey, Richard G., and Cliff Bekar, "A Structuralist View of Technical Change and Economic Growth," in *Bell Canada Papers on Economic and Public Policy*, vol. 3, Kingston, Ont.: John Deutsch Institute, Queen's University, 1995, pp. 9–75.

Lotspeich, Richard, "Crime in the Transition Economies," *Europe–Asia Studies*, 47 (4) (June 1995), 555–93.

Lukes, Stephen, "Perspectives on Authority," in Raz, *Authority*, pp. 203–17.

Lyon, David, *Postmodernity*, Minneapolis: University of Minnesota Press, 1994.

Malan, M., "Can Private Peacekeeping Deliver 'Executive Outcomes'?," *Indicator SA*, 1 (2) (1997), 12–15.

"Security Firms or Private Armies?," *The Star* (Johannesburg), 30 August 1996.

Malanczuk, Peter (ed.), *Akehurst's Modern Introduction to International Law*, 7th edn. revised, London and New York: Routledge, 1997.

Malone, Thomas W., and John F. Rockart, "How Will Information Technology Reshape Organizations? Computers as Coordination Technology," in Stephen Bradley, Jerry A. Hausman, and Richard L. Nolan (eds.), *Globalization, Technology, and Competition: The Fusion of Technology and Computers in the 1990s*, Boston: Harvard Business School Press, 1993, pp. 37–56.

Markandya, Anil, "Eco-labeling: An Introduction and Review," in Simonetta Zarrilli, Veena Jha, and Rene Vossenaar (eds.), *Eco-labeling and International Trade*, New York: St. Martin's Press, 1997.

Marshall, Alfred, *Principles of Economics*, 8th edn., London: Macmillan, 1961.

Marshall, T. H., *The Right to Welfare and Other Essays*, New York: Free Press, 1981.

Martin, D., and Johnson, P., *The Struggle for Zimbabwe*, Harare: Zimbabwe Publishing House, 1981.

Mathews, Jessica, "The Changing Role of the State," transcript from the 75th Anniversary Symposium of a keynote address at the Harvard School of Public Health, *www.hsph.harvard.edu/digest/mathews.html*.

McCloskey, Deirdre N., *The Rhetoric of Economics*, Madison: University of Wisconsin Press, 1998.

McKeown, Timothy J., "Hegemonic Stability Theory and Nineteenth-Century Tariff Levels in Europe," *International Organization*, 37 (1) (Winter 1983), 73–91.

McMahon, Darrin, *Enemies of the Enlightenment: The French Counter-Enlightenment and the Making of Modernity*, New York: Oxford University Press, 2001.

Mead, W. R., "Trains, Planes, and Automobiles: The End of the Postmodern Moment," *World Policy Journal*, 12 (4) (Winter 1995/96), 13–32.

Meidinger, Errol E., "'Private' Environmental Regulation, Human Rights, and Community," *Buffalo Environmental Law Journal*, 2000, *www.ublaw.buffalo.edu/fas/meidinger/hrec.pdf* (5/11/00).

Mengisteab, K., and B. Logan, *Beyond Economic Liberalization in Africa: Structural Adjustment and the Alternatives*, London: Zed Books, 1995.

Michalet, Charles-Albert, "Strategic Partnerships and the Changing Internationalization Process," in Mytelka, *Strategic Partnerships*, pp. 35–50.

"Transnational Corporations and the Changing International Economic System," *Transnational Corporations*, 3 (1) (1994), 6–22.

Migdal, Joel S., *Strong Societies and Weak States*, Princeton N.J.: Princeton University Press, 1988.

Miles, Raymond, and Charles C. Snow, "Organizations: New Concepts for New Norms," *California Management Review*, 27 (3) (1986), 62–73.

Milgrom, Paul, Douglass North, and Barry Weingast, "The Role of Institutions in the Revival of Trade: The Law Merchant, Private Judges, and the Champagne Fairs," *Economics and Politics*, 2 (1) (1990), 1–23.

Milner, Helen, "The Assumption of Anarchy in International Relations Theory: A Critique," *Review of International Studies*, 17 (1) (1991), 67–85.

Mishra, Ramesh, *Globalization and the Welfare State*, Cheltenham, UK: Edward Elgar, 1999.

Mitchell, Ronald B., "Sources of Transparency: Information Systems in International Regimes," *International Studies Quarterly*, 42 (1998), 109–30.

Mitrany, D., *A Working Peace System*, Chicago: Quadrangle Books, 1966.

Mittelman, James, "The Dynamics of Globalization," in Mittelman, *Globalization*, pp. 1–20.

(ed.), *Globalization: Critical Reflections. International Political Economy Yearbook*, vol. 9, Boulder, Colo.: Lynne Rienner, 1996.

The Globalization Syndrome: Transformation and Resistance, Princeton, N.J.: Princeton University Press, 2000.

Mokyr, Joel, *The Lever of Riches: Technological Creativity and Economic Progress*, New York: Oxford University Press, 1990.

Murphy, Craig N., *International Organization and Industrial Change: Global Governance Since 1850*, New York: Oxford University Press, 1994.

"Seeing Women, Recognizing Gender, Recasting International Relations," *International Organization*, 50 (3) (Summer 1996), 513–38.

Murphy, Kim, "Have the Islamic Militants Turned to a New Battlefront in the US?," *Los Angeles Times*, 3 March 1993, A20.

Mytelka, Lynn Krieger, "Crisis, Technological Change and the Strategic Alliance," in Mytelka, *Strategic Partnerships*, pp. 7–34.

(ed.), *Strategic Partnerships: States, Firms and International Competition*, Rutherford, N.J.: Fairleigh-Dickinson University Press, 1991.

Mytelka, Lynn Krieger, and Michel Delapierre, "Strategic Partnerships, Knowledge-Based Networks and the State," in Cutler, Haufler, and Porter, *Private Authority and International Affairs*, pp. 129–49.

Nathan, L., "Lethal Weapons: Why Africa Needs Alternatives to Hired Guns," *Track Two*, 6 (2) (August 1997), 10–12.

Negroponte, Nicholas, *Being Digital*, 1st edn., New York: Knopf, 1995.

Nohria, Nitin, and Robert C. Eccles, *Networks and Organizations: Structure, Form and Action*, Boston: Harvard Business School Press, 1992.

Nye, Joseph S. Jr., *Bound to Lead: The Changing Nature of American Power*, New York: Basic Books, 1990.

O'Brien, Richard, *Global Financial Integration: The End of Geography*, London: Pinter, 1992.

O'Brien, Robert, Anne Marie Goetz, Jan Aart Scholte, and Marc Williams (eds.), *Contesting Global Governance: Multilateral Economic Institutions and Global Social Movements*, Cambridge: Cambridge University Press, 2000.

Ohmae, Kenichi, *The Borderless World*, New York: Harper Business, 1990.

The End of the Nation-State, New York: Free Press, 1995.

Onuf, Nicholas, and Frank F. Clink, "Anarchy, Authority, and Rule," *International Studies Quarterly*, 33 (2) (1989), 149–73.

Organization for Economic Cooperation and Development [OECD], *Technology and the Economy: The Key Relationship*, Paris: OECD, 1992.

Transborder Data Flow Contracts in the Wider Framework Mechanisms for Privacy Protection in Global Networks, Paris: OECD, 2000.

Osborn, Richard N., and C. Christopher Baughn, "Forms of Interorganizational Governance for Multinational Alliances," *Academy of Management Journal*, 33 (1990), 503–19.

Ostrom, E., *Governing the Commons: The Evolution of Institutions for Collective Action*, Cambridge: Cambridge University Press, 1990.

Pandit, S. K., "Wired to the Rest of the World," *Financial Times*, 10 January 1995, 12.

Panitch, Leo, "Rethinking the Role of the State in an Era of Globalization," in Mittelman, *Globalization*, pp. 83–113.

Parker, Martin, "Post-modern Organizations or Postmodern Theory?," *Organization Studies*, 13 (1) (1992), 1–17.

Parker, William N., *Europe, America and the Wider World: Essays on the Economic History of Western Capitalism*, Cambridge: Cambridge University Press, 1984.

Pauly, Louis W., "Capital Mobility and the New Global Order," in Stubbs and Underhill, *Political Economy and the Changing World Order*, pp. 119–28.

"Capital Mobility, State Autonomy, and Political Legitimacy," *Journal of International Affairs*, 48 (2) (Winter 1995), 369–88.

Who Elected the Bankers? Surveillance and Control in the World Economy, Ithaca, N.Y.: Cornell University Press, 1997.

Pauly, Louis W., and Simon Reich, "National Structures and Multinational Corporate Behavior: Enduring Differences in the Age of Globalization," *International Organization*, 51 (1) (1997), 1–30.

Pech, K., "Bill to Crack Down on SA Mercenaries," *The Star* (Johannesburg), 19 September 1997.

"Executive Outcomes: A Corporate Quest," in Cilliers and Mason, *Peace, Profit or Plunder?*, pp. 81–110.

Pech, K., and D. Beresford, "Africa's New-Look Dogs of War," *Mail & Guardian* (Johannesburg), 24 January 1997.

Pech, K., W. Boot, and A. Eveleth, "South African Dogs of War in Congo," *Mail & Guardian* (Johannesburg), 28 August 1998, 7.

Picciotto, Sol, *International Business Taxation: A Study in the Internationalization of Business Regulation*, London: Weidenfeld and Nicolson, 1992.

Picciotto, Sol, and Ruth Mayne (eds.), *Regulating International Business: Beyond Liberalization*, Houndmills and Basingstoke: Macmillan, 1999.

Poggi, Gianfranco, *The State: Its Nature, Development and Prospects*, Stanford: Stanford University Press, 1990.

Polanyi, Karl, *The Great Transformation*, Boston: Beacon Press, 1957 [1944].

della Porta, Donatella, and Alberto Vannucci, *Corrupt Exchanges*, New York: Aldine De Gruyter, 1999.

Porter, Michael, *The Competitive Advantage of States*, New York: Free Press, 1990.

Powell, Walter W., "Neither Market Nor Hierarchy: Network Forms of Organization," *Research in Organization Behavior*, 12 (1990), 295–316.

Princen, T., and M. Finger (eds.), *Environmental NGOs in World Politics*, London: Routledge, 1994.

Raz, Joseph (ed.), *Authority*, Washington Square, N.Y.: New York University Press and Oxford: Basil Blackwell, 1990.

Reich, Robert B., *The Work of Nations*, New York: Alfred A. Knopf, 1991.

Risse-Kappen, Thomas (ed.), *Bringing Transnational Relations Back In: Non-State Actors, Domestic Structures and International Institutions*, Cambridge: Cambridge University Press, 1995.

Rittberger, Volker, with Peter Mayer (eds.), *Regime Theory and International Relations*, Oxford: Clarendon Press, 1993.

Rochester, Martin, "The Rise and Fall of International Organization as a Field of Study," *International Organization*, 40 (1986), 777–813.

"The United Nations in the New World Order: Reviving the Theory and Practice of International Organization," in Charles Kegley (ed.), *Controversies in International Relations Theory: Realism and the Neoliberal Challenge*, New York: St. Martin's Press, 1995, pp. 199–222.

Rodrik, Dani, *Has Globalization Gone Too Far?*, Washington, D.C.: Institute for International Economics, 1997.

Rosecrance, Richard, A. Alexandroff, W. Koehler, J. Kroll, S. Laquer, and J. Stocker, "Whither Interdependence," *International Organization*, 31 (3) (1977), 385–424.

Rosenau, James, *Along the Domestic–Foreign Frontier: Exploring Governance in a Turbulent World*, Cambridge: Cambridge University Press, 1997.

"Governance, Order, and Change in World Politics," in Rosenau and Czempiel, *Governance Without Government*, pp. 1–29.

Turbulence in World Politics, Princeton, N.J.: Princeton University Press, 1990.

Rosenau, James N., and Ernst-Otto Czempiel (eds.), *Governance Without Government: Order and Change in World Politics*, Cambridge: Cambridge University Press, 1992.

Rubin, E., "Saving Sierra Leone, at a Price," *New York Times*, 4 February 1999.

Ruggie, John Gerard, "Continuity and Transformation in the World Polity: Toward a Neorealist Synthesis," *World Politics*, 35 (2) (January 1983), 261–85.

"Territoriality and Beyond: Problematizing modernity in International Relations," *International Organisation*, 47 (1) (1993), 139–74.

Winning the piece, New York: Columbia University Press, 1996.

Russel, A., *Big Men, Little People: Encounters in Africa*, Basingstoke: Macmillan, 1999.

Sassen, Saskia, *Denationalization: Economy and Polity in a Global Digital Age*, under contract with Princeton University Press, September 2003.

　The Global City: New York, London, Tokyo, Princeton, N.J.: Princeton University Press, 2001 [1991].

　"Global Financial Centers," *Foreign Affairs*, 78 (1) (January/February 1999), 75–87.

　Losing Control? Sovereignty in an Age of Globalization, 1995 Columbia University Leonard Hastings Schoff Memorial Lectures, New York: Columbia University Press, 1996.

Schelling, Thomas, *Arms and Influence*, New Haven and London: Yale University Press, 1967.

Scherer, F. M., "Economies of Scale and Industrial Concentration," in Harvey Goldschmid, H. Michael Mann, and J. Fred Weston (eds.), *Industrial Concentration: The New Learning*, Boston: Little Brown and Company, 1974, pp. 16–54.

Scheuerman, William, "Economic Globalization and the Rule of Law," *Constellations: An International Journal of Critical and Democratic Theory*, 6 (1) (March 1999), 3–25.

Schoofs, Mark, and Michal Waltholtsz, "New Regimen: AIDS-Drug Price War Breaks Out in Africa," *Wall Street Journal*, 7 March 2001.

Scott, J., *Seeing Like a State*, New Haven: Yale University Press, 1998.

Serrano, Richard A., "McVeigh Speaks Out, Receives Death Sentence," *Los Angeles Times*, 15 August 1997, A1.

Shearer, D., *Private Armies and Military Intervention*, Adelphi Paper No. 316, New York: Oxford University Press, 1998.

Sheppard, Simon, "Foot Soldiers of the New World Order: The Rise of the Corporate Military," *New Left Review*, 228 (March/April 1998), 128–38.

Shklar, Judith, *Legalism*, Cambridge, Mass.: Harvard University Press, 1964.

Skocpol, Theda, "Bringing the State Back In: Strategies of Analysis in Current Research," in Evans, Reuschemeyer, and Skocpol, *Bringing the State Back In*, pp. 3–37.

Smith, J., C. Chatfield, and R. Pagnucco (eds.), *Transnational Social Movements and Global Politics: Solidarity Beyond the State*, Syracuse, N.Y.: Syracuse University Press, 1997.

Smith, Michael Joseph, *Realist Thought from Weber to Kissinger*, Baton Rouge and London: Louisiana State University Press, 1986.

Sodersten, Bo, *International Economics*, 2nd edn., New York: St. Martin's Press, 1980.

de Sousa Santos, Boaventura, *Toward a New Common Sense: Law Science and Politics in the Paradigmatic Transition*, New York and London: Routledge, 1995.

Spruyt, Hendrik, *The Sovereign State and Its Competitors*, Princeton, N.J.: Princeton University Press, 1994.

Stewart, Thomas A., "A New 500 for the New Economy," *Fortune*, 15 May 1995, 168–78.

Stiglitz, Joseph, "Back to Basics: Policies and Strategies for Enhanced Growth and Equity in Post-Crisis East Asia," delivered 19 July 1999, Shangri-la Hotel, Bangkok, Thailand.

"The Insider: What I Learned at the World Economic Crisis," *New Republic*, 17 & 24 April 2000, 56–60.

"Must Financial Crises Be This Frequent and This Painful?," McKay Lecture, University of Pittsburgh, Pittsburgh, Penn., 23 September 1998, *www.worldbank.org/html/extdr/extme/js-092398/*.

"Whither Reform? Ten Years of the Transition," keynote address for the World Bank Annual Bank Conference on Development Economics, Washington, D.C., 28–30 April 1999.

Stopford, John M., and Susan Strange, *Rival States, Rival Firms: Competition for World Market Shares*, Cambridge: Cambridge University Press, 1991.

Strange, Susan, "*Cave! Hic dragones*: A Critique of Regime Analysis," in Krasner, *International Regimes*, pp. 337–54.

Mad Money, Ann Arbor, Mich.: University of Michigan Press, 1998.

The Retreat of the State: The Diffusion of Power in the World Economy, Cambridge: Cambridge University Press, 1996.

"Territory, State, Authority, and Economy: A New Realist Ontology of Global Political Economy," in Robert W. Cox (ed.), *The New Realisms: Perspectives on Multilateralism and World Order*, Tokyo: United Nations University Press, 1997, pp. 3–19.

Streeten, Paul, *Interdependence and Integration of the World Economy: The Role of States*, New York: Oxford University Press, 1992.

Stubbs, Richard, and Geoffrey Underhill (eds.), *Political Economy and the Changing World Order*, 2nd edn., Oxford and New York: Oxford University Press, 2000.

Szaz, A., *Ecopopulism*, Minneapolis: University of Minnesota Press, 1994.

Taylor, I., and P. Williams, "South African Foreign Policy and the Great Lakes Crisis: African Renaissance Meets Vagabondage Politique?," *African Affairs*, 100 (399) (April 2001), 265–86.

Terpstra, Vern, and Bernard L. Simonin, "Strategic Alliances in the Triad: An Exploratory Study," *Journal of International Marketing*, 1 (1993), 4–25.

Thomas, George M., et al. (eds.), *Institutional Structure: Constituting State, Society and the Individual*, Newbury Park, Cal.: Sage, 1987.

Thomson, Janice E., *Mercenaries, Pirates and Sovereigns*, Princeton, N.J.: Princeton University Press, 1996.

Thorelli, Hans B., "Networks: Between Markets and Hierarchies," *Strategic Management Journal*, 7 (1986), 37–51.

Thoumi, Francisco E., *Political Economy and Illegal Drugs in Colombia*, Boulder, Colo.: Lynne Rienner, 1995.

Tichy, Noel M., Michael L. Tushman, and Charles Fombrun, "Social Network Analysis for Organizations," *Academy of Management Review*, 4 (4) (1979), 507–19.

Tilly, Charles, "War Making and State Making as Organized Crime," in Evans, Rueschemeyer, and Skocpol, *Bringing the State Back In*, pp. 169–91.

Turbiville, Graham H., *Mafia in Uniform: The Criminalization of the Russian Armed Forces*, Fort Leavenworth, Kan.: Foreign Military Studies Office, 1996.

"Organized Crime and the Russian Armed Forces," *Transnational Organized Crime*, 1 (4) (Winter 1995), 57–104.

Twining, William, "Globalization and Legal Theory: Some Local Implications," *Current Legal Problems*, 49 (1996), 1–42.

Underhill, Geoffrey, "Keeping Governments out of Politics: Transnational Securities Markets, Regulatory Cooperation, and Political Legitimacy," *Review of International Studies*, 21 (3) (1995), 251–78.

United Kingdom, Foreign and Commonwealth Office, *Global Citizenship: Business and Society in a Changing World*, London: Foreign and Commonwealth Office, 2001.

United Nations Conference on Trade and Development [UNCTAD], "Trends in Foreign Direct Investment," TD/B/ITNC/2, UNCTAD: Geneva, 1995.

World Investment Report: 1993, New York: United Nations, 1994.

World Investment Report: 1999, New York and Geneva: United Nations, 1999.

United States Congress, Office of Technology Assessment, *Multinationals and the National Interest: Playing by Different Rules*, OTA-ITE-569, Washington, D.C.: US Government Printing Office, 1993.

Multinationals and the US Technology Base, OTA-ITE-612, Washington, D.C.: US. Government Printing Office, 1994.

Varese, Federico, *The Russian Mafia*, Oxford: Oxford University Press, 2001.

Vogel, D., *Trading Up: Consumer and Environmental Regulation in a Global Economy*, Cambridge, Mass.: Harvard University Press, 1995.

Vogel, S. K., *Freer Markets, More Rules: Regulatory Reform in Advanced Industrial Countries*, Ithaca, N.Y.: Cornell University Press, 1996.

Wade, Robert, "Globalization and Its Limits: Reports of the Death of the National Economy Are Greatly Exaggerated," in S. Berger and R. Dore (eds.), *National Diversity and Global Capitalism*, Ithaca, N.Y.: Cornell University Press, 1996, pp. 60–88.

Wade, Robert, and Frank Veneroso, "The Asian Crisis: The High Debt Model Versus the Wall Street–Treasury–IMF Complex," *New Left Review*, 228 (March/April 1998), 3–24.

Walker, R. B. J., *Inside/Outside: International Relations as Political Theory*, Cambridge: Cambridge University Press, 1993.

Wallerstein, Immanuel, *After Liberalism*, New York: New Press, 1995.

Walzer, Michael, "Liberalism and the Art of Separation," *Political Theory*, 12 (3) (1984), 315–30.

Wapner, P., *Environmental Activism and World Civic Politics*, Albany, N.Y.: SUNY Press, 1996.

Weber, Cynthia, *Simulating Sovereignty: Intervention, the State and Symbolic Exchange*, Cambridge: Cambridge University Press, 1995.

Weber, Max, "Politics as a Vocation," in H. H. Gerth and C. Wright Mills (eds.), *From Max Weber: Essays in Sociology*, London: Routledge & Kegan Paul, 1948, pp. 77–128.

Weinberg, S., *Last of the Pirates: The Search for Bob Denard*, London: Jonathan Cape, 1994.

Weiss, Linda, *The Myth of the Powerless State*, Ithaca, N.Y.: Cornell University Press, 1998.

Wellman, Barry, and S. D. Berkowitz, *Social Structures: A Network Approach*, Cambridge: Cambridge University Press, 1988.

Willetts, Peter (ed.), *"The Conscience of the World": The Influence of Non-Governmental Organizations in the UN System*, Washington, D.C.: Brookings Institution, 1996.

Williams, Phil, "Transnational Criminal Organizations and International Security," *Survival*, 36 (Spring 1994), 96–113.

"Transnational Criminal Organizations: Strategic Alliances," *Washington Quarterly*, 18 (Winter 1995), 57–72.

Williamson, Oliver E., "Comparative Economic Organization: The Analysis of Discrete Structural Alternatives," *Administrative Science Quarterly*, 36 (1991), 269–97.

Winer, Jonathan, "International Crime in the New Geopolitics: A Core Threat to Democracy," in W. F. McDonald (ed.), *Crime and Law Enforcement in the Global Village*, Cincinnati, Ohio: Anderson, 1997, pp. 41–64.

Wolf, Martin, "Globalization and the State," *Financial Times*, 18 September 1995, 22.

Wright, Robin, "Prophetic 'Terror 2000' Mapped Evolving Threat," *Los Angeles Times*, 9 August 1998, A16.

Wriston, Walter B., *The Twilight of Sovereignty*, New York: Charles Scribners and Sons, 1992.

Young, I. M., *Justice and the Politics of Difference*, Princeton, N.J.: Princeton University Press, 1990.

Zacher, Mark W., "The Decaying Pillars of the Westphalian Temple: Implications for International Order and Governance," in Rosenau and Czempiel, *Governance Without Government*, pp. 58–101.

Zacher, Mark W., with Brent Sutton, *Governing Global Networks: International Regimes for Transportation and Communications*, Cambridge: Cambridge University Press, 1996.

Zeskind, Leonard, *The "Christian Identity" Movement: Analyzing Its Theological Rationalization for Racist and Anti-Semitic Violence*, New York: Division of Church and Society of the National Council of the Churches of Christ in the USA, 1986.

Index

Abacha, Sani, 178
Abouhalima, Mahmud, 143–6, 150
Acheson, Donald, 191
Afghanistan, 141, 152
Africa, 98, 183
  and AIDS drugs, 65
  and financial institutions, 184
  and mercenaries / private armies,
    185–97, 205
  embassy bombings, 141, 145, 148
"age of extremes," 45
AIDS/HIV, 65, 128
al Qaeda, 142, 152, 153, 154
Algeria, 142, 152
alliances, *see* transnational strategic
  alliances
American dominance, 144,149
Amnesty International, 14, 67
anarchy, 4
Angola, 185, 187, 188, 194
anti-America, 145
  satanization, 148
anti-globalization movement, 76, 115, 212
  guerrilla anti-globalists, 142, 145
anti-GMO, 128
apartheid, 190, 191, 192, 216
Arafat, Yasir, 150, 153, *see also* Israel,
  Palestinian Authority
arbitration, 95
arms dealers, 191
assassinations, 191
Association of South East Asian Nations
  (ASEAN), 67
Aum Shinrikyo, 16, 147, 150, 152
authority,
  and legitimacy, 28
  criminal organizations and state
    authority, 180
  defined, 3
  distinguished from cooperation, 27
  distinguished from power, 4

  erosion of state authority, 193
  forms of, 5
  illicit forms thrive inversely to state
    legitimacy, 180
  illicit, 164–81
  market, 6, 76, 77
  moral, 14, 146–51
  of the state, 163
  overlapping, 64, 67
  private authority: types, bases, examples,
    and sources of potential reversal of,
    218
  socially constructed, 6
  see also illicit authority, market authority,
    moral authority

Baker, Wayne, 53
Bank for International Settlements, 83
banking, secret, 169
  underground, 179
Barlow, Eben, 191, *see also* mercenaries
Berger, Samuel, 11, 46
Bhagwati, 135
Bhindranwale, Jarnail Singh, 154
bin Laden, Osama, 16, 141, 145, 146 148,
  152, 153, 154
  see also al Qaeda, terrorism
Blinder, Alan, 45
border controls, 167
borders, 45, 54, 78, 165
  diffuse in middle ages, 64
  not irrelevant, 56
Bourdieu, Pierre, 149, 151
Branch Energy, 189
Bressand, Albert, 51
Bretton Woods, 79, 83, 85
British South Africa Company, 189, 190
Brown, Clarence, 51
Bull, Hedley, 64
Burley, Anne Marie, 82
Bush, George W., 146, 147

241

CAMBRIDGE STUDIES IN INTERNATIONAL RELATIONS